THE HISTORY OF GAMBLING IN AMERICA: BALANCING COSTS AND BENEFITS OF LEGALIZED GAMING

PART OF THE
CASINO MANAGEMENT ESSENTIALS SERIES

Steve Durham
The Pennsylvania State University

Kathryn Hashimoto
East Carolina University

Prentice Hall

Boston Columbus Indianapolis New York San Francisco
Upper Saddle River Amsterdam Cape Town Dubai London
Madrid Milan Munich Paris Montreal Toronto Delhi Mexico City
Sao Paulo Sydney Hong Kong Seoul Singapore Taipei Tokyo

Library of Congress Cataloging-in-Publication Data

Durham, Steve.
The history of gambling in America/Steve Durham, Kathryn Hashimoto.
p. cm.—(Casino management essentials series)
Includes bibliographical references and index.
ISBN-13: 978-0-13-239079-8 (alk. paper)
ISBN-10: 0-13-239079-5 (alk. paper)
1. Gambling–United States–History. 2. Casinos–United States–History. 3. Gambling–Law and legislation–United States. 4. Gambling on Indian reservations–United States–History. 5. United States–Economic conditions. 6. United States–Social conditions. I. Hashimoto, Kathryn. II. Title.

HV6715.D87 2010
795.0973–dc22

2009009542

Editor in Chief: Vernon Anthony
Acquisitions Editor: William Lawrensen
Development Editor: Sharon Hughes, O'Donnell and Associates, LLC
Editorial Assistant: Lara Dimmick
Production Coordination: Kris Roach
Production Manager: Kathy Sleys
Creative Director: Jayne Conte
Cover Designer: Margaret Kenselaar
Cover Image(s): Getty Images, Inc.
Director of Marketing: David Gesell
Marketing Manager: Leigh Ann Sims
Marketing Coordinator: Les Roberts
Full Service Project Management: Yasmeen Neelofar

This book was set in 10/12 Palatino by GGS Higher Education Resources, A Division of Premedia Global, Inc. and was printed and bound by Courier Companies, Inc. The cover was printed by Courier Companies, Inc.

Pearson Education Ltd., London
Pearson Education Singapore Pte. Ltd.
Pearson Education Canada, Inc.
Pearson Education—Japan
Pearson Education Australia Pty. Limited
Pearson Education North Asia Ltd.
Pearson Educación de Mexico, S.A. de C.V.
Pearson Education Malaysia Pte. Ltd.

Prentice Hall
is an imprint of

www.pearsonhighered.com

10 9 8 7 6 5 4 3 2 1
ISBN-13: 978-0-13-239079-8
ISBN-10: 0-13-239079-5

This book is dedicated to the students of today who will become the casino managers of tomorrow.

BRIEF CONTENTS

CONTENTS

PREFACE

The casino industry has been on a wild ride for three-quarters of a century. What started as an attempt at economic development in the desert and turned into a haven for organized crime, is today one of the fastest-growing industries around the world. The success of Nevada in breaking the connection between crime and gambling has offered other jurisdictions a template for legalizing an age-old scourge while minimizing the negative impacts.

The gaming industry has grown tremendously over the past 35 years. After crime was tamed in Nevada, New Jersey legalized casinos in Atlantic City. With a second successful attempt at breaking the crime–gambling link, the floodgates opened. Today, all but two states have some form of gambling. Less than 10% of the American population lives more than four hours away from a casino.

The gaming frenzy is not just an American phenomenon. It seems new jurisdictions legalize casinos every year. And jurisdictions with established gambling are liberalizing their laws. Macau opened up its licenses to foreign companies and in 2006 it passed Las Vegas as the largest market judged by gaming revenue.

The changes have gathered speed and it seems there is something new every day. The student of the gaming industry, much less a manager, will find it difficult to keep up with the rapid pace. But no one can fully understand where the industry is today without looking at where it has been.

This book traces the history of American gaming from the first European settlers to the Nevada experiment. Along the way you will read about the impact of gaming on society and the early attempts to minimize that impact. The book then takes you through the evolution of the gaming industry in Nevada as it deals with organized crime. In the process, a template for strict enforcement of laws to ensure the integrity of the casinos emerges that benefits the industry, the state, and the customers.

The book then examines the other jurisdictions in America that legalized casino gaming—New Jersey, Indian gaming, riverboats, and land-based casinos. Each of these chapters tells the story of legalization and the state of the segment today.

A book on gaming cannot be complete without addressing the reasons for legalization and the reasons against it. We tackle the social effects first. Crime, bankruptcy, and disordered gambling are just three of the issues. But what becomes clear quickly is that the link between the negative impacts and gaming are loose at best with one exception: pathological gambling.

It cannot be denied that legalizing gaming increases the incidence of pathological gambling. People with the predisposition toward this condition are not likely to exhibit the traits without a venue in which to gamble. With the spread of gaming, more people have gaming readily available and disordered gambling has increased accordingly.

It behooves the industry to continue funding the research into this phenomenon. The purpose, of course, is to understand the root of the problem. But of more practical concern is developing a protocol for identifying someone who is overindulging in gambling. Once that is known, casinos can back off these gamblers from the tables and slot machines much the same way bartenders back off overserved customers.

The analogy with alcohol is not accidental. Alcohol also has had a checkered past in terms of impacts on society. It is only in the last 65 years that America has brought about a way to deal with the negative impacts of serving alcohol. That could be the template for dealing with problem gambling.

The future of the gaming industry is bright. With a system in place that ensures the absence of organized crime, jurisdictions can feel comfortable legalizing gaming. Although there is always the possibility of a reversal in the trend, it looks like gaming is a permanent part of the entertainment industry. As you learn more about the gaming industry, you will appreciate the achievements of the past. More importantly, you will be ready for the future.

ACKNOWLEDGMENTS

Much went into the writing of this book. To take years of experience in the industry, add research efforts, set it all in writing, and make it presentable for the reading public is not an easy process. I could not have completed this task without the assistance of many people.

First and foremost, I would like to thank Prentice Hall. Patience does not begin to cover their forbearance as this first-time author struggled with the process. Missed deadlines were my biggest sin and forgiveness their deepest well. Thank you for persevering.

I thank the reviewers for providing insightful comments. They are Priscilla Bloomquist, Ph.D., New Mexico State University; Dan Creed, Normandale Community College; Donna Faria, Johnson & Wales University; Evelyn K. Green, The University of Southern Mississippi; Paul Howe, Morrisville University; Jayne Pearson, Manchester Community College; Jack Tucci, Mississippi State University; and Jim Wortman, University of Houston.

Special thanks to Kathryn Hashimoto for bringing me into this project because she thought I had something to say. I am glad she did. As I wrote this book, I realized how much I knew. And how much I did not know. The knowledge I gained in my research for this book has given me new insights while confirming much of what I already knew. Thanks, Kathryn.

As much as I know, I do not know everything about every aspect of gaming in America. Soo Kang wrote Chapter 8 on land-based casinos in South Dakota and Colorado. She does an excellent job of exploring these experiments in small-stakes gambling targeting specific towns. Dan Heneghan authored Chapter 5 on Atlantic City because he has been there from the beginning, first as a journalist and later as part of the regulatory agency. John Marchel knows the history of riverboat gambling as well as the modern riverboat casinos on the Mississippi River. His story about the Wilson Rangers in New Orleans during the Civil War says more about card sharps than any psychological study. William Thompson is a gaming expert with knowledge on a broad range of topics. Chapter 11 on the acceptance of gaming explains the political process of legalization with knowledge and insight.

My sister, Deborah, was a source of encouragement. When I was struggling with tight deadlines and multiple demands on my time, she helped me keep my perspective. She also gently nudged me forward when I was tempted to rest. Thanks, Deb.

And finally my parents, John and Janet Durham. Clearly, I would not be the man I am today if not for them. Among the many lessons taught, I learned to persevere, to focus, and to organize. Without these traits, a book report, much less a book, could not be written. Thanks, Mom and Dad.

Steve Durham

ACKNOWLEDGMENTS

CHAPTER 1

WHY ARE THERE RULES?

STEVE DURHAM

Learning Objectives

1. To understand the connection between society's need for rules and the regulation of the casino industry
2. To understand the many unique qualities of casinos as an industry
3. To learn of the early history of gambling starting at the beginning of U.S. history
4. To learn of the continuing history of gambling through the frontier era of U.S. history
5. To understand how the many benefits of casino gambling have contributed to its growth
6. To understand how the many costs of casino gambling have affected its growth
7. To understand the development and importance of regulations to the casino industry
8. To identify possible future trends in the casino industry

Chapter Outline

INTRODUCTION

Rules take many forms. There are rules for school, work, and children's games. Laws, ordinances, and judicial rulings are another form of rules. Treaties and contracts, negotiated between two or more parties, also create rules.

Then there are all the informal rules of life. We hold a fork in our left hand and knife in our right hand. You make eye contact when greeting someone on the street; you avoid eye contact when someone is angry with you. A telephone conversation is ended with a form of "good-bye"; you do not just hang up. There are a lot of rules.

The basic need for any rule, whether formal or informal, is to facilitate human interactions. If you lived alone on a desert island, you would have very few rules. They would be the kind that would make your existence more pleasant. For example, bathing once a week might be sufficient. Bathing every day would be unnecessary since there would be no one to offend with your body odor. However, bathing once every two weeks might bring on health issues.

However, living in a community with other human beings requires a set of rules. Some rules ensure there is fairness. Minimum-wage laws ensure a level of income judged to be adequate. Other rules facilitate efficiency. Only the most qualified candidate gets the job. Still others attempt to avoid confusion and uncertainty. If two cars approach an intersection with a four-way stop at the same time, the car on the right has the right of way.

Rules create order. To the extent that everyone follows the rules, life is certain. Rules provide predictability. Rules also give structure to our society.

The need for communities to regulate individual behavior that affects the larger community is real. If a personal behavior has no impact beyond the individual or individuals participating consensually in that activity, the American response is, generally, to decline to regulate or prohibit the behavior. However, when there is a negative impact, society, rightfully, chooses to set boundaries on the offending activity.

FIGURE 1.1 Signs make our lives orderly and predictable.

Source: © Jason Stitt. Image from BigStockPhoto.com.

The struggle between individual freedom and social order is at the center of the issue to legalize gaming. Gambling has been and is viewed as an activity that, justifiably, draws the attention of government. While gaming is considered a reasonable entertainment alternative in today's society, it was not always so.

Throughout American history, gambling has been associated with crime and social disruption. Too frequently unregulated gaming led to cheats who swindled unsuspecting marks—naïve wealthy people targeted because they are easy to steal from. However, whether through cheats or just bad playing, fortunes could be lost and a once-wealthy man and his family could end up at the bottom of the socioeconomic order. Certainly, the American attitude toward cheating is not favorable.

For this basic reason, the government finds it in the interest of society to regulate gaming activity closely. **Regulations** are just another form of rules that facilitate human interaction. In this book, we will examine the evolution of gaming in America, the pros and cons of legalized gaming, and the efforts made to regulate it.

OVERVIEW

Welcome to the world of casino management. If you are like most people reading this book, you are a student enrolled in a course. Perhaps you hope to work your way to the top of a gaming enterprise and a degree will give you a head start. If not a student, maybe you are currently employed in the industry and want to increase your knowledge. Additional knowledge allows you to make better decisions that increase your worth to your employer. This can lead to an increase in pay and promotions. Or possibly, you are just curious about what makes the casino industry different and interesting. Whatever your reason for picking up this book, be prepared to learn from an inside perspective.

This book is one in a series of five books on casino management. Each book, which covers a different area within the industry, can stand on its own. However, together they will give you a complete picture of what makes casino gaming unique. Each book is written by an expert. Some authors have worked in the field; others have studied and taught it. Some have done all three. Regardless of the authors' background, each book will give you inside information.

We present only the unique characteristics of the gaming industry. We have left the discussion of management topics common to all businesses to general business management textbooks. You will find discussions on card counting and mathematical probabilities, Indian sovereignty and tribal compacts, fill slips and credit slips, whales and grind action, and a myriad of other topics found only in the gaming industry. This is the information that you want.

GAMING: A UNIQUE INDUSTRY

So, what makes the gaming industry unique?

Several factors contribute to this. The amount of money that changes hands is tremendous. The business of gambling is done strictly in cash and cash equivalents, primarily casino chips. There are no personal checks, debit cards, or credit cards—yet. Because it is a cash business, there are large inventories of cash and cash equivalents. For example, a typical blackjack table has between $15,000 and $20,000 in chips in the chip

FIGURE 1.2 Cash and chips are a constant temptation to customers and employees alike in a casino.

Source: © Yuetau Huang. Image from BigStockPhoto.com.

rack. In a 30-table pit operation, there is $450,000 to $600,000 within easy reach of customers. And, it is sitting there tempting employees as well.

Not only is there a great deal of money, but it is constantly moving. To begin a new table, it moves from the vault to the cage to the table. Then, during the course of play, it moves from dealer to player and back again. It moves between one cashier cage and another. It moves from the machines to the vault. It moves from the vault to a commercial bank. The amount of money and its movement open up opportunities for theft and embezzlement. Steps must be taken to reduce or eliminate this risk.

Therefore, the possibility of cheating by customers is ever present. The ingenuity cheaters exhibit in devising ways to take what does not belong to them would be admirable if it were focused on a legitimate purpose. Most of the procedures implemented by casinos are in response to previously successful attempts at cheating. The clearing of a dealer's hands and the prohibition of players from touching their bet once play has begun are two such rules. Electronic gaming device manufacturers continually incorporate anti-cheating mechanisms on their equipment.

However, customers are not the only ones who think about getting more money. One chip can be worth $50,000. It is the size of a half-dollar. Working with that kind of money every day is a temptation for any person. Therefore, safeguards are in place to protect employees from themselves. But what about criminals outside the casino who want to rob the house or its winners? Or, the huge amounts of cash generated by the casino attract politicians, regulators, or police to take bribes. In addition, organized crime is an ever-present threat whether for laundering dirty money or just making it. As you will see, the saga of gambling is full of people who do not follow the legal course to make money.

The history of gambling also impacts the uniqueness of the industry. The past is checkered at best. The current industry has an excellent reputation for honesty and integrity. However, prior to the tightening of Nevada regulations in the 1950s and 1960s, there was no guarantee that a casino was dealing fairly and honestly with guests. And prior to state-sanctioned casino gaming, the individual gamblers who roamed from town to town or the organized criminal element that ran illegal gambling were hardly above cheating. Not only were the players and outsiders suspect, the management of the casino was occasionally questionable. Therefore, it is not so surprising that rules and government sanctions developed to protect everyone. In addition, as you will learn, the industry itself wanted to demonstrate that it could remove the criminal element from gambling and run an honest business. So, honest gambling operators like William Harrah were instrumental in working with governments to create fair practices.

As a result of governmental regulations and sanctions, the public's perception of gambling has changed dramatically over the past 50 years. In part, the tight regulation of gambling activity has improved its image as an honest, legitimate business. A common marketing approach in the casino industry today is that gambling is a form of recreation. People can choose to go to a movie or go bowling or go to a casino. When planning a vacation, activities can include gambling. As a result, gambling can be a part of daily life. As a result, there has been a shift in accepting gambling as one of many entertainment options available to adults. While it was once viewed as a vice, it is now considered no more unsavory than going to the movies or attending the opera. However, public sentiment can reverse and gambling could be criminalized once again. Legal and political issues are constantly roiling around the industry. For all these reasons, the gaming industry is unique.

A BRIEF HISTORY

The Beginnings

The history of gambling in America has been characterized by swings between legalization and criminalization. It is also characterized by geographic movement.

The form of gaming we examine in this textbook is European-style casino gaming brought to this continent by immigrants from Europe. Casinos, as we know them today, or their early predecessors did not appear until the end of the nineteenth century.

However, our gambling heritage started earlier than that. Did you ever wonder how the Pilgrims had enough money for supplies and passage to the New World? This was an expensive proposition. The Pilgrims signed on with a sponsor who set up lotteries to fund the voyage. Unfortunately, the organizers got greedy and ended up in legal trouble, which placed them in physical danger. However, not before the Pilgrims had acquired enough money to pay for the voyage.

It took people who were less risk averse to think about moving all their belongings to a strange new world. So, it is theorized that America itself was founded by people who were willing to take a risk on winning a chance at new wealth. And, isn't that the definition of a gambler?

As the settlers organized their towns, they needed to develop new **infrastructure** like streets, public buildings, and so on. However, since there was no central government to levy taxes, the dilemma was how to raise the money to pay for these new improvements. Lotteries once again paid for new improvements for the towns. "The reconstruction of Boston's Faneuil Hall in 1762 was accomplished through the sale of lottery tickets. So, too, were construction projects for many colleges, including Harvard, Yale, Princeton, Dartmouth, Brown, and William and Mary."[1]

FIGURE 1.3 The Pilgrims' ship, the *Mayflower*, was funded by a lottery.
Source: © Herbert Greene. Image from BigStockPhoto.com.

Later in the mid-1800s, down in New Orleans, **Charity Hospital** had too many people who could not pay for services and it was going broke. So, guess what? The hospital hired a group of gamblers to organize a lottery. The deal was that the organizers would pay all the expenses for running Charity Hospital, and in exchange, they could keep the rest of the winnings. The lottery was a huge success. However, as usual, the organizers broke the law by keeping too much money, bribing officials, and the usual graft and greed. The thriving lottery became known as the Louisiana Octopus because its tentacles of corruption reached far and wide. As a result, it took federal marshalls from Washington to come down to Louisiana to bring it down.

The Frontier

Gambling activity throughout the early years of the country gravitated to the frontier. Typically, gambling was illegal or restricted in those areas of the country that had a greater number of residents in close proximity to each other. On the frontier, though, no controlling legal authority existed and personal behavior found its freest expression. As the frontier moved westward, so did gambling. From the Appalachians to the Mississippi River to the Old West, gambling moved with the men who explored new territories and worked on the frontier. However, the Mississippi River was the mecca for gamblers. As the main transportation route from north to south, the slow boat ride encouraged gambling. As a result, New Orleans became the first gambling center of America. In fact "in 1828, **John Davis** opened what has been considered the first real casino in the United States at the corner of Bourbon and Orleans Streets."[2] Davis had been to Europe and brought back luxurious decorations to create his casino to impress his society friends. His complimentary food and drinks were known as the best in New Orleans and his rooms were opulent in their splendor.

When the continent was completely settled by European Americans around the turn of the twentieth century, gambling was criminalized throughout the country. Gambling activity went underground and was operated by organized crime. This situation continued until the economic duress of the Great Depression moved the state of Nevada to legalize casino gaming.

Nevada's experiment in gaming also marked the beginning of state-sanctioned casino gaming. Prior to this, gambling occurred between individuals or at illegal gaming operations. At the end of the nineteenth century and the start of the twentieth century, there were casinos at resorts and spas patronized by the wealthy. However, these were neither state sanctioned nor regulated.

The industry in Nevada started as small saloons in a largely rural state, offering a couple slot machines and a few table games to local residents. As the market changed, the casinos evolved into increasingly complex and large operations. Today, a typical casino resort in Las Vegas offers gaming, restaurants, bars, shows, nightclubs, shopping venues, spas, swimming pools, and much more. They would hardly be recognizable to the customers of the casinos in 1930s Nevada.

Nevada had a monopoly on casino gaming for 45 years until New Jersey legalized gambling in Atlantic City. It was a short 12 years until the Indian Gaming Regulatory Act was passed and 2 more years until riverboats and other casino forms were legalized in various states throughout the United States. Prior to the opening of Atlantic City's first casino, 10% of the American population lived within a four-hour drive of a casino. Today, 90% are within a four-hour drive.

BENEFITS AND COSTS

Why this expansion of gaming?

The circumstances of legalization varied widely. The legislature in Nevada passed a law, while the voters of New Jersey passed a referendum. Native American gaming was created by a law passed by Congress in response to a series of successful lawsuits establishing the right of tribes to conduct casino gaming on tribal lands.

There were many factors involved. The key factor was the previously mentioned shift of the public's attitude toward gambling. The generation that came of age after World War II has continually exhibited a less rigid approach to issues. Without this relaxed attitude toward gambling, there would have been no considering state-sanctioned or regulated casino gaming.

But without exception, the motivators for government to legalize gaming were the need for tax revenue and economic development. Whether discussing Nevada in 1931 or the Mashantucket Pequot in 1988, the responsible political entity saw a need to generate tax revenue so that it could provide the services its constituents expected. It also saw the need to develop and diversify the economic activity within its political jurisdiction.

The need for jobs was the primary focus of economic development. Voters expect their political leaders to take steps to facilitate a stable and healthy economy. Naturally, voters are most interested in jobs. Jobs in Depression Era Nevada were desperately needed as they are today on Indian reservations.

The benefit of jobs goes beyond the immediate worker. The worker spends his money in the community, which generates more economic activity. This in turn produces jobs and greater tax revenue. While a casino may employ 1,000 people, more than that can thank the casino for their jobs. As long as the original business remains healthy, the community remains vital.

(a)

(b)

(c)

(d)

FIGURE 1.4a, b, c, and d Today's Las Vegas casinos are the result of an evolution which started with the El Rancho and the Last Frontier casinos. (a) Bellagio, (b) Paris Las Vegas, (c) the Luxor, and (d) Planet Hollywood.

However, there is a downside to legalized gaming. While there is no clear and proven connection, there appears to be an impact on the quality of life in a community once gaming is allowed. Critics of gaming often point out that social costs such as suicide rates, bankruptcy, child neglect and abuse, criminal activity, and pathological gambling increase with legalization. However, studies on these phenomena are inconclusive in making the connection. On the other hand, there have been studies that indicate that some of the problems of gambling are, in fact, social myths. For example, a number of studies suggest that there is a pattern of problems in the first two years of a new casino, but then the cycle reverses itself and problems lessen over time. In particular, this pattern is revealed in studies about crime in and around casinos and local restaurants going out of business. There has been no definitive study yet that shows how gaming impacts the social fabric of a community.

However, of the social costs identified above, one clearly and consistently increases with the legalization of gaming. Pathological gambling, or the uncontrollable impulse to gamble, always rises among some people. It is obvious that if the tendency toward this condition is dormant, it will emerge when the opportunity to gamble becomes available. With 90% of Americans living within a four-hour drive of a casino, it is clear that such a problem affects most communities. Pathological gambling has been studied increasingly since the mid-1990s, and casinos have created programs on responsible gambling to address this major concern for the approximately 1–2% of the population who are predisposed to having serious problems. Far from taking over every gambler as some critics claim, pathological gambling affects only a small portion of the population. Even a small proportion, though, requires the attention of government.

FIGURE 1.5 Organizations to deal with pathological gambling have sprung up where casino gaming has been legalized.

Many of the staunchest critics of legalized gaming are religious organizations and individuals. Their objection is based on their life belief system. Many religions frown upon gambling because it entails no direct economic effort on the part of the bettor, because there is no exchange of value-added or finished product, because of the historical connection between the one who offers a bet and crime, and because it can consume some players with pathological gambling.

Proponents, on the other hand, claim that there is value added for the gambler. Viewed as entertainment, gaming is just as rewarding as going to the movies or dining in a gourmet restaurant. In these cases, the customer does not walk away with a tangible product. However, they have been enriched by the movie or experienced pleasure at consuming superb food. In the case of gambling, the bettor has purchased a chance to win, to match his/her skill against the casino, and to be entertained in an elaborate setting.

It is not an exaggeration to say that the issue of costs and benefits of casino gaming is confusing. Whenever morality and religion intersect with public policy, there is a predictable explosion of conflict and confrontation. This creates a volatile mix of politics and emotions.

In our system of government, disparate viewpoints are taken into account. Through the legislative and judicial processes, a compromise is cobbled together that is supported by a consensus of citizens. Beyond the procedure for passing laws, legislatures also can commission studies of pressing issues facing the country. Congress did so with the National Study on the Impact of Gambling.

This study was commissioned in 1997 when widespread gaming was less than ten years old. The report was presented to Congress in 1999. It neither praised nor condemned the gaming industry. However, it settled the argument of legal gambling in favor of proponents.

REGULATION

The competing voices in the debate to legalize gaming ensured that a consensus was reached on the type of gaming, the location, and other parameters. However, legalized gaming came with strings. The government wanted to be sure to collect the proper amount of taxes. Government also needed to show it was taking steps to minimize the negative impact of gaming. Regulating gaming became part of the enabling legislation. The state of Nevada's system of regulation is held up as a model for ensuring the integrity of casino gaming. It was not always thus.

In the early years of legalization, Nevada regulation was local, lax, and limited. When organized crime moved into Las Vegas, there was incentive to improve the regulatory oversight of the state. There was also pressure from the federal government. The process of tightening regulation was slow, but by the 1960s, Nevada had an exemplary regulatory environment. By the early 1980s, the last of organized crime was eliminated from Las Vegas.

This tighter regulation served several purposes. First and foremost, it ensured that the state was receiving the proper amount in taxes. No casino can manipulate its books in order to reduce its tax liability. Secondly, it improved and protected the reputation of the industry. Customers could have confidence that the casinos would not cheat them. Third, it held the federal government at bay. In the past 50 years, there has never been a serious attempt at the federal level to outlaw gaming in America. Finally, the stability and fairness of the regulations has allowed Las Vegas to grow into the premier gaming market in the world.

More recently, as the social impact of gaming takes a more prominent place in the public's perception, regulatory bodies are increasingly addressing these issues. How successful they are in mitigating these impacts will influence the public debate on legalized gaming.

However settled the consensus process appears now, it is never complete because the government guarantees citizens the right to redress of grievances. In the future, the consensus surrounding legalized gaming can unravel and a movement to criminalize it could arise. It has happened before in American history and it could happen again.

FUTURE TRENDS

However, the future of gaming in America has some exciting possibilities, too. Technology continues to change the landscape within which the industry operates. Internet gaming, already a reality in most parts of the world, will become prevalent in the United States. The use of "ticket in ticket out" electronic gaming devices is just a layover to the use of smart cards or debit and credit cards on the casino floor. The platform for electronic gaming devices is shifting to a central processing unit in the back of the house to offer multiple games from the same unit on the floor.

Technology continues to transform other parts of the business. Hotel, restaurant, and show reservations can be made online. Digital camera technology allows the casino to record and store the entire casino to a hard drive for later recall. Slot player club cards have facilitated the targeting of very specific market segments to increase revenue and customer loyalty.

There are other market trends that call for our attention. The consolidation of industry players in Las Vegas has been remarkable. Fifty years ago, the casinos on The Strip were individually owned. Today, six major players control over 130,000 hotel rooms. Globalization has come to the casino industry. The Sands organization has opened a casino in Macao.

Atronics is a German-based electronic gaming device manufacturer with a significant presence in Europe, America, and Russia. A shift in revenue sources has occurred. Thirty years ago, rooms, food, and beverages were discounted or given away free to entice gamblers. Gaming revenue was the vast majority of total casino revenue. Today, gaming

FIGURE 1.6 Ticket In, Ticket Out or TITO is the result of new technology and has improved the customers' experiences and reduced costs for the casino.

revenues in Las Vegas represent less than 50% and casinos charge a premium for their rooms, food, and beverage. Another shift in revenue is away from the pit, which ruled the casino world throughout the twentieth century. Today, electronic gaming devices produce the lion's share of total gaming revenue.

Conclusion

So this is the exciting world of casino gaming. It has a rowdy history. The temptation to cheat and embezzle by both customers and employees is ever present. The debate of legalizing gaming is raucous and never complete. The industry and its state sponsors have responded by setting up a tight system of regulation. The rules ensure that the interaction between the various participants is fair and predictable.

You will find as you read this book and the others in this series that there are many things that make it unique. However, as you read, you will learn from an insider's perspective about the normalcy that reigns behind the facade of glamour and glitz. It is, after all, just a business where payroll must be met, customers must be satisfied, and the competitive environment mastered.

The future will bring change, as it always does. Change in the business, change in regulations, and change in the political environment. How the industry reacts to this change and adapts to the new forces that will have impact on it will determine whether and how it will survive. However, if the past 75 years are any indication, casino gaming will be with us for a very long time.

Key Words

Regulations *3*
Infrastructure *5*
Charity Hospital *6*
John Davis *6*
Atronics *11*

Review Questions

1. Explain the connection between society's need for rules and the regulation of the casino industry.
2. Describe the many unique qualities of casinos as an industry.
3. Discuss the early history of gambling starting at the beginning of U.S. history.
4. Discuss the continuing history of gambling through the frontier era of U.S. history.
5. Describe the many benefits of casino gambling that have contributed to its growth.
6. Discuss how the many costs of casino gambling have affected its growth.
7. Describe the development and importance of regulations to the casino industry.
8. Identify some possible future trends in the casino industry.

Endnotes

1. Thompson, W. (2001). *Gambling in America: An Encyclopedia of History, Issues, and Society*. Santa Barbara, CA: ABC-CLIO, 227.
2. Ibid., 231.

CHAPTER 2

HISTORY FROM PLYMOUTH PLANTATION TO THE CIVIL WAR

STEVE DURHAM

Learning Objectives

1. To understand the various reasons why people gamble
2. To learn the details of gambling in pre-Columbian America
3. To learn the details of the role of gambling in the Puritan communities of Colonial America
4. To learn the details of the role of gambling in the communities of the southern colonies in Colonial America
5. To learn the details of the role of gambling in the early American era communities
6. To understand the details of the role of gambling in the Native American communities
7. To understand the European and Native American perspectives on Indian removal in early American history
8. To understand the effects of the "Indian Wars" on American history
9. To understand the effects of the "The Trail of Tears" on American history

Chapter Outline

INTRODUCTION

Gambling is inherent in human nature. The temptation to gamble has been recorded throughout history. It has been documented in ancient civilizations and prehistoric times. Ancient cultures used drawing lots and chance events to divine the will of the gods. Even the ancient Hebrews used such methods to understand God's will. Of course, gambling was also a leisure activity. There is ample evidence in recorded history up to the current time.

However, this trait is not evenly distributed throughout the human species. Gambling behavior is a function of an individual's risk averseness. Some people are very risk averse, while others appear to have no fear. Risk-taking behavior can be expressed in different ways. Some display it through their choice of leisure activity—bungee jumping, skydiving, and amusement park rides. Others reveal their gambling behavior through their choice of employment. Entrepreneurs, typically, are more risk tolerant than non-entrepreneurs. The most risk-averse people will still take small risks, such as stopping in a tow-away zone or altering a recipe.

Betting behavior is a common way for risk-taking behavior to express itself. Again, this behavior is not evenly distributed among the population. Some enjoy the activity more than others do. But understanding why people gamble is helpful in understanding the history of gaming and the regulation of the industry.

WHY PEOPLE GAMBLE

There are five reasons why people gamble. No one exhibits all five reasons, but most gamble for multiple reasons. The most obvious reason for people gambling is the hope of winning. Clearly, the potential outcome of placing a bet is winning and some people focus on the winning potential of gaming.

Another common reason is the social nature of the activity. There are many people around who are enjoying the same game. Commiserating over a bad hand or rejoicing over a jackpot develops a natural camaraderie.

Some people view gambling as a form of entertainment. They are amused by the antics of their fellow gamblers or the bonus rounds on an electronic gaming device. The sights and sounds of the casino excite them. They see a challenge in using their intelligence to create a strategy to maximize their winnings or minimize their losses.

The most excitable gamblers are looking for exhilaration. For them, an adrenaline rush accompanies betting activity.

Finally, some people gamble because they suffer from a behavioral disorder called pathological gambling. Those with this impulse control disorder cannot control their urge to gamble.

FIGURE 2.1 Many people gamble for social and entertainment reasons.

Source: © Yuri Arcurs. Image from BigStockPhoto.com.

GAMBLING IN PRE-COLUMBIAN AMERICA

Pre-Columbian Native Americans incorporated gambling behavior into their lives. While it is inaccurate to generalize about such a large population, some common characteristics can be noted. Intra-tribal and intertribal games created a setting for small-stakes social betting. For example, some tribes in the southwest played a game with a small rubber ball in a court. The object was to get the ball through a hoop mounted on one wall of the court without using the hands. Another example is called **the hand game**. Teams of two or more were created. Individuals on a team would hold marked sticks in their closed fists. The other team would try to guess who held a certain stick. These games, whether formal or informal, generated betting activity.

As with many gamblers, luck played an important role in their betting behaviors. The original Americans believed that chance occurrences like the appearance of a wild animal or a change in the moon or sun could be a communication from the spirit world. A Hopi belief is that when it snows after someone dies, it is the deceased's way of saying "Goodbye," and that they are successfully making their way to the spirit world. Some Native American gamblers also take natural occurrences such as falling snow to be a sign from the supernatural world to reveal or assist them in the best bet.

However, Native Americans did not develop commercial gambling. It was strictly small-stakes social games or the activity was significant for religious and spiritual reasons.

We will study the style of gaming that was brought by the immigrants from Europe. To understand how gaming developed in the United States, one must know about the Europeans who settled the continent.

Early in America's history, a variety of European nationalities settled on the eastern seaboard. The English, French, Dutch, Scots, Germans, and Irish were the predominant groups. Initially, these groups were very small and focused on surviving in an alien and often harsh environment. They had to create communities from nothing. Houses had to be built, fields cleared and planted, and governments established. Their existence during the first few years was tenuous at best. Survival was the sole priority.

Some sociologists say that this is the ultimate gamble—betting your skills against your survival. Because of our heritage, it is part of the American belief system to be less risk averse than other national groups. We tend to see the upside potential and are willing to take the risk to see its fruition.

Once settlements were firmly established and their survival assured, gambling and associated behaviors started to appear. How the different communities and colonies dealt with the issue depended upon the attitude the colonists brought with them.

GAMBLING IN COLONIAL AMERICA

The Puritans

It is well known that the New England colonies were settled by groups who were characterized as religiously strict. The **Puritans** arrived in 1620 on the *Mayflower* in what is now Massachusetts. They created a settlement on Cape Cod Bay called Plymouth Plantation. It was named after Plymouth, England, where they embarked on their journey.

While the Puritans are the best known, there were different groups who settled from Maine to Connecticut with similar worldviews. They had left the Old World to avoid religious persecution and the decadence of Europe. They saw their escape to the New World as an opportunity to create a faith-based paradise on earth. They felt an obligation to God to create a society based on laws derived from the Bible as they interpreted it.

Gambling in its many forms was banned. The religious underpinnings of this ban relied on the belief that God had placed each man and woman on earth for a purpose. While each person's purpose was his/hers alone, it was guided by reading the Bible. According to New Englanders, people were created to be productive, populate the earth, and to spread belief in Christianity.

Therefore, the religions of New England felt strongly that all activity must be focused on producing value for the community or for the glory of God. Their experience of surviving the settlement of New England through hard work and perseverance reinforced their belief that **Divine Will** had brought them to America and had favored them. Nothing of value was created by gambling, God was not glorified, and the deity's name was often called in vain. Therefore, gambling was viewed as blasphemy and idleness. It was considered to have a negative impact on individuals' souls and on the community at large and was banned. Coincidentally, many social activities were also banned because they were not productive in nature.

However, it is interesting to note that despite their deeply held views on gambling, the *Mayflower*'s trip to the western hemisphere was funded by a lottery. Lotteries are a form of gambling and have not changed significantly over the centuries. Much like our state-sponsored lotteries today, an individual purchases a chance at a large prize by buying a ticket. The individual or organization running the lottery offers a prize worth less than the total expected amount collected in ticket sales. Of course, if more tickets, or chances, are sold than anticipated, there is greater profit. Perhaps because the Pilgrims' purpose was to be productive and populate the earth, the end justified the means, as the lottery was the only way by which the *Mayflower*'s passengers could have funded the expedition.

FIGURE 2.2 Punishment for crimes in the New England colonies often included being placed in a pillory in a public location.

Source: © Dennis Cox. Image from BigStockPhoto.com.

For the early settlers, there was no centralized government. However, the dilemma was how to subsidize large public service projects without the ability or resources to levy taxes. As a result, lotteries became a common method of financing large-scale ventures. Lotteries were seen as a legitimate means of fund raising if the cause was just. Consequently, many roads, canals, bridges, and so on were built by private enterprises using lotteries as a funding source.

The Southern Colonies

The southern colonies were settled by a different group of British subjects. They did not settle in America due to religious persecution. In fact, the colony of Georgia began as a penal colony inhabited by convicts from the prisons of England. Because the prisons were overcrowded in Europe, many countries offered their prisoners the choice of remaining in prison in Europe or colonizing a new world. The Scotch and the Irish who also settled the southern colonies were fleeing discrimination and lack of economic opportunity at home. As a result, the majority of settlers in the southern colonies viewed America in terms of economic opportunity.

The possibility of owning land in Europe was limited, while there was plenty of land to be had in America, the existence of Native Americans notwithstanding. In that period of history, land ownership represented economic independence and sustenance, but the price might be your life. Due to the unknown nature of the land and the cultural chasm between Europeans and Native Americans, the American continent was viewed with both fear and hope. However, it was the risk takers among the settlers who were willing to gamble on improving their lot against what they had. It is not surprising then that they had a more relaxed social code. Gambling was widely practiced in the form of small-stakes social betting. However, there were numerous laws passed by the government to ensure that the social and economic order was not upset due to gambling activities.

The New England colonies favored a more egalitarian view of humankind. They believed that God created and loved each individual and valued everyone equally. The southern colonies exhibited a more hierarchical social order. In their eyes, some men were born at a higher station of life and it was important not to upset this "natural" order. Therefore, laws were designed to protect the plantation owners from themselves and their families from losing it all in gambling debts. Consequently, the laws that regulated gambling activity dealt often with how bets were placed and how much could be collected as payment.

The colonies south of New England and north of the southern colonies were populated by a more diverse mix of ethnic groups. New York was originally called **New Amsterdam** because the Dutch settled it. Pennsylvania had a significant German segment. This diversity resulted in a less uniform attitude toward gambling. Consequently, laws were less restrictive. Essentially the issue of gambling was dealt with at a lower level of the political order than New England or the southern colonies. As a result, the laws on gambling varied widely within the middle Atlantic colonies.

As noted in the preceding text, the early years were spent surviving the harshness of settling the land. As the colonies became more populated and the Indian population was displaced, more laws were passed to facilitate the interactions among a growing population of Europeans. Increasingly, gambling was restricted or outlawed.

Law enforcement also became more effective. With increased law enforcement, gambling activity was discouraged. However, on the frontier where law enforcement was more sporadic, gambling behavior continued relatively unimpeded. This pattern of greater gambling activity on the frontier continued until European Americans completed settling the continent at the turn of the twentieth century.

THE EARLY AMERICAN ERA

After the Revolutionary War in the late eighteenth century, the 13 colonies became the United States of America. This political fact did not change the American attitude toward gambling. The New England states were still more restrictive than the southern states, with the Middle Atlantic states straddling the muddled middle ground on the issue. Regardless of their stance on gambling, law enforcement was consistent and effective along the eastern seaboard.

The Treaty of Paris, which ended the war, transferred the land across the Appalachian Mountains and east of the Mississippi to the United States. This area became territories of the new United States. There was minimal legal presence in this area. In fact, much of the land was still occupied by Indian tribes.

However, Americans began to pour into the territories in order to make a life for themselves. Between 1783 and 1860, 20 territories applied for and received statehood. All the states east of the Mississippi in addition to Missouri, Vermont, Maine, Oregon, and California entered the union.

As before history repeated itself—gambling activity was minimal when people were struggling to settle the land. Clearing land, defending against attacks by Indians, establishing towns, and building roads left little time for leisure activities. However, as their future became more assured and disposable incomes rose, gambling activity increased.

The economic development of the territories required access to markets. Cotton harvested in the South had to reach the mills in New England or in Great Britain. The corn, apples, and other produce from the northern states were destined for other regions of the New World. The Ohio and Mississippi rivers provided a natural highway for commerce. Once these rivers were secured, barges and paddle wheel boats plied the waters constantly. New Orleans, Natchez, Vicksburg, Memphis, St. Louis, Minneapolis, Louisville, and Cincinnati became major hubs of commercial activity.

These cities played dual roles. First, the primary means of transportation for individual travel was the paddle wheel steamboat. Only the wealthy could afford to travel by this means. Primarily, southern planters and northern merchants would have the income to travel by steamboat. Second, port cities were the gathering points for farm and plantation produce. A farmer or planter would send his harvest to these ports to be loaded on to a boat headed for the waiting customer. This required wealthy planters and merchants, along with the independent farmers accompanying the produce to the port, to have long periods of monotonous travel on the boat and then several days in New Orleans selling the goods, before returning home. Once the boat arrived at port, business was transacted by the ship captain and the crew would go ashore as well. While business could be transacted during these stays, it did not require all the time. Since the farmers, plantation owners, and crew had money in their pockets because they had sold their goods or just received wages for the voyage, leisure activities were in demand.

The presence of individuals looking for leisure activities created a natural environment for gambling. Cards and dice are easily transported, so card playing took place onboard the ship among the passengers. In addition, card playing in saloons in the port cities also flourished. The laws concerning gambling at cards varied among jurisdictions. However, the activity occurred without much interference from law enforcement.

FIGURE 2.3 Steamboat travel on the Mississippi River and its tributaries was common between the Revolutionary War and the Civil War.

Source: © Alon Brik. Image from BigStockPhoto.com.

Not surprisingly, card cheats were drawn to all of the port cities along the rivers, where they found tremendous opportunity to practice their trade. They could join a game in progress and use their superior skills to win. Failing that, they could cheat to win. Those who could pass muster could travel on the paddle wheel boats as if they were one of the wealthy patrons. In this way, they could join the onboard games and ply their trade. As a result, towns along the rivers became the home base of card cheats.

Initially, when the population density in an area was sparse, gambling was tolerated. However, as the population swelled, the impact of gambling on the community increased. Loss of wealth and the subsequent disruption to the social order were felt keenly. Periodically, the local population would rise up in anger and take action to restrict or eliminate gambling. Most often, such action took the form of passing laws or requiring the authorities to enforce the existing laws. However, on occasion mob violence would do the job. Suspected card cheats were run out of town or taken captive and thrown into jail. All too often, mob justice was administered and the card cheats and their allies were murdered.

Native American Gambling

Now that the European viewpoint on gambling has been discussed, let's explore the Native American gaming traditions. Like other cultures, Native populations also engaged in betting. Although there were hundreds of game variations, they fell into two major categories.

The first category was comprised of games of dexterity. Betting on archery, javelin and darts, shooting, ball games, and racing games all showed the warrior skills to hunt and survive, while proclaiming who was the best.

The second category was games of chance, including dice games and guessing games. Guessing games required one person to hold a number of sticks behind his/her back while another guessed the number. Other guessing games required one person to hide an object and another to find it. There also was a game similar to European dice. Most Native American tribes had some form of dice play. The dice stones had two distinct sides. Two individuals or groups competed against one another based on rules pertaining to who could toss the dice into a basket and which side came up.

The games of dexterity required men to test their abilities against others. Training for these games made the warriors stronger and more skilled. As a result, they were able to bring more food to the table and to protect their families. The other games appear to have been mostly those in which others, including family members, participated, which offered a form of control on betting while enhancing social relationships through fun and recreation. Later, when the federal government regulated Native American gaming, these games came to be called **Class 1 games**.

INDIAN REMOVAL

The European Perspective

As mentioned earlier in this chapter, the Treaty of Paris, which ended the Revolutionary War, gave the land west of the Appalachians and east of the Mississippi River to the United States. This territory was occupied primarily by Native Americans. As had been the custom prior to independence, the land was claimed and transferred among European powers without regard for the Indians' physical possession of the land.

This situation arose due to genuine cultural differences between the Native Americans and the Europeans. The Europeans colonized the world beginning with Columbus' discovery of the Americas in 1492. Due to European technological superiority, other countries and societies stood little chance of resisting their conquest. Europeans reasoned that they were destined to rule the earth. They had a monotheistic religion, which stated that it was the only true religion, while much of the world believed in multiple gods and a very different spiritual world. Christianity, unlike most religions, has a tenet that instructs believers to evangelize. Europeans concluded that God had given them the means to subjugate the world because they were superior to the rest of mankind and that they were to convert the world to Christianity. This attitude led to policies that segregated Native Americans from other Americans, damaged the social fabric of Native American societies, and set the stage for legalizing casino gaming on reservations in the twentieth century.

The Europeans viewed land differently than most societies they encountered. They felt that land was a commodity to be bought and sold. Like any densely populated region, ownership of land represented power, independence, and standing in society, because only the rich could afford to buy land. The division of land and the building of fences flowed naturally from these beliefs.

In order to avoid conflict, the Europeans devised ways to document and ensure rightful ownership of land. Disputes over land were settled in court or on the battlefield. While Europeans had sentimental and nationalistic attachments to the land, their basic view was utilitarian in nature. Peasants worked the land and paid taxes to the property owner. Therefore, landownership meant wealth.

When the Europeans arrived in North America, they saw a land occupied by people they felt to be inferior to them. The Native Americans did not follow a monotheistic religion. They combined limited agriculture with hunting and gathering for sustenance. They were physically different in skin tone and facial features. The technology of their weapons and tools were similar to a much earlier era of European history.

The Native American Perspective

The Native Americans' perspective on the land was also very different. While each tribe had a different relationship with the land, they all shared the concept that the land was not something to be bought and sold. It was a gift from the Creator. It was to be used communally for the good of the entire tribe. While disputes with an opposing tribe about the range over which a tribe had sovereignty were settled through negotiations or battle, individuals within a tribe did not lay claim to a specific plot of land.

When the European and Native American cultures intersected, there was conflict. The Europeans claimed the land as if the Indians were merely a herd of animals with no rights to the land. The Indians were mystified that the Europeans thought the land could be owned. One might as well own the air.

As history has shown, the Europeans prevailed. Their superior technology and their greater numbers overwhelmed the Indians, along with their occasionally devious transactions. Broken treaties, playing one tribe or coalition against another, and the distribution of plague- and smallpox-infected blankets are just a few examples of the underhanded treatment used by the Europeans to gain control. As we will see later, this attitude and tradition remain ingrained in the American mind-set.

As mentioned earlier, the European population of the young country immigrated westward into the territories. This placed pressure on the indigenous populations. A Shawnee chief named **Tecumseh** lived in the area that would become the state of Indiana. He saw that the Americans were encroaching on the Indians' territory and resisted. Beginning in 1805, he worked to create a pan-tribal alliance among all the tribes along the western frontier from Florida to New York. However, as would be true throughout American history, the tribes viewed themselves as independent and were reluctant to make common cause against the Americans.

The "Indian Wars"

The Battle of Tippecanoe was fought in 1811. The battle site was an Indian city with 200 bark houses laid out in streets and lanes. There were 100 acres of cultivated fields. It was a center of commerce among Native Americans and between Native Americans and American traders. It was a city in the European-American sense of the word. Still, the Americans considered the Native Americans as less civilized.

The battle was provoked by the governor of the Indiana territory, William Henry Harrison. He would later win the presidency with the slogan "Tippecanoe and Tyler, Too." The American forces suffered substantial losses but eventually prevailed. They completely destroyed the city.

Tecumseh was absent from the battle because he was on a mission to the Creek, Cherokee, and Chickasaws in the South to convince them to join his confederation. When he returned, he saw the destruction caused by the Americans. Relations between Great Britain and the United States had remained tense since the end of the Revolutionary War. Tecumseh had diplomatically juggled the British, who still occupied Canada as a colony, and the Americans. With this latest atrocity by the Americans, Tecumseh threw in with the British.

The War of 1812 saw Tecumseh and his confederation in alliance with the British in an effort to check the advancement of the Americans. Tecumseh lost his life in a battle near Detroit in 1813. Andrew Jackson, the future president, led an army, which routed the Creek in Georgia. The British lost the war decisively, the Indian alliance crumbled, and the Americans' claim to the land was secured. The Creek were removed from Georgia and the Indians in the Northwest were pushed farther west.

Most Americans felt that Indian removal was a legitimate policy. The feelings of racial superiority and a sense of a right to the land superseded all other considerations. However, the Indian removal movement coincided with the Second Great Awakening.

The Second Great Awakening was a religious revival whose seeds were planted in the last decade of the eighteenth century. It gained momentum in the 1820s and peaked and dissipated in the 1840s. It spread from New England to the western frontier and spontaneously arose in the backwoods of the South. While it was not one movement but many, its impact on the country was profound. Theology was revised. Church attendance rose dramatically. Political questions from slavery to Indian removal were recast in moral terms. The rise of the Religious Right in the late twentieth century and its focus on the morality of abortion and gambling has been compared to the Second Great Awakening's impact on nineteenth-century America. Throughout American history, gambling has alternated between legal activity and banned activity. It could happen again.

The "Trail of Tears"

The infamous "Trail of Tears" associated with the removal of the Cherokee nation resulted from the Indian Removal policy. The crisis was provoked when the Georgia legislature passed a law in 1829 declaring the laws and constitution of the Cherokee null and void so that Georgia's European-American residents could obtain the Cherokees' fertile land and the gold discovered on it.

The Cherokee were not just any tribe. Through the efforts of adherents to the Second Great Awakening, they had traded hunting for settled agriculture. Many converted to Christianity. Sequoyah, an ex-warrior who fought with Andrew Jackson, developed a written alphabet. The Cherokee lived in towns and developed trades. They wore clothes like the Americans. In nearly every aspect, they had assimilated into American culture.

The federal government, to which is delegated in the Constitution the responsibility to deal with Indian tribes, had to act when the Georgia legislature moved to remove the Cherokee. Andrew Jackson was elected president in 1828. Being in favor of Indian removal, he proposed to Congress the funding of a removal of the Cherokee beyond the Mississippi.

The reaction across the land was loud. Those most affected by the Second Great Awakening felt outraged at the lack of moral consideration in this decision. They were horrified that the crass greed for the Cherokees' land could negate their property rights.

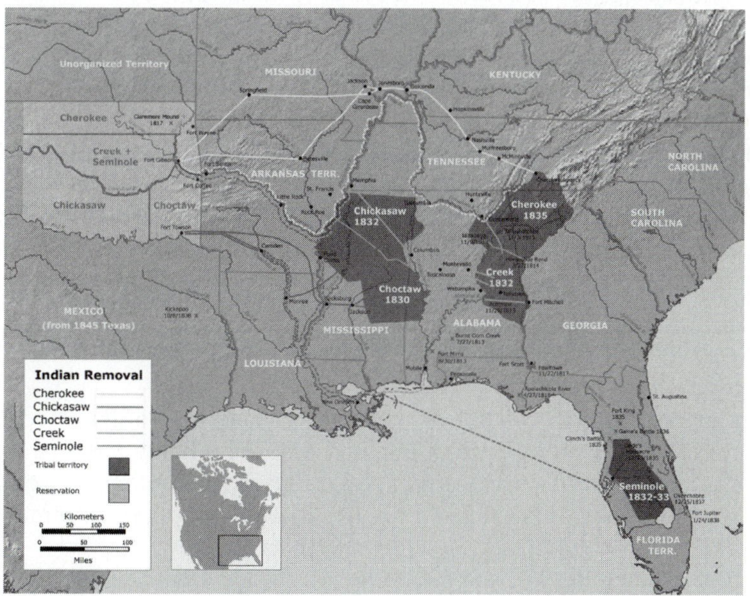

FIGURE 2.4 The removal of Indians from east of the Mississippi meant a long and deadly journey.

Petitions from all parts of the country poured into Congress in opposition to the removal. Prominent elected officials including Henry Clay, Daniel Webster, and Davy Crockett also labored against the act. All was to no avail. Davy Crockett said, "I would sooner be damned honestly than hypocritically immortalized." He also supported the Cherokees in the debate in Congress about their removal from Georgia.[1]

President Jackson made sure that Congress funded the removal by passing the Indian Removal Act of 1830. While preparation began for the process of removal, the Cherokees brought suit against the law. The lawsuit was appealed until it came before the Supreme Court. In the ruling, *Worcester v. Georgia*, the Supreme Court reasoned that prior to the arrival of the Europeans, all Indian tribes were functioning, legal entities providing for their citizens like any other national government. The Cherokees' assimilation of American customs strengthened their case. Therefore, the Cherokee Nation was a sovereign nation and the removal laws were invalid on Indian land. The ruling went on to say that the only way to remove the Cherokee was by treaty.

Unfortunately, a renegade band of Cherokee who were in favor of removal signed such a treaty in 1835. This was the tool President Jackson needed to act. In May 1838, a force of 7,000 soldiers entered the Cherokee Nation and began the removal process. Nearly all of the 17,000 Cherokee were marched to Oklahoma through the fall and winter. Due to lack of provisions and poor planning, 4,000 Cherokee died en route, hence the name **"Trail of Tears."**

Despite their efforts to assimilate and resist, the Indians of the eastern woodlands were relegated to reserved land west of the Mississippi. By 1840, 70,000 Native Americans had been removed to Oklahoma. However, their sovereignty as nations was established in law. The significance of this fact would be crucial in the 1980s when gambling was legalized as a viable economic development tool on reservations.

The United States hurdled toward civil war over the next 20 years. The simmering conflict based on the slavery question exploded into the forefront on April 12, 1861, when the state of South Carolina fired on Fort Sumter in Charleston harbor. The carnage and destruction of the Civil War disrupted the nation and changed it forever In Chapter 3, we will see the impact of the war on the development of the country and on gambling.

Conclusion

The tendency to gamble is in us all, but not to the same degree. Some like it more than others do. Some exhibit it in leisure activities while it shows up in work life choices for others. Still, it is there.

When the negative side effects of gambling affect the community as a whole, the government steps in to regulate, restrict, or prohibit gambling. What course is taken depends in large measure on the religious, moral, and social expectations of the population. As we have seen, the religious tenets of the New England colonists leaned toward banning gambling altogether. By contrast, the southern colonies were less religious and had a more relaxed social code. They allowed gambling, although with restrictions that were intended to maintain the prevailing social order.

However, gambling activity was more likely to occur where laws were nonexistent or not enforced. The frontier at the edge of European settlement saw more gambling activity than the towns and villages established on the eastern seaboard. This relationship between frontier and gambling remained until the frontier was closed at the close of the nineteenth century.

The closing of the frontier, of course, is a European-American term. The Native Americans had settled the land thousands of years earlier. However, with the tragic removal of the Indians across the Mississippi River were planted the seeds of success. The Supreme Court of the United States of America recognized Indian tribes as sovereign nations who had a government-to-government relationship with the federal government and not with the state governments. This precedent would prove to be crucial in the legal battles to legalize reservation gambling in the latter half of the twentieth century.

Key Words

The hand game *15*
Puritans *16*
Divine will *16*
New Amsterdam *18*
The Treaty of Paris *18*
Class 1 games *20*
Tecumseh *22*
The Battle of Tippecanoe *22*
The Second Great Awakening *22*
The "Trail of Tears" *24*

Review Questions

1. Detail the various reasons why people gamble.
2. Explain the extent of gambling in pre-Columbian America.
3. Detail the role of gambling in the Puritan communities of Colonial America.
4. Detail the role of gambling in the communities of the southern colonies in Colonial America.
5. Explain the role of gambling in the early-American-era communities.
6. Explain the role of gambling in the Native American communities.
7. Describe and compare the European and Native American perspectives on Indian removal in early American history.
8. Describe the effects of the "Indian Wars" on American history.
9. Describe some of the effects of the "The Trail of Tears" on American history.

Endnote

1. Retrieved July 20, 2008, from http://ngeorgia.com/history/nghisttt.html.

CHAPTER 3

HISTORY FROM THE CIVIL WAR THROUGH THE GREAT DEPRESSION

STEVE DURHAM

Learning Objectives

1. To learn about the functioning of gambling at the start of the Civil War
2. To learn the role of Wilson's Rangers in the Civil War
3. To understand the impact of the Civil War on gambling in the South
4. To learn the history of the Louisiana Lottery and its effects on gambling
5. To learn the history of the "Old West" frontier and its effects on gambling
6. To understand the effects of the Progressive Era on gambling
7. To understand the effects of the Great Depression on gambling
8. To learn of the beginnings of Las Vegas and its early role in the history of gambling

Chapter Outline

INTRODUCTION

The Civil War in America is considered by most historians to be the defining event in American history. It was the culmination of many forces and conflicts in existence prior to that time. The United States experienced continuous tension across sectional lines from the founding of the nation until the bombardment of Fort Sumter. The war resolved the conflicts and set the nation on a new trajectory.

Both sides were passionate about the rightness of their cause. The depth of their feelings was generated by the number of issues that divided them and the intensity of those issues. Abolitionists believed in the evil of slavery as strongly as Southerners believed in the necessity of subjugating African Americans for social order. The dominance of the federal government over states' rights also created a chasm between the North and the South. The agrarian South resented the tariffs on imported goods, which protected Northern industrial and mercantile concerns, but raised the price of consumer and business goods. Unfortunately, both sides demonized the other.

GAMBLING AND THE CIVIL WAR

Just prior to the start of the Civil War, gambling was booming in New Orleans. Small gaming establishments operated as farmers and plantation owners brought their wares for sale. However, John Davis had visited Europe and had a dream for opening a European-style casino in 1827. Since he was part of the upper strata of society, he wanted everything to be on a grand style. His food was reputed to be the best in town and his decorations were shipped in from Europe. Unfortunately, New Orleans banned casinos in 1835 and the elaborate casino was forced to shut down.

However, that did not prevent the lower-class gambling operations from running illegally. As a result, the antigambling movement fostered by the Second Great Awakening reached new heights. Gamblers were considered evil and run out of every town on a rail or worse. Vigilante committees formed up and down the Mississippi River and set fire to any gambling dens they could find. One such committee in Vicksburg, Mississippi, not only gathered all the gamblers together, but also lynched five of them. Despite the furor of the reform, riverboat gambling did not decline until the advent of the Civil War.

The war started in April 1861 when the South Carolina militia fired on Fort Sumter in Charleston harbor. It ended four bloody, destructive years later in April 1865 when General Robert E. Lee surrendered to General Ulysses S. Grant at Appomattox Courthouse, Virginia.

When the war started most gamblers abandoned the riverboats and sought safety in New Orleans. Many were Southerners who did not mind one-on-one combat at a card table, but to gamblers, war was another thing. **George Devol**, a professional gambler, who wrote a book called *Forty Years a Gambler on the Mississippi*, described how gamblers took to supporting the war effort when they moved to New Orleans. He said that the general public attitude was that all able-bodied men were expected to volunteer for service. Following that perception the gamblers realized they had a real public relations problem on their hands. They finally came up with the idea of a Confederate cavalry unit and named it **Wilson's Rangers**. The local paper described them as "A finer mounted troop of cavalry, we think, can hardly be found anywhere in the South than the Wilson Rangers of this city. From what we have seen of them at drill we judge them to be a valuable support to our army of gulf coast defense."[1]

However, according to Devol, there was more than a gallant ride through the streets of New Orleans on the way to drill for this unit. After riding out of sight of the city, the unit would be halted, dismounted, and "ordered" to hunt for shade and to play cards. Four or five men would group together under the fine shade of a tree and play cards until the cool of the evening. Again, orders were given to cease playing, mount, and ride back to the city. People would come out to cheer them with waving handkerchiefs and present them with bouquets of flowers. This was certainly a fine way to serve their cause and continue their professional careers.

Unfortunately for the gamblers, the unit was ordered to active service in April 1862, when Union forces attacked the city. The Rangers mounted up and rode out with the cheers and well wishes of the citizens ringing in their ears. About six miles outside of the city, Union naval forces began to shell them. They quickly retreated to the city. Upon arrival in New Orleans they dismounted, cut the buttons off their coats, buried their sabers and tried to look like any peaceful citizen overwhelmed by the events taking place. That was the end of a fine play of hand for the gamblers of New Orleans. It was said that the Southern gamblers could not bluff against the full hand held by the Union forces.

The passion of the soldiers and citizens for their cause revealed itself on the battlefield. The extent of the destruction of lives and infrastructure was greater than anything the United States had seen up to that point or since.

THE IMPACT OF THE CIVIL WAR

The overriding impact of the Civil War is that the sectional conflicts were resolved in favor of the North. There would be new problems facing the nation, but slavery and an agrarian-based economy were firmly discredited. In addition, the supremacy of the federal government over the states was established. While the history of the United States prior to the war was defined by the tension between the North and the South, the post–Civil War course of the country went off on a new trajectory largely defined by an industrial-based economy.

The impact on the South was devastating. The loss of life numbered 620,000 soldiers for both the Union and the Confederacy. This is more than all military deaths incurred in all the other wars from the Revolution to the Vietnam War. Although the exact number of civilian deaths is not known, but was significant, too.

In Table 3.1, the significance of these deaths becomes apparent. The South lost 26% of its male population in the middle of its most economically productive years. Keep in mind that America did not utilize fully its human capital because women and African Americans were not allowed to fully participate in the economic or political spheres. The loss of such a large number of white males created a significant handicap for the South.

TABLE 3.1 The Loss of Life in the Civil War.

	North	South
Population	22,000,000	9,000,000 (3.5 million slaves)
Military Age Males	4,000,000	1,000,000
Military Deaths	360,000	260,000
Percentage	9	26

The vast majority of the battles were fought on Southern soil. Railroad tracks, telegraph lines, farms, roads, public buildings, and more were destroyed as a result of battles fought or the predations of the Union Army. Sherman's march from Atlanta to Savannah, then northward through South Carolina and North Carolina wreaked complete devastation on the infrastructure in its path. The South's physical and human capital was laid waste and very little was left with which to rebuild. The need for revenue for the southern states to rebuild infrastructure was acute. Creative ways had to be found to regain a stable economic foothold for the region. This pattern was repeated in the twentieth century and is repeated today as states look for ways to raise revenue without taxing the citizenry.

THE LOUISIANA LOTTERY

Like the other southern states, Louisiana had been the site of many battles. Part of the North's strategy was to take the Mississippi River and cut the Confederacy in half, depriving the eastern half of the beef and other produce of Louisiana and Texas. Baton Rouge was captured twice by the Union army. New Orleans was occupied in 1862. There was considerable destruction of the infrastructure. In order to revitalize its economy, Louisiana desperately needed money to rebuild.

Therefore, in 1868, the legislature passed a bill that authorized a group of businessmen or a syndicate to organize and run a lottery. It was called the **Louisiana Lottery**. In exchange for the profits from the lottery, the syndicate agreed to pay the state of Louisiana $40,000 per year. The license for the lottery ran 25 years and provided the state $1 million, which was a large sum of money in the nineteenth century.

The lottery was similar in format to all lotteries. Tickets were sold for periodic drawings. The tickets were sold nationwide because there were no laws prohibiting it. The population of the United States at the time was approximately 39 million. It is not hard to see what a lucrative business a lottery could be.

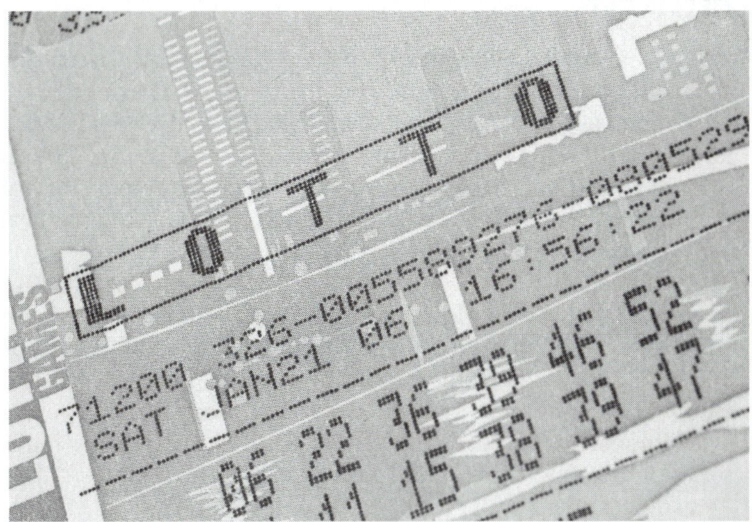

FIGURE 3.1 Lotteries have not changed much since they began. Customers purchase a ticket for a chance at a large prize.

Source: © Robert Lerich. Image from BigStockPhoto.com.

The Louisiana legislature had authorized the lottery during a time when anti-lottery sentiment was mounting. Between 1820 and 1878, corruption became rampant in privately operated lotteries. Some awarded fewer prizes than advertised; others awarded no prizes at all. It was difficult for governments to regulate the lotteries, so prohibition was considered.

Almost as soon as the Louisiana Lottery was authorized, corruption set in. Flush with cash, the syndicate bribed state and federal officials. By 1878, every state except Louisiana had prohibited lotteries either by statute or in their constitutions.

In 1879, the Louisiana legislature voided the lottery charter. However, the syndicate applied pressure and bribed officials. The legislature was reconvened and rescinded the voiding act. The thwarting of the popular will created an uproar in the state. The activity in Louisiana drew the attention of the federal government. In 1890, the Congress passed a law that banned all lottery materials from the U.S. Post Office. This had been the primary way to maintain a nationwide network for the lottery. The ban was a serious blow to the lottery's operations.

In 1892, the Louisiana legislature voted down the renewal of the charter with the syndicate. The syndicate moved the operation of the lottery to Honduras, but retained the name "Louisiana Lottery." However, in 1895 Congress cited **the Interstate Commerce Clause** of the Constitution and prohibited the import of lottery materials. The Louisiana Lottery soon ceased operation. However, the funding of the Louisiana Lottery did provide the war-ravaged state with the needed reconstruction money.

Many people might think that the lottery corruption was a terrible price to pay. That legacy of corruption lives on in recent memory with the conviction of former Governor Edwin Edwards in 2001. He was convicted of accepting bribes in exchange for issuing casino licenses. His reputation for corruption began during his first two terms in the 1970s when he made frequent trips to Harrah's Lake Tahoe.

THE OLD WEST

The territory west of the Mississippi had been attracting American settlers since the turn of the nineteenth century. The Oregon Trail, the Mormon Trail, and the Old Spanish Trail led pioneers to the western lands. Most were headed to the West Coast because the interior was considered too arid and desolate to support farming. The discovery of gold in California in 1848 set off the largest mass movement in the history of North America. As with the Pilgrims and settlers of the East Coast, life was a gamble and the settlers were proficient risk takers of all kinds.

> Following that great gold rush, California soon became a gambler's paradise, since in no other part of the world was gambling carried on more openly or on a larger scale. Far from the restraining Eastern influences of home, family and church, the California pioneers soon found themselves wagering on practically everything in sight . . . this "anything goes" era was under the domination of a series of bosses who maintained complete political control.[2]

Metals needed for the industrializing nation were discovered in other parts of the west. For example, in the 1860s, two Irish gold prospectors found some gold surrounded by a heavy bluish mud. When they took the gold in for assaying, they found that the mud was more valuable. The mud became one of the largest silver strikes in the world, the Comstock Lode. As a result, miners flocked to Virginia City, Nevada, to find their fortune and to gamble their nights away. Discoveries like these spawned similar sudden immigration throughout the second half of the nineteenth century. Boomtowns grew in remote areas of the West.

After the Civil War, there was increased migration to the West. The Civil War disrupted the South's social order and destroyed its infrastructure. Many southerners, both black and white, felt it was easier to start again in a new place than try to rebuild on the old. The Homestead Act of 1862 offered land for free or a very low price to anyone who would farm it. This fueled increased migration to the West by Americans as well as immigrants from Europe.

The **Transcontinental Railroad** was completed in 1869. It was possible to travel from Chicago to San Francisco in a matter of days rather than weeks. A trip from the West Coast to the East Coast did not require a trip around the southern tip of South America. More importantly, goods and produce could be shipped across the nation in a shorter time and at less cost. The availability of railroad service provided incentive to settle the farther reaches of the West.

All of these factors moved people into areas previously unsettled by European Americans. As with the westward movement of the frontier before the Civil War, gambling activity followed. With gambling reforms in the eastern portion of America and men pouring into the mining towns in California, gambling dens opened up to cater to the men who were sure that their luck was great. With the people pouring into California, San Francisco became the new gambling center. Unfortunately, that only lasted until 1855 when reformers won and legal gambling was gradually shut down. By 1860, all the house-banked games were banned in California, leaving poker games as the only legal gambling.

FIGURE 3.2 The Comstock Lode in Virginia City, Nevada contained gold and silver. Its value allowed Nevada to become a state in 1864 and helped the Union win the war.

Source: © Dave Eckenberg. Image from BigStockPhoto.com.

However, because there was no controlling legal authority or the enforcement of laws was so lax, gambling activity thrived.

Gambling was primarily a miner and cowboy phenomenon. It was an informal activity. A saloon would provide tables for patrons to start poker or other card games. The house rarely received money for the gambling, but instead profited from the alcohol consumption that accompanied these games. In 1891, Colorado introduced its first elegant casino, the **Broadmoor Casino Resort**. It was reputed to bring in 15,000 people per day.[3] However, despite the large number of gamblers, the casino did not make its money from gambling because people played against each other, rather than against the house.

Gambling also occurred in the mining camps, on the ranches, or on trail rides. Card games were prevalent in these venues. However, cowboys would also compete and bet on their abilities at the skills required in their jobs. The skills exhibited in today's rodeos were needed by cowboys in the Old West. Calf roping, bull riding, horse taming, and other skills were a regular part of the cowboy's job. They would compete among themselves to see who was the best. Naturally, gambling on the outcome of these contests occurred.

While most of the time this form of gambling was uneventful, it could turn violent. Especially when alcohol was consumed, the results could be bloody and fatal. The history of the Old West is full of stories of gunfights and stabbings over disputes that arose in card games. It was during this time that one of the most colorful female gamblers, **Poker Alice**, played. It was said that she smoked long black cigars and spoke with a distinctive English accent. Like other gamblers, she drank hard, but she never drank when she gambled and she never gambled on Sunday. However, most important, she was known to be a regular winner with a dexterity that rivaled the best.

As the century wore on, the Native Americans were conquered and removed from their lands. The Indian Wars were fought throughout the West, but they came to an end in 1886 when Geronimo, a Chiricahua Apache from Arizona, surrendered. He had been placed on a reservation three times and three times he escaped. He spent his time off-reservation leading raiding parties on American and Mexican citizens. After his final capture, he was placed on the reservation at Fort Sill, Oklahoma, where he stayed until his death in 1909.

European Americans had settled the lower 48 states. By 1900, only Oklahoma, New Mexico, and Arizona were still territories. By 1912, they would become part of the country. With the closing of the frontier, gambling became an increasingly important issue.

THE PROGRESSIVE ERA

The last half of the nineteenth century and the early decades of the twentieth century are called **the Progressive Era**. Due to the changes in the American economy, in the size and composition of the population, and in the concentration of the population in different areas of the country, there was popular agitation for government to tackle social and economic problems.

The American economy was already industrializing in the Northern states prior to the Civil War. With its higher degree of industrialization, the North's victory over the South proved the superiority of an industrial economy over an agrarian economy. The country as a whole embraced industrialization.

With the spread of the railroads, a national market emerged. Businesses could sell their products from coast to coast. With an expanded market came the opportunity for

FIGURE 3.3 Once trains spanned the country, the economy quickly industrialized.

Source: © Andrew Lundquist. Image from BigStockPhoto.com.

economies of scale. Major companies could reduce their costs per unit and charge lower prices than smaller local firms could.

The smaller firms would go out of business or be acquired by the larger companies. Frequently, a company would acquire or start businesses that provided it with products or through which it sold to consumers and other businesses. Called vertical integration, this led to monopolies or oligopolies. Competition was limited and prices could be set arbitrarily. Economic abuse attracted the attention of reformers.

The population of the country exploded from 40 million in 1870 to 100 million in 1916. Almost half or 25 million of the increase was due to immigration, mostly from Europe. The immigrants typically concentrated in large urban areas. New York, Chicago, Boston, Philadelphia, and similar cities were magnets for them. Slums with tenements developed in these cities where overcrowding and unhealthy conditions were the rule.

The influx of immigrants to the cities as well as the movement of Americans from the farms to the cities in search of jobs led to a shift in the concentration of population. While only 25% of the American population lived in an urban area in 1870, nearly 50% did in 1916. America had become an industrialized urban nation in less than two generations. Reformers also tackled the horrific social conditions of the cities.

It was during the Progressive Era that referendums were introduced as a method for legislative action. Referendums placed a proposition before the public for a vote. The spread of suffrage beyond white landowners at the founding of the United States to nearly all white males by the turn of the twentieth century led to a belief that citizens should participate more fully. Through referendums, the voters could bypass vested interests and tell the legislatures what laws to pass. Reformers used referendums to advance their causes. It was just such a referendum that legalized casino gaming in New Jersey in 1976.

It was during these changes in America, that a new form of gambling appeared in San Francisco. In 1887, **Charles Fey** created a three-reel Liberty Bell that accepted nickels

FIGURE 3.4 The original slot machines were very simple and intended to be an amusement game.

Source: © James Cottingham. Image from BigStockPhoto.com.

and with the pull of a handle, novelties could be won. Conversion to monetary payoffs occurred later.

However, it was really **Herbert Mills** who made the slot machine popular. He owned the Mills Novelty Company of Chicago, which already had a nationwide presence, and when the slot machines were added to his line, sales took off. He was known as the Henry Ford of slot machines because he incorporated mass production techniques to building slot machines. His salesmen covered the country selling inexpensive slot machines.

In the beginning people had to stand while playing. However, in New York City, so the story goes, a young boy wanted to put his nickel into the machine, but could not reach high enough. Realizing that the store was losing money because of this problem, the owner put a stool in front of the machine so that young children could play (this was before there were laws about the minimum age for gambling). Since this also improved the comfort and length of time that people could play, the stools became a major piece of equipment. These innovations and his sales force convinced Mills he had a certain winner on his hands, and so, he paid for extensive advertising and mail order catalogs. In fact, slot machines became so popular that they are thought to have created such common phrases as "It's a lemon" when referring to bad products and "jackpot" when discussing big wins.

Gambling was a popular activity across America at the turn of the century.[4] In 1902, the Old Saratoga Club House in Saratoga Springs, New York, was purchased by a very famous gambler, Richard A. Canfield. He renamed it the Monte Carlo of America. In 1904, the first totally dedicated ship for gambling was launched on Lake Michigan. The city of Traverse was built by a famous gambler, Big Jim O'Leary. There were many different forms of gambling that were introduced during this time.

Part of the focus of reformers in the Progressive Era was on gambling. By 1895, all lotteries, including the Louisiana Lottery, were outlawed. In fact, all forms of gambling were prohibited or severely restricted in all states by the turn of the twentieth century.

In 1911, Nevada joined the nation and banned gambling. With the closing of the frontier and more effective law enforcement in sparsely populated areas of the country, the ban was effective nationwide.

However, gambling activity did not cease. Due to its illegality, gambling was offered through organized crime groups. Located in urban areas, these groups offered gambling in a variety of venues depending upon the gambling activity. Betting on horses or numbers did not require a fixed facility or location. Gambling that required equipment such as a table or slot machine had to be operated in a facility. Ostensibly, legitimate entertainment clubs were opened, but offered gambling to a select clientele to avoid detection by the police.

The **Eighteenth Amendment to the Constitution** banned the sale, manufacture, or import of alcoholic beverages. The amendment was another product of the Progressive Era. A movement to limit or ban alcohol had been prominent in America since the early days of the country. When the amendment went into effect in 1920, there was another reason to go to the clubs. The organized crime groups found tremendous profits in providing alcohol and gambling to the consuming public.

Naturally, corruption followed gambling. Police and judges were bribed so that the gambling activity could continue. Raids were staged as a way to deceive the public into thinking something was being done. The organized crime groups became wealthy from the profits they made. There were frequent violent turf wars between groups resulting in deaths. Clearly, banning gambling did not eliminate it. And the negative side effects of banning it were undesirable.

THE GREAT DEPRESSION

In October 1929, the stock market crashed. The value of stocks lost $8 billion in just one day. This triggered an economic crisis that grew into the Great Depression. The economic distress of the 1930s cannot be exaggerated. Gross National Product contracted by 34% between 1929 and 1932. Today, a decline between 2% and 4% is considered a severe recession.

Unemployment stood between 25% and 33%. The exact figure is not known because economic data were not tracked in detail. However, it is estimated that 6 million were out of work in 1930 and 12 million in 1932. Unemployment increased because factories and mines reduced production or shut down. In the face of reduced demand, other employers cut back. Farmers lost their farms to foreclosures and were thrown out of work.

Bank failures numbered 5,741 between 1929 and 1932. Depositors lost their money when a bank closed because there was no federal insurance. This prevented people from making loan payments or drawing on their savings for living expenses when unemployed, which further fed the crisis. Nearly every sphere of economic life was distressed.

Economic calamity put stress on governments, too. Reduced economic activity suppressed tax revenues just when the government was called on to assist the public. There was an outcry for action.

It was in the context of the Great Depression that Nevada legalized gambling in 1931. Nevada was merely recognizing what was already occurring in the saloons of the many small towns in the state. Rather than suppress gambling, the state sought to generate tax revenue and to create jobs.

At the same time that they legalized gambling, the legislature liberalized the marriage laws and the residency period for divorce. The legislature also legalized local option for

FIGURE 3.5a and b Farms were abandoned and people faced life-threatening conditions during the Great Depression.

Source: Copyright © 2008 Steve Durham. Permission is granted to copy, distribute and/or modify the following photos under the terms of the GNU Free Documentation License, Version 1.2 or any later version published by the Free Software Foundation; with no Invariant Sections, no Front-Cover Texts, and no Back-Cover Texts. A copy of the license is included in the section entitled "GNU Free Documentation License".

prostitution. Each county could decide whether to allow prostitution within its borders. As a result, Reno, the largest city in Nevada at the time, became a tourist mecca.

When Nevada legalized gambling, it left regulation in the hands of the country sheriff. This may sound naïve today, but at the time casinos consisted primarily of a few slot machines and a blackjack or craps table in the back of a saloon. The saloon owner was known to the community and most customers were local residents. No one anticipated the rise of Las Vegas as the epicenter of worldwide gaming.

LAS VEGAS

The city of Las Vegas was founded in 1905. It was a Mormon outpost in the Mohave Desert. The train ran through the Las Vegas valley and acted as a lifeline for the community.

Las Vegas would remain a dusty sleepy town until the construction of **Hoover Dam** between 1930 and 1935. The dam was designed to retain water for use by the lower Colorado River states, generate electricity, and enhance flood control. It was an engineering marvel at the time and was the highest dam in the world when completed. The dam contains more masonry than the Great Pyramid at Giza. Its remote location made this accomplishment all the more impressive.

The influx of 16,000 men and women over the construction period provided economic activity for Las Vegas. All business benefited, including the saloons with their gambling. Even after the dam opened in 1935, many of the men and women decided to stay. Employment opportunities elsewhere were still limited due to the Great Depression.

Conclusion

America changed drastically between the Civil War and the Great Depression. A rural population became an urban population. An industrial economy took hold and made America a world power. The federal government became more actively involved in the economy through regulations and infrastructure projects like the Hoover Dam.

America's social policies changed, too. The Progressive Era ushered in a belief that government could and should actively manage national life so that progress toward an ideal state could be achieved. Alcohol was banned with the eighteenth amendment, but that was repealed in 1933 when it was obvious that the ban had failed. Gambling remained prohibited except by Nevada at the end of the 1930s despite the evidence that gambling still existed and thrived illegally.

The stage was set for the future. Nevada's experiment in legalized gaming began as an effort to generate tax revenue and to create jobs. It would lead to the creation of a model for legalized, regulated gaming that possessed the integrity to gain widespread acceptance among the American public.

Key Words

George Devol *27*
Wilson's Rangers *27*
Louisiana Lottery *29*
The Interstate Commerce Clause *30*
Transcontinental Railroad *31*
Broadmoor Casino Resort *32*
Poker Alice *32*
The Progressive Era *32*
Charles Fey *33*
Herbert Mills *34*
The Eighteenth Amendment to the Constitution *35*
Hoover Dam *36*

Review Questions

1. Explain the functioning of gambling at the start of the Civil War.
2. Detail the role of Wilson's Rangers in the Civil War.
3. Discuss the impact of the Civil War on gambling in the South.
4. Discuss the history of the Louisiana Lottery and its effects on gambling.
5. Detail the history of the "Old West" frontier and its effects on gambling.
6. Explain the effects of the Progressive Era on gambling.
7. Explain the effects of the Great Depression on gambling.
8. Discuss the beginnings of Las Vegas and its early role in the history of gambling.

Endnotes

1. Devol, G. (1996). *Forty Years a Gambler on the Mississippi River.* Carlisle, MA: Applewood Books, 116.
2. Fey, M. (1994). *Slot Machines*. Reno, NV: Liberty Belle Books, 13.
3. Thompson, W. N. (2001). *Gambling in America.* Santa Barbara, CA: ABC-CLIO, 12.
4. Hashimoto, K., Kline, S. F., & Fenich, G. G. (1996). *Casino Management: Past, Present, Future.* Dubuque, IA: Kendall-Hunt Publishing, 29.

CHAPTER 4

THE MODERN ERA—NEVADA

STEVE DURHAM

Learning Objectives

1. To learn about the shifting of gambling from Reno to Las Vegas
2. To learn about the role of Bugsy Siegel in the history of Las Vegas and gambling
3. To understand the factors leading to and the importance of Nevada's legalization of gambling
4. To learn the details of the rise of organized crime in Las Vegas
5. To understand the beginnings and roles of the Nevada Gaming Control Board
6. To learn the details of the casinos' response to the beginning of government regulations
7. To learn the details and significance of the rise of theme resorts in Las Vegas
8. To understand the extent of the revitalization of the casino industry in the 1970s

Chapter Outline

NOTE FROM THE AUTHOR

In 1980, the author enrolled in a master of business administration program at an eastern university. At that point, he had worked for three years at Harrah's Reno as a financial analyst. Prior to that, during his college years, he had worked in the summers in food and beverage at Harrah's. He was intrigued by the casino business and had decided to make it his life's work.

When he introduced himself to his classmates and professors, inevitably someone would ask if he worked with Italian-surnamed mobsters. He resented this line of questioning because it implied the lack of legitimacy of casino gaming. It totally ignored the strict regulatory environment in Nevada and the approaching success of completely eliminating organized crime from Las Vegas. At the same time, it provided a certain personal mystique. He could claim to be an insider of the industry from where he could set the story straight.

In reality, he worked with one Italian American. His name was Rome Andreotti. Andreotti was the executive vice president of gaming. He had worked with Bill Harrah in the early days and gained his trust and worked his way up the organization. Andreotti was in the military during World War II and saw action in Europe. Contrary to the stereotype, he stood 6 feet tall and spoke perfect English. His standards for integrity and honesty were rigid and unbending. He held himself and his subordinates to his standards. There was nothing the least disreputable about him.

When asked about mafia influence, the author originally spoke at length about Andreotti and the overall integrity of the industry. However, the explanation fell on deaf ears. People wanted to believe the myth of mob rule. The explanation became shorter and shorter until the author merely gave a disapproving look and simply said, "No."

People still believe the mafia is somehow involved in Las Vegas. It is no wonder the ad campaign "What happens in Vegas, stays in Vegas" resonates with the American public.

INTRODUCTION

When the state of Nevada legalized casino gambling in 1931, it was an attempt at economic development. The hope was that jobs would be created and a source of tax revenue generated. There was no vision that the state would become an exemplar of regulated gaming activity. The initial legislation established the **Nevada Gaming Commission**. The purpose of this body was to address issues facing gaming activity in the state as they arose.

The primary responsibility for regulating gaming activity fell to the county sheriff. While this seems naïve today, it was more than adequate for the first 15 years of legalized gaming in Nevada. Casino operators were local residents. In the smaller towns, a casino was really just a couple slot machines and tables in a saloon. In Reno, the largest city in the state, casinos lined Virginia Street from the Truckee River north to the railroad tracks. However, these were modest affairs. Again, the bar featured prominently. However, there were a greater number of slot machines and table games. Bingo and keno were offered as well.

THE SHIFT FROM RENO TO LAS VEGAS

In the early days of Nevada, Reno was a tourist destination because it was better situated than any other Nevada city. San Francisco and the Bay area are only 200 miles away. In the days before air conditioning, the climate was more hospitable than the climate of southern Nevada. In addition, Lake Tahoe had been a summer vacation spot for many years.

However, the center of tourism activity started to shift in the 1940s. As mentioned in Chapter 3, the construction of Hoover Dam brought an influx of workers and their families. Many stayed on after the completion of the dam because there were jobs and economic opportunity. The construction of the dam also had led to the building of infrastructure, especially roads. What had been a dusty way station on a railroad was now a full-fledged town.

In 1941, the **El Rancho Vegas** opened on what would later become The Strip. It was located on Sahara Avenue. A central building held the casino, restaurants, and other public spaces. Wings off the central building contained 65 motel rooms. There were surface parking lots to accommodate the cars of locals as well as visitors from southern California.

The Last Frontier opened in 1942, just south of the El Rancho Vegas. It was a Wild West–themed casino resort, which included the standard casino, motel rooms, restaurants, and so on. However, it also featured a western town recreated to resemble a "typical" town from the Wild West era, roughly 1860–1900. The town included a museum, retail shops, jail, saloon, post office, and train cars. It certainly evoked the era.

Both resorts were located over two miles from downtown Las Vegas. At that time, Las Vegas consisted of only the downtown business/casino district and residential neighborhoods surrounding it. There was open desert between downtown and the two casino resorts.

This was a considerable distance. Cars were only beginning their rise to be the preeminent form of transportation. The American mentality was still oriented toward walking and other slower means of travel such as bicycles, horses, and public transportation. The general perception was that these resorts were taking a huge risk. Why would people drive to visit just one casino when they could park downtown and visit numerous casinos on foot?

FIGURE 4.1 There was nothing but desert surrounding Las Vegas when the El Rancho and the Last Frontier opened more than two miles from downtown.

Source: Copyright © 2008 Steve Durham. Permission is granted to copy, distribute and/or modify the following photos under the terms of the GNU Free Documentation License, Version 1.2 or any later version published by the Free Software Foundation; with no Invariant Sections, no Front-Cover Texts, and no Back-Cover Texts. A copy of the license is included in the section entitled "GNU Free Documentation License".

The El Rancho Vegas and the Last Frontier were commercially successful. The possibility that location on an isolated patch of land was not a handicap to success opened the eyes of budding entrepreneurs. **Billy Wilkerson** from southern California felt he could build a luxurious casino on The Strip along the lines of the Beverly Hills Hotel whose target market was the wealthy elite of Los Angeles. He envisioned a hotel that was elegant and exclusive and positioned well above what Las Vegas had to offer.

BUGSY SIEGEL AND THE RISE OF LAS VEGAS

However, his personal capital was inadequate and he could not fully fund the project. He turned to Benjamin **"Bugsy" Siegel** for funding. Siegel was a member of an organized crime outfit in New York. He was known for his violent temper and womanizing. Through his involvement in numerous illegal activities in New York including gambling and bootlegging, he became a significant member of his outfit.

He was assigned the task of going to Los Angeles to oversee some small gambling operations and other illegal activities shared with a local organized crime group. He quickly took over the outfit. He also acquired a girlfriend by the name of Virginia Hill, an actress with the nickname of "The Flamingo."

When Wilkerson came to Siegel, the latter fronted for other investors, primarily his organized crime outfit, which included Meyer Lansky. He soon pushed Wilkerson out of the project and brought in The Del Webb Company, an up-and-coming construction and development company based in Phoenix, Arizona. He became intimately involved in the design and construction of the casino resort. He worked from his knowledge of gambling operations in New York and Los Angeles. He also observed what worked for the El Rancho Vegas and the Last Frontier.

However, he took Wilkerson's concept of luxury and elegance even further. He wanted nothing but the best and envisioned bringing the glamour of Hollywood to the desert. The cost for the project originally was estimated at $1 million, an extraordinary sum in the 1940s. Due to changing and often erratic demands on Siegel's part as well other factors, the cost ballooned. The exact cost is not known, but estimates range from $3 million to $7 million.

The Flamingo opened on December 26, 1946. By all accounts, it was a disaster. The weather was rainy and cold. Although the top movie stars of the day were invited, only secondary celebrities attended. The motel rooms were not ready for occupancy. Casino guests gambled, but stayed elsewhere. To make things worse, the inexperienced dealers made many mistakes and the gamblers won. Since they could not stay at **the Flamingo**, they went to the El Rancho Vegas and Last Frontier where they gambled their winnings away. The casino lost money.

The casino soon closed its doors in order to complete construction. Reopening in March 1947, the Flamingo quickly became profitable. However, Siegel was murdered in June 1947. The murderers have never been identified nor their motive. Legend has it that Siegel's crime outfit ordered his death due to the cost overruns and alleged skimming by him and Virginia Hill. It is equally possible that an enemy from his past ended his life. He antagonized many people in his crime career, people who might have wanted to seek his death. Some have even speculated that other Nevada casino operators recognized that Siegel's reputation and behavior might attract greater law enforcement. This might have been motivation enough to have Siegel killed.

FIGURE 4.2 The Flamingo today is owned by Harrah's and may soon be demolished to create a megaresort on the corner of Las Vegas Boulevard and Flamingo Road.

The mythology surrounding Benjamin "Bugsy" Siegal is legendary. His reputation has been immortalized in books and in movies. He is credited as being the first to envision the completely self-contained casino resort on The Strip. He is also credited with conceptualizing a luxurious casino resort with a Hollywood connection. As mentioned previously, the El Rancho Vegas and the Last Frontier were ahead of Siegel by five years in building self-contained casino resorts on The Strip. The idea of building a luxurious casino resort with a direct Hollywood connection came to Billy Wilkerson first. Siegel took his idea and made it a reality; but only after creating exorbitant cost overruns and displaying inept management skills.

While it is clear Bugsy Siegel does not deserve credit for creating the modern casino resort, he was part of a wave of criminal underworld influence in Las Vegas. While this created headaches for the state of Nevada, it resulted in the model regulatory environment for government-sanctioned gaming.

ORGANIZED CRIME AND LAS VEGAS

Through the late 1940s and 1950s, organized crime groups from throughout the nation invested in Las Vegas casinos. They gravitated to Las Vegas because gambling operations in other parts of the country were being shut down or severely restricted by the legal authorities.

In 1950, **Estes Kefauver**, a U.S. Senator from Tennessee, chaired the Special Committee to Investigate Organized Crime in Interstate Commerce. The Committee existed from May 1950 to May 1951. The Committee held hearings in Washington, D.C., Las Vegas, New York City, Chicago, and Los Angeles among other cities.

Senator Kefauver was convinced that a single crime group ran all gambling operations throughout the nation. He used the Committee to establish this fact. In reality, the organized crime elements were not cohesive. In fact, they were in competition with each other. And despite popular perception, organized crime was not efficiently run. The instability of relationships that accrues when individuals are in association outside established social norms was apparent in these organized crime groups.

Regardless of the reality of organized crime, their pursuit of illegal gambling operations in the major cities of the country became the focus of law enforcement. It became increasingly difficult to provide gambling activities. As a result, these underworld figures moved their money and expertise to Nevada. Frequently, they also moved to Las Vegas.

Typically, they invested in groups called syndicates. They pooled their money and provided the funding to build or expand the casinos. Not all casinos were involved with criminal syndicates. However, the well-known Strip casinos had funding from these sources.

Casinos used this source of funding because traditional sources were not willing to make loans or investments. The risk of casinos was twofold. First, the control of the cash and cash equivalents in order to avoid theft and embezzlement was a daunting task. In addition, a bad run of luck could have a substantial impact on profit. There were other industries with less operational risk. The second source of risk was the viability of the industry. Gambling had only been legal since 1931. And the pressure exerted by the publicity of the Kefauver Committee was tremendous. There was no guarantee that gambling would remain legal. To invest or loan millions for a building which might sit without purpose a couple years hence was an unacceptable risk.

In addition, the cost to build a casino which could compete with the existing casinos had risen considerably since Bugsy Siegel's extravagant spending on the Flamingo. Crime syndicates were finding it increasingly difficult to invest and individuals rarely had adequate resources. It was becoming clear that other legitimate sources had to be found because the popularity of Las Vegas as a destination was increasing. By 1956, there were 9,000 rooms in southern Nevada. The Sahara, Sands, Dunes, and Riviera were added to The Strip. Several had expanded and hotel rooms in high-rise towers were added to the motel rooms of the previous decade.

(a)

(b)

FIGURE 4.3a and b The Sahara and the Riviera today are second-rate properties because they could not keep up with the change in the market.

Source: Copyright © 2008 Steve Durham. Permission is granted to copy, distribute and/or modify the following photos under the terms of the GNU Free Documentation License, Version 1.2 or any later version published by the Free Software Foundation; with no Invariant Sections, no Front-Cover Texts, and no Back-Cover Texts. A copy of the license is included in the section entitled "GNU Free Documentation License".

The Nevada law legalizing casino gaming came from an era where individuals owned and operated casinos. There was no provision for licensing corporations or investor groups known as **syndicates**. Consequently, members of organized crime groups would find a front man for their syndicate of investors who could qualify for a gaming license. The members of the syndicate would not be subject to licensing because they were not involved in the day-to-day operation. At least, that was the impression given on paper.

In reality, they were involved to varying degrees. Regardless of any other involvement, they all skimmed money from the operations. Money skimming is achieved by removing cash from the accounting cycle before it is counted. Essentially, the drop was counted after an amount was diverted to the pockets of the syndicate. For example, if the drop was $100,000, maybe $10,000 was diverted to the organized crime investors and $90,000 was reported as drop.

This was significant to the state because the gaming tax was levied on revenue, not profit. If the casinos were reporting less in drop, they were reporting less in hold. *Hold* is revenue for public reporting purposes. Hence, reported revenue was less than actual revenue and the state was losing tax revenue correspondingly.

Kefauver created an incentive for more active regulation by the state. The perception created by the Kefauver Committee generated the real possibility that the federal government would act to make gaming illegal nationwide. Since gaming was an integral and significant part of the Nevada economy, the state needed to establish and maintain the integrity of the industry.

NEVADA GAMING CONTROL BOARD

The original legislation legalizing casino gambling assigned the chief responsibility for gaming regulation and control to the Tax Commission. In reality, the counties executed these responsibilities in the beginning of legalized casino gaming. The Tax Commission assumed these duties in 1945, but they were not equipped to provide the oversight necessary. The volume of the Las Vegas casinos was beyond anyone's imagination.

In 1955, **the Nevada Gaming Control Board** was created within the Tax Commission. The Nevada Gaming Control Board was charged with the responsibility of removing undesirable individuals from the ownership and operation of casinos as well as to establish the standards of licensing and regulation. It was to focus on enforcement. The Gaming Control Board wields tremendous power. Its most significant powers are its ability to deny or revoke a license and to close a casino. These powers have been upheld in courts all the way to the Supreme Court. Without these powers, it would be difficult for the state of Nevada to maintain the integrity of legal gaming.

Four years later, the Nevada Gaming Commission was created. It assumed the licensing and taxing function. The Nevada Gaming Control Board became subordinate to the Nevada Gaming Commission. The Board continued to focus on investigation and enforcement, while the Commission set policy. The elimination of the undesirable element in Nevada gaming was a gradual process. It would be the 1980s before the last scandal surrounding organized crime involvement in Las Vegas casinos occurred. Other changes were evolving at the same time Nevada sought to eliminate the undesirable element in legal gaming.

In 1967, the gaming laws were revised to allow licensing of corporations to invest and to operate casinos. Instead of licensing individual owners, anyone felt to have influence on the day-to-day operation was considered a licensee. Key management personnel and significant shareholders were required to submit to the licensing process.

The change in the law drew more investment funding to Nevada. By this time, the casino industry was firmly established. Nevada had moved into a more activist stance in order to protect its most important form of economic activity and source of tax revenue. Investors and the public in general began to view the casinos less and less as an experiment. Casinos were perceived as an ongoing business that would not be ruled illegal.

At the same time, the casinos were becoming more professionally managed. The state wanted to ensure that the proper amount in taxes was paid and that the integrity of the industry was maintained. The skimming of revenue had to end. In order to comply with the state's requirements, casinos had to develop detailed procedures that had to be approved by the state. Special attention was paid to procedures involving cash and cash equivalents. As you can imagine, most procedures involved cash and cash equivalents.

THE CASINO RESPONSE TO REGULATIONS

The casinos gladly complied with this intrusion by government into their operations. They recognized that it was in their self-interest to maintain a high level of integrity in the industry. A major scandal, especially one involving cheating of customers, would destroy the confidence of customers. After all, no one will gamble in a casino where they feel the house will cheat them.

With the increased participation of corporations in legalized gaming, there were additional pressures to improve the industry's integrity. Publicly traded companies must answer to their shareholders and other governmental agencies. The most important agency is the **Securities and Exchange Commission**, which regulates the stock markets to ensure their integrity.

Public corporations are scrutinized by both the state and the federal government. This applied more pressure to ensure the honesty of the casino operators. Corporate managers were not going to do anything to destroy shareholder value. Since they often were shareholders of company stock, it was in their best interest to maintain a clean operation.

An additional impact of allowing corporations to be licensed and operate casinos was the opportunity for privately held casinos to go public. The individually owned casinos represented a great deal of wealth to the owners. Many who started in the business in the 1930s and 1940s were aging in the 1960s. They were looking for ways to exit the industry. Making a public offering on the stock exchanges allowed an owner to extract value from his business.

In 1971, William Harrah, who founded Harrah's in Reno, Nevada, in 1937, went public on the New York Stock Exchange. He had a reputation for requiring meticulous bookkeeping at his casinos. In fact, the Nevada Gaming Control Board utilized his procedures as a template for approving the procedures submitted by other casinos. His personal integrity as well as the integrity of his gaming operations were above reproach. Consequently, the public's confidence in his stock offering was very high. Harrah's was the first strictly casino company to be listed on the New York Stock Exchange.

As the integrity of the industry improved and more and more corporations, banks, and other more traditional sources invested in Las Vegas, the public perception of gaming evolved. Gradually, people lost the impression that organized crime operated the casinos. More and more, legal gambling is viewed as just another entertainment choice.

THE RISE OF THEME RESORTS

Something else happened in the 1960s. The evolution of the casino resort continued. The basic formula established by the El Rancho Vegas and the Last Frontier was expanded upon, but not refined for 20 years. Then in 1966, Caesar's Palace opened.

The shift in the industry was startling. **Caesars Palace** was the first comprehensively themed casino. Previous attempts at themes had been halfhearted at best. Superficial touches were used to evoke a time or place. Caesars went all out to create an ancient Roman ambience. Everything from the design of the building and entry driveway to the uniforms to the gaming chips to the choice of restaurant names and menu items was tied to the theme. Italian marble was imported. Fountains were placed around the property. Italian cypress trees were used in the landscaping.

Caesars also was the first casino to incorporate a convention center into its design. The convention business had been developing since the mid-1950s. The casinos recognized that the vacation and weekend trade was not enough to fill their hotel rooms or keep their casinos busy 24/7. They turned to conventions.

Conventions provided large numbers of people with known arrival and departure dates. Meetings were held during the day, which left the evenings open for gambling. The casinos could negotiate room rates, food and beverage service, and other convention necessities knowing the gambling hold would cover any losses. Once the individual casinos

FIGURE 4.4 Caesars Palace carried the theme into the details of their cards and chips.

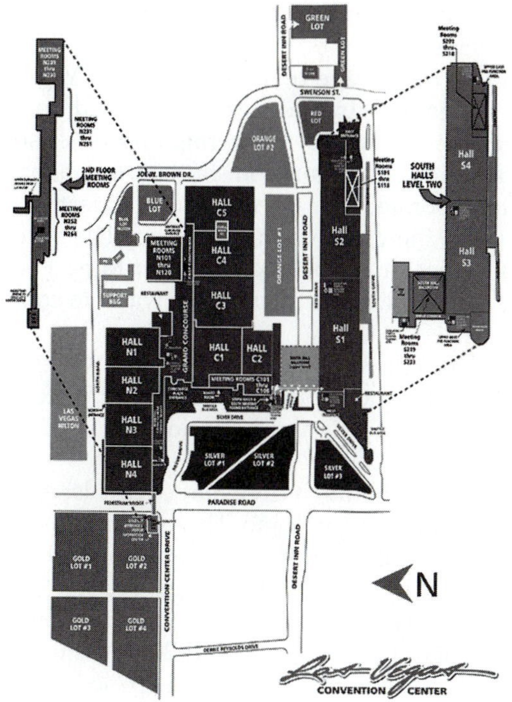

FIGURE 4.5 The Las Vegas Convention Center has grown to over three million square feet. It is one of the largest such facilities in the world.

Source: Provided by the Las Vegas Convention & Vistiors Authority.

realized this source of business, they added convention space to their facilities. Through the 1950s and 1960s, each casino resort built meeting space and expanded it when business demanded it. However, these additions looked and felt like additions. By incorporating convention space into its design, Caesars Palace created a seamless flow from casino to hotel room to meeting to restaurant. The new standard for Strip resorts was set.

The Las Vegas Convention Center was opened in 1959 to encourage convention business for the entire city. This was a municipally owned and operated entity, which drew conventions larger than could be hosted by an individual property. The Convention Center has expanded numerous times over the past 60 years. It now offers 3.2 million square feet covering 16 exhibit halls, 144 meeting rooms, and a lobby and concourse. Some of the largest conventions in the world meet there.

REVITALIZATION IN THE 1970S

By the 1970s, casinos in Las Vegas had outdistanced the casinos in the rest of the state. Las Vegas had become the epicenter of gaming in Nevada and by default in America. But the 1970s were also a time of consolidation and evolution. More and more corporations took control of the casinos and built the new casinos. Management became more professional. Organized crime continued to be driven from Las Vegas. These legitimizing forces made gambling, and a trip to Las Vegas in particular, more acceptable to the American public.

It was also during the 1970s that legal gaming spread outside Nevada. New Jersey voters approved a referendum in 1976 to allow casinos in Atlantic City. The activity surrounding this new jurisdiction distracted operators from Las Vegas as they prepared to take advantage of the opportunity. Their attention and capital spending were effectively diverted to Atlantic City until the mid-1980s.

The 1989 opening of Steve Wynn's **The Mirage** revitalized the Las Vegas market. Wynn took the concept of creating a theme to a dramatic extreme. Based on a tropical theme, he incorporated plants throughout the casino. Carpeting and other soft goods reflected the tropics through patterns and designs. Plantation shutters, bamboo furniture, and other totems of tropical life were incorporated into the furnishings. Most spectacularly, he built an erupting volcano between the casino and The Strip. The volcano was realistically designed. It was generally conical in shape and appeared to be a South Seas island complete with vegetation on its sides. It was surrounded by water to complete the island look.

The volcanic effects were achieved by releasing natural gas underwater. As it rose swiftly to the surface, it erupted from the water and exploded into flame. Pyrotechnics and flames shot from the summit of the volcano. The roar and explosion of gas was heard up and down The Strip.

Erupting periodically during the evening hours, it drew large crowds. A trip to Las Vegas was not complete without seeing the erupting volcano. The volcano was a gimmick to create awareness in the public's mind. It was also a draw to bring people into the casino. Once they watched the volcano erupt, people would visit the casino.

Through the 1990s and the early twenty-first century, the construction of super-themed casinos was nothing but spectacular. Between 1989 and 2001, casinos based on Paris, New York, a medieval castle, Egyptian pyramids, and Arabia opened, among many others. The detail to which the casinos went to recreate their targeted theme was without precedence. The Paris required its telephone operators to greet guests with the phrase, "Bonjour." The floor and retail area of the New York-New York are faux cobblestones. The interior of the Luxor is a pyramid-shaped atrium with elevators moving diagonally along the ceiling to the different floors of the hotel. Every effort was made to transport the customer to another place or time.

FIGURE 4.6 Steve Wynn hit upon the idea to build an erupting volcano on the Strip to lure people into his new casino, The Mirage.

While Las Vegas reestablished its status as epicenter of the gaming industry, legalized gaming expanded across the country and the globe. The legalization of casino riverboats on the Mississippi River and Ohio River, land-based casinos in the middle section of the country, and casinos on Native American reservations in the late 1980s and 1990s spread gaming across the country. In the 1970s, 10% of the population was within a four-hour drive of a casino. Today, 90% of Americans are within a four-hour drive. That is a phenomenal reversal given the short time frame.

The expansion of gaming presented an opportunity for casino companies to grow. They started expanding in the 1970s when the Atlantic City market opened. As each new jurisdiction legalized gaming, the casino operators found more opportunity. Today there are Harrah's in 11 states. The Sands Macao cracked the international market for American gaming companies in 2004.

The expansion of casino companies generated economies of scale and expertise. The sophistication of today's casino company is light years ahead of that of the individual owners of the 1950s and 1960s. This expansion also led to a consolidation of the industry. Larger companies acquired smaller companies. Today, only a handful of companies are represented on The Strip. Harrah's Entertainment owns Harrah's, Caesars, Paris, Bally's, and Rio Suites. MGM/Mirage offers the MGM Grand, New York-New York, Monte Carlo, Bellagio, The Mirage, TI, Circus Circus, Mandalay Bay, Luxor, and Excalibur.

Conclusion

Nevada gaming has come a long way. What started as an effort to develop the economy and generate tax revenue during the Great Depression has transformed into a multibillion-dollar industry that extends well beyond Nevada's borders. The dusty gambling halls of Nevada have become themed megaresorts on The Strip.

Along the way, the state stepped up to each new challenge. To ensure the integrity of the industry and its survival, regulatory oversight was improved and tightened. Laws were rewritten to adapt to the new reality.

In the process, the image of Nevada's premier industry among the public has turned around. Whereas gaming suffered a black eye from the Kefauver Committee in 1950 and 1951, today it is considered just another option for Americans' entertainment dollar. No other industry can claim to having gone from social pariah to mainstream acceptance except, possibly, the alcoholic beverage industry. But then, it is no coincidence that alcohol is an integral part of the casino experience.

Key Words

Nevada Gaming Commission *39*
El Rancho Vegas *40*
Billy Wilkerson *41*
Bugsy Siegel *41*
The Flamingo *41*
Estes Kefauver *42*
Syndicates *44*
The Nevada Gaming Control Board *44*
Securities and Exchange Commission *45*
Caesars Palace *46*
The Las Vegas Convention Center *47*
The Mirage *48*

Review Questions

1. Describe the history and effects of the shift of gambling from Reno to Las Vegas.
2. Detail the role of Bugsy Siegel in the history of Las Vegas and gambling.
3. Describe the factors leading to and the importance of Nevada's legalization of gambling.
4. Detail and explain the rise of organized crime in Las Vegas.
5. Describe the beginnings and roles of the Nevada Gaming Control Board.
6. Detail the casinos' response to the beginning of government regulations.
7. Tell of the details and significance of the rise of theme resorts in Las Vegas.
8. Discuss the extent of the revitalization of the casino industry in the 1970s.

CHAPTER 5

MODERN ERA—NEW JERSEY

DANIEL HENEGHAN

Learning Objectives

1. To learn about the history of Atlantic City prior to the legalization of gambling
2. To learn the detailed history of the referendum that legalized gambling in Atlantic City
3. To learn the details of the development of Resorts International and Caesars in Atlantic City
4. To learn the details of the development of Bally and Brighton/Sands in Atlantic City
5. To learn the details of the development of Harrah's in Atlantic City
6. To learn the details of the development of the Golden Nugget/Grand Hilton and Playboy/Atlantis in Atlantic City
7. To learn the details of the development of Claridge and Tropicana in Atlantic City
8. To learn the details of the development of Trump Plaza, Trump Marina, and Trump Taj Mahal
9. To understand the details of the development of Showboat and Borgata in Atlantic City
10. To understand the evolution of regulations in Atlantic City
11. To learn about the later regulations applied to Atlantic City casinos

Chapter Outline

- Trump Marina
- Showboat
- Trump Taj Mahal
- Borgata
- Evolution of Regulation
- Later Regulations
- Conclusion

INTRODUCTION

After Las Vegas, **Atlantic City** is the second largest gaming market in the United States. The seashore resort has a dozen enormous casino hotel complexes that have transformed a once-dying resort into a thriving resort destination that attracts more than 35 million visitors a year and generates more than $5 billion in gaming revenue.

To understand why the people of New Jersey approved casinos for Atlantic City, this chapter will describe the history of Atlantic City. After that, it will detail the development of the city's 12 gaming halls as well as the evolution of the New Jersey Casino Control Act and the state's philosophy toward gaming.

HISTORY OF ATLANTIC CITY

Atlantic City was founded in 1854, just a couple of months before the first railroad started offering service from Camden, which is right across the Delaware River from Philadelphia. With rail service, and a doctor trumpeting the medicinal benefits of salt air and seawater, the city quickly became a tourist destination and a place for Philadelphians to escape the summer heat. Hotels sprang up first along Atlantic Avenue, the main street in the city. But over time, more and more of them started opening along the beach.

The first boardwalk was built in 1870 and the city's first ocean pier opened in 1882 as a measure to keep guests from bringing sand into the hotels. The original boardwalk was a temporary walkway that was taken up at the end of the summer season. Over time, it grew into a permanent fixture and a major thoroughfare. Big-name entertainment was offered in

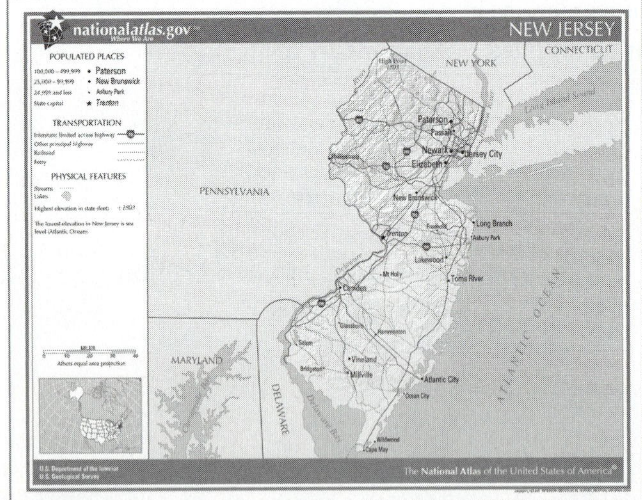

FIGURE 5.1 Atlantic City is a short drive from Philadelphia and New York City.

Source: National Atlas of the United States, April 29, 2008, http://nationalatlas.gov.

hotel showrooms and on the piers. Opera great Enrico Caruso was a regular visitor to Atlantic City and the famous Zeigfield Follies debuted there before moving to Broadway. It was a regular stop for John Philip Sousa and his band for many summers. In later years, it was the Glenn Miller Orchestra, the Dorsey Brothers, Frank Sinatra, Count Basie, Louis Armstrong, and even The Beatles. It was a city that had entertainment for every taste.

Atlantic City was a city where vice was a way of life. Prohibition was a business opportunity, and there was plenty of casino-style gambling decades before casino gambling was legalized. It was a "wide open" city that was controlled by a series of corrupt political bosses and a place where organized crime bigwigs felt secure enough to have their own conference in 1929.

Atlantic City actually peaked in the 1930s. By the time World War II started, the city was already losing population. But the decline was masked by the war effort. Atlantic City was converted into a combination training camp and R&R base for the military. Convention Hall became the Army Air Forces Basic Training Camp #7 and an indoor exercise facility. Recruits practiced landings on Atlantic City's beaches, while the wounded were treated in some of the city's finest hotels, which had been temporarily renamed the Thomas M. England General Hospital.

When the Army pulled out in 1946, the landscape had changed dramatically. GIs returning home were buying houses in suburbs and, more importantly, they were buying cars. Their vacation plans were no longer tied to where the trains went. The development of the interstate highway system gave people easier access to other vacation alternatives. And the development of affordable air transportation made a trip to Miami just a little longer than a drive to Atlantic City for many people in the Northeast. Compounding the city's decline were the efforts of reformers to shut down the illegal gambling operations. In the early 1950s, Senator Estes Kefauver brought his U.S. Senate Crime Committee to Atlantic City to expose the corruption that allowed gambling to flourish. Over the next several years, reformers tried to shutter the gambling dens. As forces outside Atlantic City pushed to clean up the town, locals started thinking more and more about simply legalizing gambling.

Perhaps Atlantic City's turning point came in 1964 when the Democratic Party chose the city to host its convention. While Atlantic City was controlled by Republicans, they saw the value that a major political convention could bring to the city. They knew the media attention could give the city millions of dollars worth of free publicity, and they wanted to show the rest of the nation what a great vacation resort it was.

That effort failed miserably. Instead of basking in positive publicity, the city's shabbier side was put on display for all to see. The national media played up the city's shortcomings and highlighted the inadequacies of the hotels. The result was a dramatic decline in Atlantic City that pushed it to the edge of an economic abyss.

A study done for the Atlantic City Housing Authority and Urban Redevelopment Agency in 1976 noted that between 1966 and 1976, the city lost almost 6,000 hotel rooms. Many of the city's fine old hotels were shuttered, demolished, or converted to apartments mainly for senior citizens. By 1976, the city only had 3,239 "first class" hotel rooms, and it counted among its finest hotels the Holiday Inn and the Howard Johnson's Regency Motor Lodge.

REFERENDUM

It was against this backdrop that the people of Atlantic City turned to casino gambling.

The idea of legalizing casinos for Atlantic City actually went back to shortly after the city's illegal casinos were shut down. But the effort did not gain much momentum until the early 1970s. Atlantic City's decline was well documented by then. In an effort to get support from around the state, legislators in 1974 drafted a proposed constitutional amendment that was designed to permit state-owned casinos anywhere in the state as long as it was also approved by a local referendum. But they misgauged public reaction. Fearing casinos in their backyards, voters turned down the referendum.

Within a year, local leaders were trying to devise a way to bring the issue back to the voters. Under New Jersey's Constitution, if a proposed amendment is defeated, the same question cannot be put before the voters for at least three years. To get around this, backers decided to go for privately owned casinos that would be limited to Atlantic City. Once a judge ruled that this was not the same question put to voters in 1974, efforts to get the question on the ballot in 1976, a presidential election year, shifted into high gear.

They formed the Committee to Rebuild Atlantic City (**CRAC**) and named Joseph Lazarow, Atlantic City's mayor, as its chairman. The committee included many of the city's business leaders, including prominent attorneys, bankers, insurance executives, hoteliers, and restaurateurs. They hired a campaign strategist and crafted the slogan "Help Yourself, Help Atlantic City." In brochures distributed around the state, they promised that casinos would balance taxes, create jobs, boost the economy, cut down on street crime. The CRAC committee raised more than $1 million—at times by trying to embarrass local business people who did not contribute—to finance the campaign. The largest contributor was Resorts International Inc., a company that had already bought the Chalfonte-Haddon Hall for $5.2 million and put down a $100,000 deposit on a vacant 56-acre urban renewal tract in the city for a second casino hotel. The second largest contributor was the local newspaper, the *Press of Atlantic City*, which contributed $45,000.

In comparison, the opponents had little money and relied on moralistic arguments that could not carry the day. This time around, the effort was a success. On November 2, 1976, New Jersey residents voted 57% to 43% to permit gambling in Atlantic City and to dedicate all of the taxes from gaming to support programs for seniors and people with disabilities. There literally was dancing in the streets of Atlantic City on election night. The headline in the *Press of Atlantic City* the next morning summed it up: "CITY REBORN."

Legislators worked for the next seven months to write the **Casino Control Act**, which would create a new regulatory system that would attempt to harness and direct the

FIGURE 5.2 The referendum would lead to a revival of business for Atlantic City.

Source: Photo by Dan Heneghan.

economic engine that casinos would create while imposing strict integrity standards on an industry that was better known for its unsavory ties. On June 2, 1977, then Governor Brendan T. Byrne signed the Casino Control Act in a ceremony on Atlantic City's Boardwalk. Before signing, he voiced the concern many people had about casinos, warning mobsters against trying to muscle in on the action: "I've said it before and I will repeat it again to organized crime: Keep your filthy hands off Atlantic City. Keep the hell out of our state!'"[1]

THE EVOLUTION OF THE GAMING MARKET

New Jersey currently has a dozen different casino hotels, which opened over the last 28 years. Each has its own character and its own story. Over time, they have evolved from existing hotels that were retrofitted to include a casino, to casinos that annexed existing hotels in order to comply with state mandates, to brand new casino complexes that had a hotel, restaurants, and a showroom, to full-scale resort casino hotels in a destination resort. This section will go over each of the properties and discuss their evolution.

Resorts International

Resorts International took a big bet when it bought the Chalfonte-Haddon Hall several months before the referendum. But on election night 1976, it won big. It was the only Atlantic City hotel that would be large enough to meet the requirements that would be spelled out in the Casino Control Act. Even before the bill became law, the company started a $45-million project to convert a large exhibition hall into a casino. It opened to gamblers on May 26, 1978 and was immediately overrun with business. Rather than worry about marketing to draw people, Resorts had to worry more about crowd control. The day it opened, and for weeks thereafter, there were lines of people snaking down Atlantic City's Boardwalk for blocks, waiting to get in.

They were heady days. The casino took in money faster than it could be counted. The "soft count" in the opening days usually took 20 to 24 hours. Coin booths on the casino floor often ran out of coin to sell simply because it couldn't be collected, counted, and rewrapped fast enough. In the approximately seven months it operated in 1978, the casino won an incredible $134 million.

Resorts operated on a temporary permit while a full investigation by the New Jersey Division of Gaming Enforcement (**DGE**) was underway. In December 1978, the DGE submitted its findings and recommended to the Casino Control Commission that Resorts' license application be denied because of ties to organized crime. After a six-week hearing in early 1979, the commission disagreed and voted 5–0 to grant Atlantic City's first casino license.

Over the years, the casino changed hands several times. First, control of the company was sold to **Donald Trump** in 1987. He later split the company and sold the property to Merv Griffin while keeping the company's second casino project, which would eventually become Trump Taj Mahal. Resorts ended up going through Chapter 11 reorganization twice while Griffin was in control. It was sold again in 1996 to Sun International, a company with its roots in South Africa, but it could not succeed in the highly competitive market in Atlantic City and was sold again to a unit of Colony Capital L.L.C. in 2000.

FIGURE 5.3 Resorts International was the first casino to open in Atlantic City.

Source: Photo by Dan Heneghan.

Caesars

Resorts maintained its monopoly for 13 months until June 1979 when Caesars Boardwalk Regency opened as Atlantic City's second casino hotel. Caesars World Inc. had purchased the Howard Johnson's Regency Motor Lodge in Atlantic City and then built a small hotel tower to give the complex the minimum of 500 rooms to complete Caesars Boardwalk Regency Hotel Casino.

Like Resorts, Caesars faced licensing problems. The DGE forced company chairman and vice chairman Clifford and Stuart Perlman to take a leave of absence in order for the company to get a temporary permit to open its casino in June 1979. The regulators were concerned about a series of personal and corporate business dealings with alleged associates of underworld financier Meyer Lansky. **Clifford Perlman** was, at that time, considered a marketing genius and was one of the leading figures in the gaming industry. But he and his brother could not pass muster in New Jersey, and they were forced to resign and sell their stake in the company that they had built. They appealed, but every court they turned to supported the regulators.

Over the years, the casino's parent company was bought several times, first by ITT Corporation, then by Starwood Hotels and Resorts Worldwide. Starwood later sold it to Bally Entertainment Corporation and the company was renamed Caesars Entertainment. In 2005, the company was sold to Harrah's Entertainment.

Bally

When Bally Manufacturing Corporation came to Atlantic City, it was the nation's largest manufacturer of slot machines. But it had decided to branch out away from its manufacturing

FIGURE 5.4 Caesars is one of the brands that transferred to Atlantic City successfully.

Source: Photo by Dan Heneghan.

base and open and operate its own casino hotel. Bally bought two of the city's most famous, old hotel complexes.

The first was **the Marlborough-Blenheim Hotel**, a two-building complex that traced its roots back to start of the twentieth century. The wooden Marlborough was built in the Queen Anne style with a slate mansard roof. Right across the street was the Moorish-style Blenheim, which was one of the first hotels in the world constructed with poured concrete. The project had been overseen by Thomas Edison who had invented the construction method. Because of its significance, the Blenheim was listed on the National Register of Historic Places. But that meant little to Bally. The Marlborough could never meet fire codes and the Blenheim was inefficient. They were both demolished to make way for what looked like a massive granite-sheathed box.

Bally also bought the Dennis Hotel, which was right next to the Blenheim. The Dennis had started as a small guesthouse in the 1860s and grew into one of the city's largest hotels by the start of the twentieth century. Bally kept the facade intact, but completely gutted the interior to build rooms large enough to comply with the 350 square-foot requirement in the Casino Control Act. It could not squeeze enough rooms into the shell of the old Dennis, so Bally added a handful of rooms atop a new parking garage it had built. Construction of Bally's Park Place was in overdrive, and the company threw enormous amounts of money at the project to open the facility by the end of 1979.

But Bally, too, faced licensing obstacles. Its chairman, William T. O'Donnell, had a number of business dealings with a reputed mobster in northern New Jersey. At a hearing in late 1980, he could not convince the Casino Control Commission that he met its high standards, and he was barred from the company and had to sell his stock in the firm. In time, Bally's went on to be one of the most profitable gaming halls in the city as well as the largest. In 1989, it opened a tower with more than 700 new rooms and, in 1997, it opened the Wild Wild West casino expansion.

FIGURE 5.5 Bally's is an example of a casino that has expanded as it succeeded in the Atlantic City market.

Source: Photo by Dan Heneghan.

In 1997, Bally was acquired by Hilton Hotels Corporation. Hilton spun off all of its gaming operations into a new company named Park Place Entertainment in 1999. Park Place Entertainment was purchased by Harrah's Entertainment in 2005.

Brighton/Sands

As 1980 dawned, casino construction was going fast and furious. A group of local and Philadelphia-area investors had banded together and bought a parcel of land back off the Boardwalk that had been the site of the Brighton Hotel decades earlier. They put together a project that was comparatively modest and designed to be somewhat sedate and named it in honor of the famous old wooden Brighton that had stood there before. It turned out to be undercapitalized, poorly designed, and in a poor location. It opened in August 1980 and suffered from financial problems from the outset. The property was sold in 1981 even before the original owners could go through the licensing process. The new owners also bought the famous Sands Hotel and Casino in Las Vegas and renamed the Atlantic City property Sands, as well. The ties to its Las Vegas namesake did not last long, but the agreement to use the name continued.

For a small property, the Sands did reasonably well for years, but profits took a nosedive in 1996 in a bitter marketing war in the city. Its parent company, which evolved from Inns of the Americas, Inc., to Pratt Casino Corporation, which was affiliated with Hollywood Casino Corporation, looked to cut its losses and in January 1998, the casino filed for reorganization. That led to a string of executive changes and changes in direction for the facility. Investor Carl Icahn held a significant amount of the casino's debt, and, as a result, he became the owner of the casino hotel in 2000, but the management changes continued and operations continued to founder. The hotel annexed the nearby Madison House in 2001, which allowed the Sands to expand its gaming area, but operations continued to suffer.

In early 2006, Icahn bought an adjacent 7.7 acre parcel where the Traymore Hotel once stood, which could be used for possible expansion. In addition, there were discussions about buying the Post Office across Pacific Avenue from the Sands for potential expansion. Instead, Icahn sold the property for $250 million to Pinnacle Entertainment Inc. in the fall of 2006. The Sands was closed in November and Pinnacle announced plans to tear it down and replace it with a 2,000-room complex that Chairman Dan Lee told the media would rival the Borgata or Wynn in Las Vegas.

Harrah's

Governor Byrne knew that in order for Atlantic City to succeed, it had to attract major hotel chains to invest there. He personally went to Memphis to meet with executives of Holiday Inns Inc. to convince them to build a casino hotel in Atlantic City. Holiday Inns, at the time, was firmly rooted in the Bible belt, and it was a big change in direction for the company to get involved in the gaming industry. But it agreed to look into Atlantic City, and it bought a parcel in the city's Marina district and started work on the Holiday Inn Marina Hotel Casino.

In 1979, it agreed to acquire Harrah's Inc., which had casinos in Reno and Lake Tahoe in Nevada. With the merger, a project Harrah's had hoped to build directly across the street from the Holiday Inn Marina was scrapped and the Holiday Inns project was renamed as Harrah's Marina. When it opened in November 1980, the property tried to distance itself from its Boardwalk competitors by saying it was in "the other Atlantic City." The marketing program resonated with visitors who did not want the ballyhoo of the Boardwalk, and the property became one of the more profitable in the city. Harrah's was one of the first properties to expand, adding a tower of rooms in 1985. The industry slowed, however, and the next expansion did not open until 1997. By then, Atlantic City was booming and the company soon started on another tower that opened in 2002, and the casino started work on its largest expansion—a 954-room addition with a dramatic domed pool and spa area—in the spring of 2006. Parts of the new addition opened in 2007 and the room tower, which is the tallest building in Atlantic City, was completed in 2008.

FIGURE 5.6 Harrah's is represented in nearly all the gaming markets across America and in Indian country as well.

Source: Photo by Dan Heneghan.

The company expanded its Atlantic City operations in other ways, too. In 1998, the company bought Showboat Inc., which gave it two Atlantic City casinos. In 2005, Harrah's bought Caesars Entertainment and expanded its holdings in Atlantic City to four casino hotel complexes. In 2006, two private equity firms, Apollo Investment Corporation and Texas Pacific Group reached an agreement to buy Harrah's for $17 billion or $90 a share.

Golden Nugget/Grand Hilton

Steve Wynn first came to Atlantic City in the summer of 1978. The chairman of Golden Nugget Inc. was on the East Coast and wanted to stop in Atlantic City and see what the hubbub was about Resorts International. He stood in the casino's Rendezvous Lounge overlooking the casino and was amazed by what he saw. There was an incredible mass of humanity crammed onto the gaming floor. The crush around tables and slot machines was beyond belief. He saw an incredible demand for gambling, a thirst that this one casino could not quench, and he told his staff to go out immediately and find a site for a Golden Nugget casino. Before he left town, he had a contract to buy an aging motel, which he would tear down and replace with a 500-room casino hotel.

Like other Las Vegas CEOs before him, Wynn faced licensing problems that required him to temporarily give up his position as chairman of the company's New Jersey subsidiary. But at the end of a hearing, the DGE did not object to Wynn and the company and its chairman were licensed in October 1981.

The property was enormously profitable, but officials at the DGE kept raising questions about organized crime. The casino was a favorite hangout for reputed organized crime figures. In addition, Golden Nugget hired an executive with ties to Anthony "Fat Tony" Salerno, then the head of the Genovese organized crime family. The executive was the son of a notorious Miami bookmaker and son-in-law of a reputed front for Meyer Lansky. Regulators also scrutinized Wynn's dealings with junk bond king Michael Milken. Wynn reportedly grew frustrated with the constant questioning and, in 1987, sold the property to Bally's Entertainment, which renamed the property Bally's Grand and later, after Bally was acquired by Hilton Hotels Corporation, the Atlantic City Hilton.

Gross operating profits fell under Bally's ownership from $88.5 million in 1986 to $29.9 million in 1996. It was not until a tower of new hotel rooms opened in 1997 that profits turned around. In 2005, the property was sold to a unit of Colony Capital, which also owned Resorts by that time.

Playboy/Atlantis

William Whitner and a number of other investors had faith in Atlantic City well before the casinos arrived. They had decided in the early 1970s to invest in Atlantic City and reached a deal with the Atlantic City Housing Authority and Urban Redevelopment Agency to build a hotel adjacent to Convention Hall. But that was when Atlantic City was at its worst and the project never got off the ground. Even though they missed every deadline to build in their agreement with the housing authority, Whitner and his partners were able to keep control of the land for years. After gaming was legalized, they struck a deal with Playboy Enterprises Inc. and Elsinore Corporation to build a casino hotel there.

Playboy, however, had serious licensing problems. The casino opened in April 1981, right around the same time that the company's London casinos lost their licenses. But the bigger problem was with Playboy chairman Hugh Hefner. When the commission

FIGURE 5.7 The Atlantic City Hilton is an example of a resort property that has had more than one owner.

Source: Photo by Dan Heneghan.

held a full licensing hearing in 1982, a controlling minority concluded that Hefner was not completely candid when he testified about a decision to pay bribes 20 years earlier to get a liquor license for a New York City club. Playboy then sold its interest to partner Elsinore.

But Playboy's role haunted the project. From the outset, Playboy was the lead partner in the Playboy Hotel Casino. The casino was patterned after Playboy's highly successful casino in London and was spread over three floors of the narrow hotel building. But Playboy clearly misjudged the U.S. market, which preferred casinos on a single floor and with mass-audience appeal. Playboy's disqualification left Elsinore to run a casino it had not designed and the decision to buy out Playboy's interest saddled the project with an unsupportable level of debt.

The property was re-themed and renamed the Atlantis Hotel Casino, but it could not overcome the crushing debt on its balance sheet. In 1985, the casino became the first to file for Chapter 11 reorganization in U.S. Bankruptcy Court. It developed a reorganization plan and emerged from bankruptcy in 1989, but the commission, which had renewed the casino's license while it was in bankruptcy, ruled it was no longer financially stable and refused to renew the license. On the day the license was to expire, Elsinore sold the property to Donald Trump who would use it as a non-casino adjunct to his nearby Trump Plaza. When Trump had his own financial problems, the hotel reverted to the banks, but Trump

FIGURE 5.8 The Atlantis started its life as the Playboy Hotel Casino.

Source: Photo by Dan Heneghan.

bought it back and was able to reopen the casino as part of Trump Plaza. However, it still was not economically viable and Trump closed it down and it was demolished.

Claridge

Atlantic City's Claridge Hotel was planned in the city's heyday in the late 1920s. But when the "Skyscraper by the Sea" opened in 1930, the country was in a depression. Unfortunately, the hotel's inauspicious beginnings would haunt it for decades to come.

A group of Connecticut investors, led by Frank "Hi-Ho" D'Addario bought the Claridge in 1977 and brought in the Del E. Webb Corporation as a 10% partner and casino operator. As the cost of the project increased, D'Addario and his group could not come up with the money needed to continue the project. Instead, they sold more and more of the project to Del Webb until it owned a half interest.

When it came time for the casino to get a temporary permit in June 1981, there was a problem. Del Webb was under indictment for criminal conspiracy and could not be licensed. Officials constructed a deal where Del Webb's interest was sold back to D'Addario in a paper transaction. Several months later, after the company was acquitted, it bought back its interest and went on to be found suitable by casino regulators in July 1982.

Financially, the casino was never very successful. In 1983, the struggling complex was packaged as a tax shelter and sold to a limited partnership. Year after year, the casino lost money. Del Webb stayed on for some time to manage the property, but it too wanted out. In 1988, Golden Nugget expressed an interest in buying the property, but the deal fell apart. So too did a deal with a former Golden Nugget executive who formed a partnership to buy the building.

Claridge stumbled along for some time until it slipped into bankruptcy in 1999. Two years later, Bally bought the property and absorbed it into the sprawling Bally's Park Place complex.

Tropicana

Ramada Inns Inc. seemed an unlikely entrant to the casino industry. The Phoenix-based company bought the shuttered Ambassador hotel in 1978 and developed plans to convert it to a casino hotel that it would call "The Phoenix." But Governor Byrne made it clear that he believed Atlantic City needed new construction, and he was openly critical of projects that were "patch and paint" jobs. That sent Ramada back to the drawing board. Several months later, after buying the Tropicana in Las Vegas, it unveiled a new plan that called for knocking all of the bricks and concrete off of the Ambassador's old steel superstructure and building a new hotel around it. In hindsight, decision to save the old steel was a bad one and the cost of the project ballooned to approximately $330 million.

But the company, which morphed from Ramada to Aztar Corporation, was a leader in recognizing the value of adding more hotel rooms. Tropicana added new hotel towers in 1988 and again in 1996. The most significant expansion came in 2004 with a 500-room tower and a dining, entertainment, and shopping arcade called The Quarter, which was designed like several of the shopping arcades at Las Vegas casino hotels. It was one of the projects that helped to redefine the city as more of a destination resort. The Quarter showed that people would come to Atlantic City for shopping and dining as well as for gambling.

Aztar's Atlantic City property and its Las Vegas counterpart, turned out to be very attractive to other companies interested in getting into those markets. In March 2006, Pinnacle Entertainment entered into an agreement to buy all of Aztar for $38 a share. The offer set off a bidding war for the company that ended in the summer when Aztar accepted a $54 a share offer from Columbia Entertainment of Fort Mitchell, Kentucky. The deal closed in January 2007.

FIGURE 5.9 The Tropicana has continually expanded over the years and has profited for it.

Source: Photo by Dan Heneghan.

Trump Plaza

But by late 1981, things were not looking as bright for the casinos. Revenues were strong, but profits were down and, for the first time since 1977, there was no casino construction taking place. High interest rates had already killed a number of projects. It was in that environment that Donald Trump came to Atlantic City and agreed to take over a project that two others had failed to get off the ground. He breezed through the licensing process and quickly partnered with Harrah's to develop what would become Harrah's Hotel Casino at Trump Plaza when it opened in 1984. Trump's business partnerships turned out to be as volatile as his personal ones and Trump and Harrah's broke up after the casino opened, leaving Trump in charge.

The property was on a very small parcel of land in a prime location right off the end of the Atlantic City Expressway, but it initially had no parking garage. The city sold air rights over a public street to the casino, which enabled it to build a 60,000 square foot casino on a single level. While it initially performed reasonably well, business softened by the end of the 1980s. Trump Plaza was tied up with all of Trump's financial problems in the early 1990s and filed for reorganization in U.S. Bankruptcy Court in 1992. It emerged from bankruptcy and was folded into a new public company named Trump Hotels and Casino Resorts.

In November 2004, Trump Hotels and Casino Resorts had to seek protection in bankruptcy court. The balance sheet again was restructured and the company came out with less debt, a new name, money for potential expansion, and someone other than Donald

FIGURE 5.10 Donald Trump wanted a casino on the Boardwalk and at the marina. The Trump Plaza is on the Boardwalk.

Source: Photo by Dan Heneghan.

Trump as the CEO. In 2006, the company unveiled plans to reposition all of its properties. Trump Plaza was to be re-themed to lure a hipper, New York City type of customer.

Trump Marina

Hilton Hotels Corporation decided to build a casino hotel in Atlantic City in 1980, but high interest rates made the company put off the project for several years. It built in the city's Marina district with a target opening for May 1985. Legislation permitting temporary permits had expired, so it was to be the first casino to open after a full licensing hearing. In a stunning decision, however, the Casino Control Commission rejected Hilton's license application. Trump swooped in and bought the property and renamed it Trump's Castle. Hilton returned in 1991, after several top executives left the company, and was found qualified to hold a license. It later acquired Bally Entertainment.

Within months of the purchase, Trump refinanced Trump's Castle and left it very highly leveraged. When casino business and Trump's personal fortunes sagged by the end of the 1980s, the casino had financial problems as well. At one point, Trump's father bought over $4 million in gaming chips so his son could make a bond interest payment. In early 1992, it had to file for reorganization in bankruptcy court in order to effectuate a restructuring of the casino's balance sheet.

It emerged from bankruptcy and, like the other Trump casinos, became part of a new public company named Trump Hotels and Casino Resorts. The complex was renamed Trump Marina to reflect the fact that it also managed a large state-owned marina adjacent to the complex. Like the other Trump properties, it suffered from lack of capital improvement over the years and it lagged behind as the neighboring Harrah's continually upgraded and expanded.

FIGURE 5.11 The Trump Marina has survived Donald Trump's bankruptcies.

Source: Photo by Dan Heneghan.

In November 2004, Trump Hotels and Casino Resorts sought protection in bankruptcy court. The balance sheet again was restructured to reduce the company's interest expense and place it on a firmer financial footing. In 2006, the company announced it would reposition the property to appeal to a middle-class, suburban market.

Showboat

In the early 1980s, **Showboat** Inc. was a small casino company that ran a popular locals casino in Las Vegas that featured a large bowling center. It could barely afford to get into the Atlantic City market, but was able to lease land from Resorts International in the urban renewal tract that firm had tied up in 1976. Officials effectively bet the company on the success of the project—a bet that paid off handsomely. The opening of its Atlantic City casino in 1987 thrust a small Nevada gaming company into the big leagues.

There was some concern about the company and the affiliation that some of the directors had with the less reputable elements from Las Vegas. For example, one director had been a part owner of a major Las Vegas casino at a time when the mob controlled it. But he convinced regulators that his stake was so small and he had no real contact with the mobsters and that he really was qualified under New Jersey's law. The regulators, who were clearly aware that investment in the city had slowed to a trickle, found all of the company's officers and directors qualified.

Showboat initially marketed the property to a mass audience—the quarter slot player. It attracted people with blue hair, not blue blood, and did quite well. Instead of a theater, like other casino hotels, it had a bowling center that it hoped would attract the locals, just like it did in Las Vegas. But what worked in Vegas did not work in Atlantic City. The bowling center was never successful, and the company turned its attention to expansion as a way of generating more business. It opened a new hotel tower in 1994, just at the time the city and state were looking for more rooms to support a new convention center that was being built. Four years later, the company was acquired by Harrah's, which started another expansion that opened in 2003. As the market changed and the competition started drawing a younger crowd, Harrah's cut a deal with the House of Blues to open a venue within Showboat. The result was a facility where Wayne Newton fans felt comfortable rubbing elbows with fans of Eminem and Nine Inch Nails. The expansion and new focus on drawing a younger crowd apparently

FIGURE 5.12 The Showboat originally attracted a sedate, older demographic, but now appeals to a younger crowd.

Source: Photo by Dan Heneghan.

worked. Revenues increased, and the property started to shed a dowdy image without alienating its existing customer base.

Trump Taj Mahal

Plans for the Trump Taj Mahal actually dated back to 1976 when Resorts International put a deposit down on the city's vast urban renewal tract even before it purchased Chalfonte-Haddon Hall. For a variety of reasons, development was delayed and ground was broken for a 1,000-room hotel in October 1983. But work progressed at a snail's pace. The project was redesigned, the company's chairman died, and control was sold to Donald Trump. Trump split the company, keeping what would become the Taj Mahal.

By the time the property opened in 1990, Resorts and Trump had spent over $1 billion on the 1,250-room casino hotel. But that proved to be too much and the casino had to file for bankruptcy protection in early 1991 at a time when Trump faced enormous financial problems. The reorganization plan gave half of the property to bondholders, but allowed Trump to buy it back, which he eventually did. Subsequently, all of Trump's casinos were combined into a new public company called Trump Hotels and Casino Resorts. But that company never had the financial strength to compete against many of the other operators in Atlantic City. Buffeted by competition and stymied by the inability to expand and meet the competition, Trump Hotels and Casino Resorts filed for reorganization as well, emerging as Trump Entertainment in 2005. The second reorganization gave the company access to funds to build an 800-room addition and modernize the tired property. By mid-2006, work started on a 45-story addition, which would include 800 new hotel rooms for the complex.

Borgata

Wynn decided to come back to Atlantic City in 1995. He struck a deal to acquire approximately 150 acres in the city's Marina district and got the state to agree to build a controversial highway and tunnel through a residential neighborhood to make it easier to get to the site. He also cut a deal to partner with Boyd Gaming of Las Vegas to build a 1,000-room hotel on the site, adjacent to one that Wynn's Mirage Resorts would build. Wynn, however, decided to sell his company to MGM Grand Inc. The new MGM Mirage dropped plans to build and got Boyd to agree to increase the joint-venture project to 2,000 rooms—a hotel that would become The **Borgata**.

The Borgata transformed Atlantic City in much the way the Mirage changed Las Vegas when it opened in 1989. Atlantic City had been a place that drew day-trippers and senior citizens. It struggled to broaden its appeal until the Borgata arrived in 2003. In anticipation of the Borgata, competitors invested more than $1 billion to upgrade their facilities.

Borgata turned out to be more successful than imagined and soon dominated the Atlantic City market. It was a new, hip place to go to that quickly became a hit with younger customers from New York and Philadelphia, and it proved to be more profitable that anyone imagined. Within six months of opening, Boyd started planning a major expansion of the complex. Just three years after opening, Borgata unveiled an enormous expansion with new gaming space and new signature restaurants. In 2007, it opened an 800-room hotel tower called the "Water Club" with a new spa.

FIGURE 5.13 The Borgata raised the standard in Atlantic City when it opened in 2003. Other casinos have moved to add retail, upscale dining, spas, and other amenities not associated with Atlantic City casinos before.

Source: Photo by Dan Heneghan.

EVOLUTION OF REGULATION

The development of the casino hotels in Atlantic City has been quite impressive. But the industry could not have evolved to this point without a regulatory environment that was also able to evolve. At the outset, New Jersey developed a regulatory system that was significantly different from Nevada's. It created the **Casino Control Commission**, which was an independent agency with members appointed by the governor and a staff that included inspectors in each casino around the clock. But the investigative and enforcement functions were given to the DGE, which was an arm of the New Jersey Attorney General's Office.

When New Jersey legalized casino gaming, there was a major scandal brewing in Nevada with allegations that organized crime controlled a number of gaming halls and that in many circles, casinos and the mob seemed to go hand in hand. (The scandal later formed the basis of the Hollywood movie *Casino*.) Governor Byrne wanted to break that link, and he helped push through legislation that created a very strict licensing system that was designed to make it all but impossible for the mob to move into Atlantic City's new industry. Earlier in this chapter, the state's efforts to force companies to sever ties with questionable executives in an effort to purge the industry of ties to organized crime are described in some detail. In 1977, the Governor's Staff Policy Group concluded that if organized crime could not infiltrate casinos through its ownership structure, it would do so by controlling the vendors that served the casinos. To protect against that, the Casino Control Act extended licensing on all casino employees and also on all vendors who did regular and continuing business with casinos, regardless of whether it was gaming or nongaming related business.

Within months of passing the Casino Control Act, efforts were underway to amend it. In early 1978, it became clear that renovation work on Resorts would be completed long before the DGE completed its investigation. Thus was born a process for issuing temporary permits to allow companies to operate a casino before the thorough background investigation was complete.

The newly formed Casino Control Commission started developing regulations to implement the provisions of the gaming law in order to process the initial application and open the first gaming hall. It was a trek through uncharted waters and regulators wanted to err on the side of caution. When there was only one casino, and when people were lined up outside casinos waiting to get in, some of the restrictions were not a problem. But it did not take long for casinos to start complaining. Early requirements to fall by the wayside included requirements for $2 and $5 blackjack tables, for live theater-style entertainment every night, early surrender at blackjack, and for state approval of all advertising prior to publication or broadcast.

Efforts to streamline the regulatory process hit a roadblock when the Abscam scandal broke in 1980, and the commission's vice chairman had to resign. The commission was overhauled and the power of the chairman was reduced and any efforts to change the system to ease regulation of the industry came to a screeching halt. Government did not want to touch casinos with a proverbial 10-foot pole. When Tom Kean became governor in 1982, he too took a hands-off approach to casinos, rarely even going into a casino hotel and never supporting any legislative relief to help the industry.

The industry withered under an unchanging regulatory system. Operators complained of an unresponsive system. Gross operating profits had grown at double-digit rates through 1983, but then slowed precipitously. In 1988, profits increased by less than 1%. The next year was even worse, for in 1989, profits fell for the first time by 2.4%. Profits fell again the next year by 1.7%. Casino gambling was spreading across the country, and casino companies and Wall Street investment bankers were opting to invest in other states where the financial and political climate was friendlier.

FIGURE 5.14 The Boardwalk is still the center of attention in Atlantic City. It continues to evolve in response to competition within the city and from other gaming jurisdictions.

Source: Photo by Dan Heneghan.

LATER REGULATIONS

When **James Florio** became governor in 1990, he and his advisors recognized that the casino industry needed help, and they started a 15-year process of regulatory and legislative reforms that revitalized and reinvigorated the industry. Sweeping changes to the Casino Control Act made it much easier to introduce new table games, made it easier for institutional investors to hold casino securities, and got the state out of regulating nongaming areas of casino hotels. The state also approved simulcasting of horse racing into casinos, eliminated a requirement that a casino be a "single room," and, probably the most important change, permitted casinos to operate 24 hours a day. From 1990 forward, state legislators and regulators completely overhauled the regulatory system, dramatically reducing the cost of regulation while focusing on maintaining integrity.

It did not take long for the changes to have an impact. After two years of declines, gross operating profits increased by 9.2% in 1991, another 10.3% in 1992, 5.8% in 1993, by 4.1% in 1994, and by a strong 15.1% in 1995 when a series of new reforms took effect. Operators then went overboard with marketing programs that cut operating profits by 19.2% in 1996. That caused a shock to the industry, which then cut back on promotional costs, and the industry started on a trend to report increases in eight of the next nine years.

The impact of the changes filtered their way to Wall Street and to Las Vegas. So, in 1994, when Atlantic City offered to sell the former landfill next to Harrah's, Steve Wynn was willing to take the risk on property that the city had been unable to sell in the past. Wynn's willingness made others consider investing more in Atlantic City as well. Wynn brought Boyd to Atlantic City, which resulted in the 2,000-room Borgata. But he also helped convince Tropicana, Resorts, and others to expand their facilities in order to effectively compete against what Borgata would be. The state continued to look at changes that could make it easier for casinos to operate without relaxing the state's strict integrity requirements.

By 2006, it was clear that Atlantic City was a hot market. Borgata, Harrah's, and Trump Taj Mahal were all building massive additions to their properties. Companies like Morgan Stanley, Pinnacle Entertainment, and Penn National Gaming Inc. were all interested in building or buying a casino there. The city also was attracting hundreds of millions of dollars in non-casino investment in condominiums and shopping and entertainment facilities.

Conclusion

Casino gambling was legalized in Atlantic City as a "unique tool of urban redevelopment," which was designed to bring Atlantic City back to its self-proclaimed position as the "Queen of Resorts." What happened to Atlantic City was much grander than casino supporters ever dreamed of prior to the referendum.

By the end of 2006, casinos had invested over $12 billion into a tiny city, transforming it from a decaying resort into an exciting, vibrant destination. They had converted the 2,500 acres of developable land into the most valuable real estate in the state of New Jersey. The casino industry also invested more than $1 billion through the Casino Reinvestment Development Authority into projects in Atlantic City that made it a more attractive place to live, to visit and to work. Casino gaming has clearly met the public policy goal of rebuilding Atlantic City.

That transformation was accomplished, in part, because New Jersey started out with a pervasive regulatory scheme that initially covered virtually every aspect of casino operations. New Jersey took an industry that was generally associated with unsavory elements and imposed high standards for good character, honesty, and integrity—standards that showed Wall Street and Main Street that casinos and the mob were not synonymous. The combination resulted in a revived resort city that now draws more than 35 million visitors a year, generates more than $5 billion in annual gaming revenue and pays about $1 billion a year in taxes to all levels of government.

Key Words

Atlantic City *52*
CRAC *54*
Casino Control Act *54*
DGE *55*
Clifford Perlman *56*
The Marlborough-Blenheim Hotel *57*
Steve Wynn *60*
William Whitner *60*
Donald Trump *55*
Showboat *66*
Borgata *67*
Casino Control Commission *68*
James Florio *70*

Review Questions

1. Explain the history of Atlantic City prior to the legalization of gambling.
2. Detail the history of the referendum that legalized gambling in Atlantic City.
3. Detail the development of Resorts International and Caesars in Atlantic City.
4. Explain the development of Bally and Brighton/Sands in Atlantic City.
5. Detail the development of Harrah's in Atlantic City.
6. Detail the development of the Golden Nugget/Grand Hilton and Playboy/Atlantis in Atlantic City.
7. Explain the development of Claridge and Tropicana in Atlantic City.
8. Explain the development of Trump Plaza, Trump Marina, and Trump Taj Mahal.
9. Detail the development of Showboat and Borgata in Atlantic City.
10. Explain the evolution of regulations in Atlantic City.
11. Explain the later regulations applied to Atlantic City casinos.

Endnote

1. Governor Brendan T. Byrne (1977). Press Office, State of New Jersey Archives S53PR001, v16.

CHAPTER 6

NATIVE AMERICAN GAMING

STEVE DURHAM

Learning Objectives

1. To understand the various needs of Native American reservations and how they may relate to gambling
2. To learn the details and issues of sovereign nation in regard to Native American gambling
3. To learn the details and effects of the Indian Gaming Regulatory Act (IGRA)
4. To understand the workings and function of the IGRA
5. To learn the details of the successes and failures of Native American casinos
6. To understand the impact of gambling on Native American reservations
7. To understand the myths about Native American gaming
8. To learn about contemporary issues associated with Native American gambling
9. To learn about future issues facing Native American gambling

Chapter Outline

Introduction
Needs on Reservations
Sovereign Nation and IGRA
The Workings and Functions of IGRA
Success and Failure of Native American Casinos
Impact on Native American Reservations
Myths about Native American Gaming
Contemporary Issues
Future Issues
Conclusion

INTRODUCTION

You have learned the history of gaming in America from colonial times to the advent of gaming in Atlantic City, New Jersey, in 1978. While gaming in its many forms appeared off and on during American history, it was not until 1931 that state sanctioned and regulated gaming was legalized in Nevada. This was the starting point for all modern gaming in the United States.

After the success of Atlantic City became established, other jurisdictions began to look at gaming as a possible source of tax revenue and economic development. They saw how casinos had benefited Nevada and New Jersey. With the final purge of organized crime from Las Vegas in the early 1980s and the establishment of a clean industry in New Jersey, the automatic link between gaming and organized crime infiltration was broken. Voters and politicians were willing to consider casinos as a legitimate business. This opened the door for gaming across America.

However, one sector of society was most in need of tax revenue and economic development: Indian reservations. As you will recall from Chapter 2, Native Americans were pushed out of the eastern United States in the years before the Civil War. The government policy in the nineteenth century toward indigenous peoples was that of removal from prime locations.

This policy was pursued until all tribes were forced onto reservations. Since most Native Americans did not want to live among their enemies (nor did most non-Native Americans want Native Americans among them) and some Native Americans preferred the traditional ways of life, the U.S. government set aside land as reservations for tribes. Reservations were intended as a solution for conquered tribes. They had the added benefit of concentrating tribal populations, which simplified administrative processes.

Treaties were signed which traded ancestral lands ceded by the tribes for reservation land and assistance from the federal government in perpetuity. According to the many treaties, education, health care, and other essential needs are the responsibility of the federal government. Typically, though, the reservation lands were in remote locations and of very little use for economic activity of any kind. This created a hard life of subsistence and poverty for Native Americans who remained on the reservations. Even today, there is a great deal of hardship among Native Americans.

NEEDS ON RESERVATIONS

According to the 2000 census, twice as many Native Americans as other Americans are poor.[1] The percentage of Native Americans living below the poverty line was 25.5%, whereas the poverty rate among all Americans was 12%. The median household income among Native Americans was $30,693 versus $41,994 for all Americans. In other words, Native American households make 73% of what other Americans make. If income is broken down on a per capita basis, Native Americans have 60% of what other Americans earn. In the U.S. Census Bureau's 2006 survey, there was more bad news. With an unemployment rate of 12%, Native Americans experienced nearly double the amount of unemployment compared to all Americans whose rate was 6.4%. Many Native Americans have moved off the reservations and live in cities. These individuals have, typically, done very well. The poverty and unemployment is concentrated among those who remain on the reservations.

TABLE 6.1 The 2000 Census Revealed the Extent of Economic Distress Among Native Americans

	Native Americans	U.S. Population
Population	1,865,118	281,421,906
Individuals below Poverty Line	475,118	33,899,812
Percentage below Poverty Line	25.5%	12%
Median Household Income	$30,693	$41,994
Per Capita Income	$12,923	$21,587
Unemployment Rate	12.0%	6.4%

Like any government, tribal governments would like to remedy the situation. Imagine the voter backlash if the government of Michigan did nothing to bring industry and business into the state while the auto industry imploded and the unemployment rate soared to twice the national average. It is a given that one of the purposes of our elected officials is to provide for the general welfare.

Tribal governments are no different. But, their options are limited. Property taxes are the backbone of local governments throughout the United States. The majority of property taxes are paid by businesses, although homeowners pay a substantial amount. Because tribal land is held in trust and not individually owned, there is no way to levy taxes because most taxes are based on economic activity. Because there is very little business on reservations, there is no point in levying taxes on it. Taxes just do not offer a substantial or sustainable flow of revenue for tribal governments.

The solution has been to seek economic activity owned and managed by tribal governments. While many businesses have been attempted over the years, few succeeded. Several tribes experimented with bingo halls in the 1970s and 1980s. They attracted players from off the reservation, created jobs, and generated revenue for tribal government. While they were small, they were not noticed or ignored by state authorities. However, when they started expanding and generating large sums of money, the host states took notice. However, it was not clear what a state could do about gaming activities on a reservation within its borders.

SOVEREIGN NATION AND IGRA

The concept of **sovereign nation** has been discussed in Chapter 2. The Supreme Court ruled in 1836 that the Cherokee and all Indian tribes, according to the Constitution, were sovereign nations before the arrival of Europeans and that they would remain a nation. As nations, their relationship was with the federal government. The Supreme Court further concluded that the state of Georgia had no jurisdiction over the Cherokees and their land. Unfortunately, this did not stop the executive branch of the federal government from assisting the state of Georgia from evicting the Cherokee from their land and driving them to Oklahoma along the "Trail of Tears."

Although the outcome in the eighteenth century was a humanitarian tragedy, a series of lawsuits grounded in the concept of sovereign nation status and decided by the Supreme Court in the twentieth century led to the passage of the Indian Gaming Regulatory Act (**IGRA**). IGRA introduced Native American gaming on a wide scale, a

(a)

(b)

FIGURE 6.1a and b Geronimo went from defender of his homeland to prisoner at Fort Sill, Oklahoma, as a result of the movement to place Native Americans on reservations.

Source: Copyright © 2008 Steve Durham. Permission is granted to copy, distribute and/or modify the following photos under the terms of the GNU Free Documentation License, Version 1.2 or any later version published by the Free Software Foundation; with no Invariant Sections, no Front-Cover Texts, and no Back-Cover Texts. A copy of the license is included in the section entitled "GNU Free Documentation License".

much more beneficial outcome. The first lawsuit was *Bryan v. Itasca County* that was decided in 1975. The ruling held that a county as a subsection of a state had no authority on an Indian reservation. The second lawsuit was ***Butterworth v. Seminole Nation*** in 1979. This lawsuit turned on the issue of whether the state of Florida had jurisdiction on the Seminole reservation. The ruling reaffirmed the sovereignty of tribes and that a state had no jurisdiction on Indian land. For example, this meant that state police could not enter a reservation without a working agreement with the tribe. In addition, any economic activity on the reservation was not taxable by the state.

Finally, in February 1987, ***California v. Cabazon Band of Mission Indians*** specifically ruled that a state could not prohibit gaming activity on an Indian reservation, if the gaming activity was allowed for any purpose to anyone in the state. Like other tribes across the country, the Cabazon Band ran a high-stakes bingo game and poker room. Like the Indian casinos in the future, except on a smaller scale, the operation provided jobs for tribal members and funding for tribal government. However, California argued that the bingo game and poker room violated state law and that the state had the right to prohibit activities on the reservation, which were considered criminal by state statute. They based this right on a 1953 law passed by Congress giving states a right to criminal jurisdiction over tribes within their borders. This jurisdiction was not absolute, but opened the door for states to interfere in the functioning of tribes on reservations.

The tribe argued that they were a sovereign nation as defined by the Constitution and according to case law. As such, their relationship was with the federal government, and the state had no right to interfere in activities conducted on tribal lands. In addition, they pointed out that California had relaxed its laws in recent years and allowed various forms of gambling including casino nights for charities. The state even ran a lottery that placed it squarely in the gambling business.

The Supreme Court ruled in the tribe's favor. The existence of the state lottery plus other forms of gambling which the state allowed proved to the court that gambling per se was not illegal in California. The 1953 law could not be used to prohibit gaming on the reservation. And, there was no basis in law for the state to regulate the gambling activity on tribal lands.

Congress quickly realized that the wide variety of gambling activity already allowed throughout the United States including casino nights held by charitable organizations would open the door to wide-open gaming in Indian country. They also recognized that there was no legal framework for regulating Native American gaming. The specter of organized crime infiltrating the reservations added impetus to the Congress' debate and in 1988, the IGRA was passed.

The purpose of IGRA was explicitly included in the legislation. IGRA was to encourage economic development on reservation lands, strengthen tribal government, and promote tribal self-sufficiency. Due to the remoteness of most reservations, there have been very few business activities that have proven profitable due to a lack of a market. With very little economic activity for tribal taxes, tribal governments have relied on funding from the federal government. Unfortunately, this funding source has not been reliable. Without economic development and no reliable source of funds, tribal self-sufficiency was an illusion at best.

Up until the passage of IGRA, gaming had begun to prove itself a viable business that would create jobs, generate a funding source for tribal activities, and foster self-sufficiency. The gaming was limited primarily to bingo halls because this was the most common form of gaming allowed in many states, particularly for churches and charities. However, with the passage of IGRA, Native American casinos evolved into full-fledged casinos offering an array of gaming and entertainment options.

This evolution was neither smooth nor preordained. The irony of IGRA is that it placed states in the middle of Native American gaming. Imbedded in IGRA was a requirement that a tribe negotiate a compact with the state within which it resided in order to offer Class III gaming. *California v. Cabazon Band of Mission Indians* ruled that states could not interfere with tribal gaming, but with IGRA, the tribes were required to negotiate in good faith to reach reasonable agreements. The tribes can appeal the process to the federal government if it is determined that the state is not negotiating in good faith. Congress also gave states restricted regulatory power over Native American gaming.

THE WORKINGS AND FUNCTIONS OF IGRA

IGRA defines three types of gaming. Class I is small stakes and social gaming. This is not regulated by the tribe or the state. We discussed Class I gaming or traditional Native American games in Chapter 2. Class II is bingo, pull-tabs, and similar forms of gaming. Only the tribe and the National Indian Gaming Commission (**NIGC**) regulate Class II. Class III is all other forms of gaming including, but not limited to table games and electronic gaming devices. Class III gaming is essentially all the games offered in modern casinos. They are regulated by the tribe, the state, and the NIGC. They also require a compact with the state.

Compacts address all the issues that are of concern to the state and the tribe. The number of machines and table games, regulation, audits, penalties, licensing and certification, revenue sharing, facility access, and more are spelled out in the compacts. They run into hundreds of pages including appendices that specify in detail items and concepts mentioned in the compact itself. The negotiation of such a complex document would be difficult under the best circumstances. However, the state and the tribe approached the issue from diametrically opposed points of view. Generally speaking, states did not want gaming inside their borders. On the other hand, tribes wanted a vehicle to provide for their members. Finding a common language and framework took many sessions and in some cases, many years.

The entire compact negotiation process was fragmented. The process and end result varied from state to state, and even varied within a state. It was not unusual for different tribes within a state to have different arrangements with the state. Hence, different compacts within a state could be markedly different.

The ability of the state to regulate Native American gaming was hindered by this fragmentation. Just the difficulty of remembering which details applied to which tribe created nightmares. With different compacts, the state certification process can be different. An employee applying to one casino would need different forms to apply to other casinos within the state.

Some states have since moved to standardize the compacts. Usually, when they are up for renewal or when a referendum on Native American gaming passes in a state, the state has renegotiated the compacts with the tribes as a group. The resulting standardization made regulation easier and ensured the integrity of each casino. In most states, all tribes had identical compacts within the state by the advent of the twenty-first century.

Because the American economy has a long tradition of free enterprise and capitalism, most Americans do not fully understand the legal status of Native American casinos. The casinos are not owned by individuals or corporations. They are owned and operated as a tribal enterprise. Although they may legally be a corporation, they are a government entity.

In American society, we allocate certain activities to government. Trash collection, water purification and distribution, and road building and maintenance are typical examples of activities we expect the government to control. The reasons are historical and cultural. Other activities are left to the private sector. What we call private enterprise, including retail stores, manufacturing companies, medical care, and so on, is left to individuals and corporations.

The confusion comes about because we see Native American casinos as the type of activity we associate with private enterprise. However, as stated earlier, tribes need funds for government activities such as building and maintaining roads on the reservation, collecting trash, and providing fresh water to residents. While the casino is run like a business, 100% of its profits are transferred to the tribal government to pay for government responsibilities. In a sense, casinos pay a 100% tax on profits. Some of this revenue returns to the casino in the form of capital investment to maintain, expand, or improve the casino. However, the primary focus and purpose of the casino is to generate revenue for the tribal government to fulfill its obligations to tribal members.

SUCCESS AND FAILURE OF NATIVE AMERICAN CASINOS

By and large, the casinos have been very successful. There are 562 federally recognized tribes in the United States, but only 225 tribes operate casinos. Because IGRA allows larger tribes to negotiate for multiple sites, there are 423 tribal gaming operations. Native American casinos

(a)

(b)

(c)

FIGURE 6.2a, b, and c Larger tribes can operate up to three casinos such as the Gila River Indian Community near Phoenix, Arizona. Their three casinos are strategically located to take advantage of residential and business patterns in the Phoenix area.

are located in 28 states, have created 670,000 jobs, and generated $25.7 billion in gaming revenue in 2006.[2] These funds have had a major impact on conditions on the reservations.

Not all Indian casinos are created equal. They vary greatly in size and thus in their ability to provide revenues. The largest and most successful casino in the world is Foxwoods in Ledyard, Connecticut. It is owned by the Mashantucket Pequot. The casino has 340,000 square feet of casino space with 380 table games, 114 poker tables, and 7,200 electronic gaming devices. A typical Las Vegas Strip casino has around 100,000 square feet, fewer than 100 table games, and under 3,000 electronic gaming devices. As you can see, Foxwoods is larger by a factor of three or four. And, it is growing. An expansion opened in 2008 that added an MGM Grand and an additional 2 million square feet of hotel and casino space. It will be some time before another casino anywhere in the world can catch up. As you can imagine, the tribe receives more than adequate funding for their needs.

FIGURE 6.3 Foxwoods is the largest and most successful casino in the world.

Source: Copyright © 2008 Steve Durham. Permission is granted to copy, distribute and/or modify the following photos under the terms of the GNU Free Documentation License, Version 1.2 or any later version published by the Free Software Foundation; with no Invariant Sections, no Front-Cover Texts, and no Back-Cover Texts. A copy of the license is included in the section entitled "GNU Free Documentation License".

However, not every tribe has a Foxwoods. Some tribes have opened casinos only to close them. The Havasupai in Arizona are one such tribe. Their reservation is located in Havasu Canyon, a side canyon of the Grand Canyon. The way in is limited to hiking or taking a mule down an eight-mile trail, helicoptering in, or arriving by boat on the Colorado River and hiking 10 miles into Havasu Canyon. In other words, it is very remote and not many outsiders visit the reservation. Their casino was open less than a year before they realized it was not going to be profitable. It closed without any beneficial effect for the Havasupai.

Foxwoods and the Havasupai are the extremes. Most Native American casinos have provided much-needed revenue, but the profitability of the casinos varies. Generally speaking, the nearer to an urban area or destination resort area, the more successful the Native American casino. Clearly, tribes located near a major city are at an advantage as far as generating funding for tribal government. They have a ready supply of customers. The tribes and the states recognized the inequality in this situation. Some states have attempted to remedy the situation. In California, tribes with casinos contribute a portion of their gaming revenues to the Revenue Sharing Trust Fund. The money in the fund is distributed to nongaming tribes. In Arizona, any tribe can lease its machine allotment to any other tribe within the state. The tribes near urban areas can increase the number of electronic gaming devices in their casinos. They gain more profit and make payments to the nongaming tribes. Both schemes allow less-fortunate tribes to benefit from the presence of tribal gaming.

IMPACT ON NATIVE AMERICAN RESERVATIONS

The impact on reservations from tribal gaming has been remarkable. Few Americans realized that some homes on reservations still lacked water, telephone, and electricity before the advent of IGRA.That these third world conditions existed in the largest and wealthiest economy is hard to believe. Although primitive conditions still exist on Indian reservations today, there has been improvement over the past 20 years.

(a)

(b)

(c)

FIGURE 6.4a, b, and c Tribal casinos near urban areas such as Sycuan Casino near San Diego fare much better than tribal casinos in remote locations such as Golden Acorn on I-8 east of San Diego or Paradise Casino in Yuma, Arizona.

There has been no comprehensive study completed that analyzes the entire U.S. Native American gaming industry. However, in 2007, Marks and Spilde Contreras published a study that analyzed the effect of tribal gaming on California tribes.[2] Contrasting conditions between 1990 and 2000, they studied the impact of the gaming industry on the tribes, on the surrounding communities, and on California as a whole.

Their findings confirmed that Indian gaming has broad benefits. Poverty on reservations has not been eliminated, but it has been reduced. In 1990, the per capita income on gaming and nongaming California reservations was nearly identical at $8,080 and $8,183, respectively. The nongaming tribes were slightly higher. In 2000, the per capita income on gaming reservations was $12,526 versus $9,410 for nongaming reservations. Not only did they switch rank order, but also the gaming tribes far exceeded the nongaming tribes. The percentage of families living below the poverty line on reservations of gaming tribes dropped from 36% in 1990 to 26% in 2000. For nongaming tribes, the rate remained nearly identical, moving only from 30% in 1990 to 29% in 2000.

While these results are astounding, it should be noted that these rates are significantly worse than the national averages. U.S. per capita income in 2000 was $23,634, almost double the figure for California gaming tribes and two-and-a-half times for nongaming tribes. The percentage of families living in poverty at the national level is between 9% and 10%, clearly superior to the results of Indian reservations in California. Gaming has helped tremendously, but much needs to be done.

There is more good news about Indian gaming. Because casinos create more jobs than there are tribal members able and willing to fill them, local economies are aided by the additional employment. Because many Native American reservations are located remotely, Indian casinos are located in rural areas that are typically poorer than urban areas. The same is true in California. What Marks and Spilde Contreras found was that the surrounding population of non-Native Americans also experienced an improvement in socioeconomic status. Of the 670,000 jobs created by tribal gaming nationwide, 75% are filled by non-Native Americans.

In 1990, the areas around Indian casinos had a median family income of $32,515.[3] The median family income in areas away from Indian casinos was $46,255. This sizable gap narrowed significantly by 2000. Median family income near casinos rose by 55% or $16,063, to $48,578. The median family income rose by 33% or $11,877, elsewhere. If one takes the difference in increase ($16,063 – $11,877 = $4,186) and multiplies it by the number of families living near a California Indian casino, the total impact on family income was $3.4 billion. While other factors surely helped with this improvement, Indian casinos were the most significant factor in this increase in these remote, economically disadvantaged regions.

TABLE 6.2 Median Family Income by Proximity to Gaming Reservation in California[4]

	Within Ten Miles of Gaming Reservation	Not Within Ten Miles of Gaming Reservation
1990	$32,515	$46,255
2000	$48,578	$58,132
Dollar Change	+$16,063	+$11,877
Percentage Change	+55%	+33%

There was also a significant reduction in the number of people living in poverty due to the presence of casinos. The study looked at per capita income levels within the areas near casinos. They noted that while all income levels saw an improvement between 1990 and 2000, the lower income levels showed the greatest decrease in poverty. For example, the number of individuals earning $1,000 per year in 1990 was reduced by 17% in 2000. The number of individuals who earned $5,000 declined by 7%. Those in higher income brackets increased in numbers. Everyone benefited, but especially those at the bottom of the economic ladder.

As we can see, there was a double benefit to Native American gaming in California. Both Native Americans, the intended beneficiaries of tribal gaming, and non-Native Americans living near the casinos saw their socioeconomic status improve. There was also a very progressive aspect to the improvement because the poorest individuals experienced the most dramatic improvement in their socioeconomic conditions.

There was yet another benefit discovered. Education attainment improved near Indian casinos. As we know, to sustain and improve one's financial well-being, an education is essential. In general, education attainment is lower in areas where there are fewer job prospects. That description fit most areas near casinos prior to their introduction. The percentage increase in individuals with high school diplomas was 11% in gaming areas, but only 1% in nongaming areas when comparing 1990 to 2000. Likewise, the number of individuals with post-secondary degrees increased by 24% in areas near casinos, but only 16% in other areas. Clearly, something about the presence of a casino encouraged people to obtain higher levels of education.

A concrete example of Indian gaming fostering education is provided by the Sycuan Band of the Kumeyaay Nation. The tribe has a casino in El Cajon, California, in the eastern portion of the San Diego region. In 2006, they donated $5.5 million to San Diego State University to establish the Sycuan Institute on Tribal Gaming as part of the School of Hospitality and Tourism. The purpose of the Institute is to offer for-credit courses oriented toward Indian gaming and to perform research into the impact of and best practices for Indian casinos.

The benefit of tribal gaming in California has been shared widely among the population near the casinos. Incomes increased, poverty declined, and education levels rose. Those who needed the help the most benefited the most. Because education levels have improved, the future for these areas is brighter. An educated workforce can transfer its skills to other jobs and industries. This bodes well for both Native Americans as well as non-Native Americans. A shift in employment needs will not strand these individuals. They will be able to find work elsewhere with the skills and education they have accumulated thanks to Indian gaming.

MYTHS ABOUT NATIVE AMERICAN GAMING

There is a poor understanding among the American public regarding Native American gaming in general. Among the misperceptions is that Native Americans do not pay taxes. This is patently false, but like most misunderstandings, there is a kernel of truth. Because reservations are sovereign nations separate from and not subject to the jurisdiction of states, there is no sales tax on reservations except that imposed by the tribal government and the federal government. Most tribes do not have a sales tax, but federal taxes such as on cigarettes and gasoline still apply. Non-Native Americans can take advantage of this

FIGURE 6.5 The Sycuan Institute at San Diego State University was established by funds provided by the Sycuan Band of the Kumeyaay Nation and their casino.

Source: Copyright © 2008 Steve Durham. Permission is granted to copy, distribute and/or modify the following photos under the terms of the GNU Free Documentation License, Version 1.2 or any later version published by the Free Software Foundation; with no Invariant Sections, no Front-Cover Texts, and no Back-Cover Texts. A copy of the license is included in the section entitled "GNU Free Documentation License".

situation by shopping on the reservation. However, there are few stores or other services located on reservations.

Income taxes are a more complex situation. All Native Americans must pay federal income tax on their earnings. If a Native American earns his living off the reservation, he must also pay state income tax. However, if he lives on the reservation and earns his income on the reservation, his wages are not subject to state income tax. Naturally, whenever a Native American shops off the reservation, he pays state sales tax like anyone else. As you can see, the only tax benefit to being Native American is to earn and spend your income on the reservation while living on the reservation. Given that there are few job opportunities on the reservation and limited shopping alternatives, this benefit is neither large nor widely enjoyed.

There is a belief among some that Indians are now rich because the casinos make so much money. This could not be further from the truth. It is true that some individual Native Americans have benefited from employment in the casinos. Their income has increased considerably and they have more disposable income. However, by and large, Native Americans are not creating a new wealthy class. As you saw earlier, poverty and low income are still substantial problems on reservations.

What feeds this myth is the existence of a per capita payment instituted by some tribes. A per capita payment is a decision by a tribe to distribute part of the profits from a casino directly to tribal members. The amount varies widely by tribe and over time. It is based on a percentage of the profits. As profits vary, the per capita varies.

However, only 25% or 73 of the gaming tribes have established a per capita payment. The tribe cannot just vote itself a per capita payment. Per capita payment plans must be approved by the U.S. Secretary of the Interior and only receive approval once the tribe proves that all of its other obligations are fulfilled. In most cases, the amount is not enough to supplant income earned from employment.

Perhaps the perception that Native Americans have more to spend also reinforces the myth. With higher disposable income, Native Americans are increasingly seen in shopping malls, restaurants, new car dealerships, movies and sporting events, and so on. In addition, tribal casinos sponsor sports teams and enter into marketing agreements with major league sports teams in their hometowns. Whereas their presence would have been limited 20 years ago, it is not unusual to see them today. This lends credence to the impression that they are wealthy now.

However, as stated earlier, only some have begun to benefit from casino revenues. It will take a couple generations for the opportunities to be fully utilized throughout the tribe.

CONTEMPORARY ISSUES

You have just read about the advent of Native American gaming and its impact on tribes and tribal members. Clearly, there have been many benefits derived from the legalization of gaming in Indian country. A once impoverished subpopulation of the United States is gaining a better foothold on the economic ladder.

However, this advancement has raised the visibility of Native Americans. With this visibility have come issues that face Indian gaming today. The most important issue is the revision of the Indian Gaming Regulatory Act. Since passage in 1988, the economic, political, and social landscape has changed dramatically. Some tribes are now among the wealthier contributors to political campaigns. However, the Jack Abramoff affair has tarnished Native American tribes active in politics. As the collective wealth of Native Americans rises and the size and sophistication of their casinos increase, the mythology of the "rich Indian" has grown. As casinos have proliferated to nearly all corners of the country, those who are morally opposed to gambling have become more vocal.

IGRA has been the object of revision attempts over the years since its passage in 1988. The gaming opponents have entered into these legislative battles. They recognize that IGRA will not be repealed, but they attempt to place restrictions on tribes. The easiest target is where and how tribes conduct gaming. In 2006, IGRA was reviewed. Despite attempts by a variety of interests including gaming opponents, only minor changes were made that effectively strengthened the law.

Another significant issue is the advance of technology in electronic gaming devices. **Class II gaming** includes bingo and pull-tabs. Pull-tabs are a mathematical variation of bingo. When Class II gaming was done with paper products, there was no confusion with the electronic gaming devices envisioned as Class III. No one prior to the 1990s would have confused a slot machine with a bingo game.

However, innovation and technology now allow patrons to play bingo on an electronic device as well as purchase pull-tabs. There is no piece of paper anymore because everything is done electronically. A bingo machine is indistinguishable from an electronic gaming device to a customer. Mechanically and electronically, there is very little difference as well.

Once the similarity was recognized, a controversy around how to categorize these new devices erupted. Tribes take the stand that bingo, regardless of how it is played, is

FIGURE 6.6 Members of Congress could revise IGRA or issue mandates to the NIGC at any time.

Class II. Opponents claim that the game is irrelevant. It is the technology of the game that determines the category.

This is a significant issue. Class II is not regulated by the state, only by the Tribe and by the NIGC. Reclassifying a large number of machines into Class III means more intrusion by the state into the affairs of the tribe. In addition, many compacts now have revenue sharing arrangements with the host state, but the revenue sharing only occurs on those machines regulated by the state. Obviously, reclassifying Class II machines into Class III means the tribe will have to pay much more to the state as part of their revenue sharing agreement on top of the increased scrutiny. This is money taken away from the needs of the reservation.

FUTURE ISSUES

This leads to the final two issues that will concern the Native American gaming segments over the next several years. It was noted earlier in this chapter that the compacting process was fragmented resulting in different compacts for different tribes, even within a state. This situation has been resolved, as states have renegotiated the compacts to make them consistent. However, states can reopen negotiations on compacts when they expire or if a referendum passes in the state.

The initial terms of the compacts was relatively short because the state did not know what to expect and they wanted the option to update the compacts relatively soon after they were approved. Many of the first rounds of compacts have expired and have been renegotiated. However, there are many more that will expire in the next ten years.

Any renegotiation would cause concern, but when a compact expires, all terms are open to revision. Because these negotiations have heavy political implications, the process becomes even more difficult. As politicians take stands for the voting public, it becomes harder to reach agreement on the terms. If the mood in the state swings back to an anti-gaming view, forms of gambling currently legal in the state may be made illegal. The logic behind *California v. Cabazon Band of Mission Indians* was that an activity legal in the state should be allowed to tribes. If gaming becomes illegal, a state has the right to prohibit such activities through the compacting process.

Tribes want very much to protect this source of income, since it is the only manner in which a reliable and substantial amount of funding has been available to tribes. To go back to the days of sporadic assistance from the federal government is not acceptable.

The last issue to face tribes over the next several years is the increasing energy with which the NIGC regulates tribal gaming. For the first 20 years of IGRA, the NIGC played a very minor role in regulating Indian gaming. Congress has not provided enough funding to hire enough staff to oversee the 423 gaming operations scattered throughout the 28 states. Essentially, the tribe and the host state fulfilled their regulatory obligations. However, that is set to change.

The visibility of Indian gaming has increased. Indian casinos are nearly ubiquitous. The money generated by the casinos is felt on the reservations and the surrounding communities. Some tribes are now large contributors to political campaigns. The industry has grown to be larger than any other segment of the industry including Las Vegas and Macau. It is increasingly felt that more regulation is needed to ensure that the integrity of Indian gaming is maintained and the positive impact of Indian gaming is greater than the negative. As a result, NIGC has lobbied for and received increased funding from Congress. This has resulted in NIGC becoming vocal on issues concerning Indian gaming and it has taken center stage on the issue of Class II versus Class III. Look for its presence to increase over the next ten years.

Conclusion

Anyone familiar with Indian country knows the poverty and deplorable conditions that many Native Americans experience. Due to the history of persecution and exclusion, Native Americans have been shut out of the American dream. Many options were tried, but nothing worked, until gaming. Gaming has consistently proven to create jobs and generate funding for tribes in a satisfactory quantity.

Today the outlook for Native Americans is vastly improved. Tribal governments are able to provide the services all governments are meant to provide. Poverty and primitive living conditions on the reservations are still present, but to a lesser degree. Each year, the impact of gaming is reducing these factors. Gaming has also created job and career opportunities that did not exist 20 years ago. Instead of a life of subsistence and survival, tribal members have hope of earning a living and providing for their families like other Americans.

The road to gaming involved several twists and turns. The lawsuits that helped establish the right of tribes as sovereign nations to pursue casino gaming pushed states out of the picture. Nevertheless, Congress passed IGRA in response to the lawsuits. Ironically, IGRA planted states in the middle of the gaming issue through the compacting process. The first decade saw a fragmented approach to creating the compacts for Native American casinos. Today, there is greater consistency because both states and tribes have learned what works and what does not work.

Tribal gaming continues to evolve. It began small, but is today the largest segment of the gaming industry. The largest most successful casino in the world is Foxwoods, owned and operated by the Mashantucket Pequot. Other tribal casinos are as large and lavish as any in Las Vegas. As the market changes, Indian gaming will adapt and improve. Although the forces aligned against gaming may still influence legislation, Indian gaming in some form or fashion is here to stay.

Key Words

Sovereign nation *74*
IGRA *74*
Butterworth v. Seminole Nation 75
California v. Cabazon Band of Mission Indians 75
NIGC *76*
Class II gaming *84*

Review Questions

1. Explain the various needs of Native American reservations and how they may relate to gambling.
2. Explain the details and issues of sovereign nation in regard to Native American gambling.
3. Explain the details and effects of the IGRA.
4. Discuss the workings and function of the IGRA.
5. Discuss the details of the successes and failures of Native American casinos.
6. Describe the impact of gambling on Native American reservations.
7. Detail various well-known myths about Native American gaming.
8. Discuss various contemporary issues associated with Native American gambling.
9. Explain some future issues facing Native American gambling.

Endnotes

1. U.S Census Bureau, 2000 Census. Census 2000 Demographic Profile Highlights: Selected Population Group: American Indian Alone. http://factfinder.census.gov/servlet/SAFFFactsCharIteration?_submenuId=factsheet_2&_sse=ons Accessed 2/28/09. Select "American Indian alone" to display table
2. Marks, Mindy and Spilde Contreras, Kate (2007). Lands of Opportunity: Social and Economic Effects of Tribal Gaming on Localities, *Policy Matters*, 1(4), 1–11.
3. Ibid., 6.
4. Ibid., 7.

CHAPTER 7

OTHER JURISDICTIONS—RIVERBOAT GAMBLING

JOHN MARCHEL

Learning Objectives

1. To learn the general reasons why riverboat gambling is popular today
2. To learn about the early history of riverboats beginning in 1812 and its effects on the country
3. To learn the details of the beginnings of gamblers traveling on riverboats
4. To learn the details of everyday life on American riverboats in the nineteenth century
5. To learn how poker was introduced on American riverboats
6. To learn how "sharpers" began to prey on riverboat travelers
7. To understand how the Civil War affected riverboat gambling
8. To understand how the westward frontier expansion of the United States affected riverboat gambling
9. To understand the workings of modern riverboat gambling
10. To become familiar with recent developments in riverboat gambling

Chapter Outline

INTRODUCTION

Today, riverboat gambling conjures up romantic thoughts of grand shallow-drafted paddle-wheeled steamboats moving majestically and slowly up the Mississippi River and other inland waterways of America. When riverboat gambling returned to the Mississippi River in 1991, after being absent for almost 100 years, some believed fondly that these old-fashioned excursions would help transport patrons back in time to the early 1800s of river boating with Mark Twain and Huckleberry Finn. Others might wonder how gambling on riverboats today could bring on this type of nostalgia. When we look into the past, we find that the great inland rivers in America were really the first highways in the country carrying vast numbers of people and goods near and far. It can also be seen that gambling on those boats became so interrelated during that period of time, it could be considered an integral part of American history as much as the westward expansion of the country. Throughout the nineteenth century, riverboats and gambling together played a big part of life on the American frontier.

THE HISTORY OF RIVERBOAT GAMBLING

Starting in January 1812, when the first steamboat, **the *New Orleans***, appeared on the Mississippi, riverboat gambling also became part of that American story. As commerce developed on America's inland waterways, gambling also expanded and moved from the city of New Orleans and the river towns and began to travel by boat up and down the Mississippi, Arkansas, Missouri, Illinois, and Ohio Rivers. In 1820, there were approximately 70 steamboats on those rivers. By 1860, just before the start of the Civil War, that number had jumped to over 700.

FIGURE 7.1 The Mississippi River system created the first interstate highway system allowing goods and people to move around the interior of the new nation.

Source: Copyright © 2008 Steve Durham. Permission is granted to copy, distribute and/or modify the following photos under the terms of the GNU Free Documentation License, Version 1.2 or any later version published by the Free Software Foundation; with no Invariant Sections, no Front-Cover Texts, and no Back-Cover Texts. A copy of the license is included in the section entitled "GNU Free Documentation License".

FIGURE 7.2 Steamboats allowed traffic to move upstream as well as downstream. Travel and commerce were revolutionized.

Source: Copyright © 2008 Steve Durham. Permission is granted to copy, distribute and/or modify the following photos under the terms of the GNU Free Documentation License, Version 1.2 or any later version published by the Free Software Foundation; with no Invariant Sections, no Front-Cover Texts, and no Back-Cover Texts. A copy of the license is included in the section entitled "GNU Free Documentation License".

All in all, over a 48-year period in the 1800s over 6,000 steamboats were constructed. That number might seem large; however, it should be noted that the average life of a riverboat on those early inland waterways was only three years. There were no lights or buoys and no locks or dams to control river levels in those early days. It was not that uncommon for boats to be wrecked on sandbars or run into submerged logs or trees, along with experiencing devastating fires and boiler explosions.

There was really no oversight on construction standards or safety during this expansion period. Boats were built in shipyards throughout the country and put into service as quick as possible. The average cost to build and outfit a steamboat ranged from $15,000 to $50,000. Yet a skilled captain hauling freight and passengers could expect to recoup the entire cost within one year of operation. Operating a riverboat was a hugely profitable business and could earn owners thousands of dollars from a single journey. It was not until 1852 that the government finally cracked down by imposing regulations on the construction of those craft and more importantly the design and maintenance of the riverboat boilers.

The important fact is that riverboats in the 1800s revolutionized passenger and commercial travel in America. It changed the flow of down-stream-only travel into a two-way highway on the inland waterways. The boat's speed, grace, and comfort, along with the amazing ability to oppose the river's current, opened one of history's most exciting and productive chapters. Almost all the lands that Lewis and Clark had explored in their 1804 through 1806 expedition were now easily accessible to many. The riverboats began to carry thousands of new settlers, mostly from Europe, to a new life west of the Allegheny Mountains. Travel to those new lands became an inexpensive, routine, and usually trouble-free passage for those early pioneers.

GAMBLERS ONBOARD

Gamblers in those very early days of river travel might have had a high opinion of themselves and their fellow associates as "skilled" professionals. However, the general public viewed gamblers very much with disdain, and considered them as contributing nothing to society. This certainly was a reasonable judgment when the vast majority of gamblers practiced their trade by cheating unsuspecting travelers. Many Americans looked upon "sharps" or "**sharpers**," as gamblers were called in those days, as a breed apart from other travelers. The name itself, "sharper" was an old term, common since the seventeenth century. It was used to describe thieves who use trickery to part an owner from his money or possessions. Most folks in the 1800s were aware that those sharpers did exist and were known to travel on the waterways of the inland rivers.

This view of gamblers was pointedly demonstrated in 1817 when a boiler on the riverboat ***Constitution*** exploded and killed 11 passengers. Among those travelers was a known gambler who was identified, singled out, and buried separately from the other victims.

During the first days of riverboat travel, professional gamblers were rarely tolerated. If their occupation was discovered, many captains saw fit to put them ashore at the first opportunity. Later, by the 1830s, the gamblers began to be recognized as "frequent" travelers, similar to frequent business travelers we see today, and a different opinion of them began to emerge. Gamblers on some boats were treated almost as crewmembers. They became so integrated with the movement of riverboat travel that some captains went so far as to claim it would be bad luck to sail without a gambler aboard. That point of view might be looked at with some skepticism, since it had become the practice by this time for gamblers to give captains and even some of the crew a piece of the action. In effect, most gamblers looked upon this payoff to the captains and crew as simply a type of license fee to operate on their boats.

Later, the gambler began to present a different picture of himself by changing his outer appearance. He was no longer seen as the fat red nosed individual with a waistcoat stained with food and drink looking like a hinterland farmer or preacher. His new professional appearance found him in knee-length broadcloth coat, tailored black pants, ruffled white shirt, and a dark slouch hat. Included on his person would be expensive boots imported from France and a vest with an intricate design and ornate buttons. Outlandish gold, ruby, or diamond rings on both hands were common. Most would display a large glittering stick pin in his ruffled tie, and a long gold chain connected to a European-made Jurgensen's watch costing as much as $1,000 would finish off his dashing appearance.

FIGURE 7.3 Gamblers were not viewed positively by the public or the steamboat captains.

Source: Copyright © 2008 Steve Durham. Permission is granted to copy, distribute and/or modify the following photos under the terms of the GNU Free Documentation License, Version 1.2 or any later version published by the Free Software Foundation; with no Invariant Sections, no Front-Cover Texts, and no Back-Cover Texts. A copy of the license is included in the section entitled "GNU Free Documentation License".

Gamblers by this time were an integral part of river travel. Some captains still did not overwhelmingly approve of those "frequent" travelers on their boats and would post signs at gateways that read, "All gamblers and fancy women must sign up with captain before boat leaves for New Orleans." Other notices would appear in newspapers and leaflets warning passengers to be wary. These notices typically read, "Thieves, con agents, and gamblers ride the steamboats. Many of these undesirable citizens hang around levees, wharves, hotels, and taverns in the river towns. Travelers are advised to buy bank drafts. Some prefer letters of credit from their own bank. If you need to carry a large sum of money, wear a money belt. Avoid games of chance on the riverboats." The word was out, but there were many travelers who did not take the advice.

LIFE ON A RIVERBOAT

The working area for these professional gamblers, as well as the social environment for cabin passengers, was the Grand Saloon. The saloon itself was as large as the cabin deck, some as long as 200–300 feet. It would be from 17–20 feet in width and as high as 12–14 feet. The saloon would be richly decorated and elaborately furnished on the better riverboats. One would have found Brussels or Persian carpets covering the deck, good quality furniture, game tables, and even a piano on some of the larger boats. The cabin dining room would be at one end of the saloon, while a superb well-stocked bar and smoking area for gentlemen travelers could be found at the other end. Even the freight carrying riverboats could provide good accommodations for the most part for the cabin passengers.

Deck passenger travel on the other hand was a completely different environment. Life on a riverboat as a deck passenger, by any standard, was crude and unpleasant. The savings on fare was the only good feature of deck passage. Cost for deck passage was usually half of what a cabin passenger paid. The ratio between deck passengers and cabin passengers would normally be three to one, and sometimes even as much as five to one. In the years of heavy immigrant flows, a boat may have had 40 cabin passengers and 200 deck passengers.

While cabin travelers had private rooms with beds and dressers, deck passengers would have to make do on the deck itself when it came to sleeping. They would also be required to bring their food with them or purchase meals from the boat's cook at about 25 cents each. Gamblers would only travel as cabin passengers, not only because conditions were better, but also that was where the cash-laden passengers could be found.

It is interesting to note that the term "**stateroom**," which is used to identify specific cabins aboard nautical vessels, comes directly from early American riverboat travel. Henry Miller Shreve, born in 1785, who was the inventor of the backhoe dredger, was also a riverboat captain and owner. Shreveport, Louisiana is named in his honor. When he became captain of the riverboat *Washington* in 1816, he named each cabin on his boat after a state, and other riverboat captains followed suit. Hence, the origin of the word "stateroom," which is still used today on passenger vessels to identify sleeping rooms.

Although travel by riverboat today is viewed as a romantic excursion or an exciting casino visit, its history tells us that travel in the early days was, at times, extremely dangerous due to the frequency of accidents. In the first 40 years following the introduction of the steamboat by Robert Fulton, it was estimated that approximately 500 boats were lost to accidents with a death toll of nearly 4,000 people. The worst riverboat accident occurred at the very end of the Civil War in April 1865, when the steamboat *Sultana*, carrying an excess capacity load of returning Union prisoners recently freed from Confederate prison camps, had its boiler blow up, causing over 1,700 deaths.

INTRODUCTION OF POKER

Another interesting footnote about riverboat gambling was the introduction of the card game poker, which came into its own during the riverboat era of the nineteenth century. It was a game that had roots in France and was brought over to New Orleans and was played in the saloons and gambling houses of that major port on the lower Mississippi Valley. History tells us that in its heyday around 1840, New Orleans, the "Paris of the Bayous," with 40,000 inhabitants was the major city in that part of America. However, it was also the gambling center, with an estimated 500 establishments located throughout the city offering poker along with other games of chance and employing over 4,000 people in the gaming business. New Orleans has been considered by many to be America's first gambling capital long before Reno or Las Vegas.

The game of poker itself was originally known by the French name of ***poque***. The pronunciation is just like "poker" without the "r," and the sound and spelling is thought to have become corrupted by the unique accent of Southerners. The game was quite different from what we know poker to be today. First, it was played with only 20 cards. The deck had 10s, jacks, queens, kings, and aces only. There were no 2s through 9s in the deck and there was no drawing of additional cards. Second, the maximum number of players that could play the game at any one time was four. Lastly, they were dealt five cards each and then bet, raised, and bluffed with only the cards they were originally given. Bluffing, and betting high stakes while holding poor cards to deceive opponents, was considered an integral part of the game.

SHARPERS' STRATEGY

When sharpers moved to the riverboats, poker moved with them and became the dominant card game on the river. In the mid-1800s, it was estimated that there were between 1,500 and 2,000 gamblers cruising on riverboats in the waters of Middle America. Travelers needed to take care when sitting down to a friendly card game in the main saloon of a Mississippi riverboat with a perfect stranger. On many occasions there might be as many as three gamblers working together as a team to fleece an unsuspecting cotton merchant or Texas cattle rancher out of their fortunes. Cards were marked, gamblers worked together to cheat, and sometimes an innocent looking bystander watching a game in progress was really a team member, who would signal his partner as to what other players were holding in their hands. Poker was a game that the uninformed traveler could not win. Nevertheless, some historians have gone so far as to say that the 25 years preceding the Civil War was the golden age of riverboat gambling.

By the mid 1800s, "how to fleece an unsuspecting traveler without getting caught" could have been the title of a riverboat gamblers' textbook. The system used by sharpers was a proven one that had been tried and tested during many excursions on the riverboats. Gambling team members would get on a boat at different stops and pretend not to know each other. After an enjoyable evening meal, one member might start up a conversation with a traveling planter at the bar. The gambler might innocently suggest cutting cards on who would buy the next round of drinks. Friendly talk about crops and the cost of bringing them to market might then prevail. As the evening progressed, another team

FIGURE 7.4 Melrose Plantation in Natchez, Mississippi, is typical of the size and grandeur of planters' and ranchers' homes.

Source: Copyright © 2008 Steve Durham. Permission is granted to copy, distribute and/or modify the following photos under the terms of the GNU Free Documentation License, Version 1.2 or any later version published by the Free Software Foundation; with no Invariant Sections, no Front-Cover Texts, and no Back-Cover Texts. A copy of the license is included in the section entitled "GNU Free Documentation License".

member would appear and join the conversation. All too soon someone would suggest that a game of cards be started to pass the time away.

Now everything would be in place to fleece the unsuspecting traveler. One gambler would call to the bartender to provide a new deck of cards and make a show of opening the new sealed pack. Unbeknownst to the unwary player, the cards were marked. They had been brought aboard earlier by one of the gamblers and given to the bartender with instructions to issue them at the appropriate time. Now it was only a matter of time to build up the stakes and then give the unknowing planter a powerful hand. However, one of the other team members would have received a stronger hand and proceed to take the "sucker" for all the money that he might be carrying. The team would then get off at the next landing and catch a boat going the other way and start all over again setting new traps for wealthy river travelers.

THE CIVIL WAR AND RIVERBOAT GAMBLING

The method described in the preceding two paragraphs was the standard practice of riverboat gamblers at the time. It was a tried-and-true method that had been perfected over the years by many professionals. However, when war broke out between the North and South in April 1861, virtually all passenger and commercial river travel abruptly diminished along with any gambling on the waterways. This was due to the fact that both sides yielded to the necessity of using the boats for the conflict. The inland riverboats became very valuable to the military of both sides mostly because they could be used to provide an effective means for transporting large numbers of troops and supplies over long distances.

This was demonstrated in the federal preparations for the battle of Shiloh, which was close to the Tennessee River. The Union used 174 riverboats to transport men and supplies during the campaign and battle. Other riverboats were converted to hospital ships that provided much-needed medical facilities on a large scale to help with the many casualties of the war. One boat, **the *Red Rover***, originally built as a commercial steamer at Cape Girardeau, Missouri, in 1859 was called into Confederate service in 1861. Federal river forces captured her in April 1862. She then became the first federal hospital ship in June 1862 and continued to serve in that role throughout the remainder of the Civil War. Her medical staff included the first female nurses to serve on board a U.S. Navy ship. They were the Sisters of the Holy Cross of Indiana, which is still operating a health-care service today. There were many losses of boats on both sides, and a study conducted by Montana State University–Bozeman showed that of the more than 1,000 total steamboat losses on the Missouri River, at least three dozen occurred on that river alone between 1861 and 1865.

GAMBLING MOVES WESTWARD

The war became a real turning point for riverboat passenger travel and gambling. The number of boats and gamblers had hit an all-time high just prior to the start of the war, but both declined noticeably afterward. With the war finally over in 1865 and the West beginning to open, many sharpers moved on to practice their trade in the cow towns that were springing up across the country and to California where gold had been discovered. At the same time railroads had begun to crisscross the country, and they started to become the prime mover of commerce.

Many gamblers moved to this new form of transportation and continued to practice their skill on new travelers. There were still riverboats that supplied a large amount of trade for the midsection of America, but a steady decline in passengers could be seen. The Civil War, the collapse of the plantation economy, and the coming of the railroads all spelled the end of passenger river trade. All these actions helped direct many gamblers to move on and leave the rivers behind.

During the late 1800s and into the early twentieth century, one could still find a few gamblers on the boats that sailed the inland waters, however, gambling was nowhere near the level it once was. Dams, levies, and dredging had tamed the rivers themselves. Passenger travel by boat was recognized as being too slow compared to trains. Freight became the dominating cargo, and barges became the primary method of transporting that cargo. Passenger travel on those boats was reduced to negligible levels thus ending the wistful romance of gambling on the riverboats. Gambling on America's rivers would become completely dormant and would not be seen again for almost 100 years.

MODERN RIVERBOATS

It was during the two decades just prior to the beginning of the twenty-first century that public opinion about gambling in America started to change dramatically. Survey after survey began to report that most American adults, over 90% in some reports, said casino gambling was acceptable for themselves and over 60% said it is acceptable for anyone. Most of those surveyed thought of gambling as just another form of entertainment. With the number of visitors to Las Vegas and Atlantic City approaching 30 to 35 million annually, gambling was proving it was no longer considered an undesirable pastime for Americans. States around the country began to react to this public opinion and loosen their gambling laws. Many states reintroduced lotteries to help raise funds in lieu of raising taxes. Another major event that happened during this period was Congress' enacting Public Law 100-497, the Indian Gaming Regulatory Act (IGRA), on October 17, 1988. This law allowed gambling casinos operated by Native American tribes throughout the U.S. Legislators began to recognize that riverboat casinos would not only bring in new tourist monies, but also create thousands of new jobs that would also generate additional tax revenue. In the mid-1990s, states along the Mississippi and Ohio Rivers decided to once again open the waterways to gambling and rake in "sin taxes" that were being enjoyed by other communities in the country.

The revival of riverboats with casinos was first sold to the public as tourist magnets and economic development engines for river towns suffering from shuttered industries and decaying downtowns. The draw of gambling money, which makes it easier to avoid raising taxes or cutting government programs, has inspired a never-ending struggle between those who have gambling in their communities and those who want it.

The first state to legalize casino riverboats was Iowa in 1989. Other states along the large rivers quickly followed suit. The Illinois Riverboat Gambling Act was enacted in February 1990, making it the second state in the nation to legalize riverboat gambling. Mississippi also authorized it in 1990, Louisiana approved it in 1991, Missouri came on line in 1992, and Indiana approved riverboat gambling on Lake Michigan and the Ohio River in 1993. As those casino riverboats started to operate in the early years of 1994 and 1995, they were able to generate $57.3 million in gaming tax revenue for education alone. In Aurora, Illinois, the Hollywood Casino riverboat generates roughly $15 million a year for the city. And with about 900 workers, it has helped bring down the city's unemployment rate, which has improved since the boat launched in 1993. This was just the kind of monies that state authorities had hoped for.

FIGURE 7.5 Modern riverboat casinos are permanently moored to a dock.

Source: Copyright © 2008 Steve Durham. Permission is granted to copy, distribute and/or modify the following photos under the terms of the GNU Free Documentation License, Version 1.2 or any later version published by the Free Software Foundation; with no Invariant Sections, no Front-Cover Texts, and no Back-Cover Texts. A copy of the license is included in the section entitled "GNU Free Documentation License".

The arrival of a riverboat into a community is viewed as both a tourist attraction and a major employer. Besides the captain and crew to operate the boat, there is a staff of reservation clerks, ticket takers, and restaurant and bar workers. There are also the typical casino jobs like dealers, pit bosses, cashiers, and slot machine mechanics, plus back-of-the-house personnel like accounting, marketing personnel, and other staff. These were all new jobs that were created when a riverboat arrived. It was estimated that a single boat could employ up to 500 people and have an affect on 2,000 additional jobs in the area. This provided a welcome economic impact to every community where the boats anchored.

The cost of building a riverboat in modern times is quite different from the cost of one in the last century. The biggest boat in the United States, the 5,223-passenger, four-deck, side-wheeler *Glory of Rome* at Caesars casino in Indiana, is also the biggest in the world. Built in 1989, this 452-foot-long, 100-foot-wide, majestic riverboat cost $50 million to construct. It has nine restaurants, a 93,000 square-foot casino with 2,425 slot machines and 146 table games.

Other new riverboats were less costly; however, they still required millions of dollars to build the craft and millions more to establish its operating facilities. These new riverboats do not carry cotton cargo like the early boats did. Instead, they typically carry thousands of slot machines and maybe 70-plus table games, which are considerably more profitable to the owners.

Originally, casino boats had to be fully capable of sailing even if tied permanently to a dock. In 1990, Mississippi passed legislation to allow gambling boats to eliminate the cruise requirement of vessels and allow "dockside" gaming on the Mississippi River and Mississippi Sound. Boat builders recognized that the word "riverboat" was omitted from the bills, therefore providing an opportunity to create a different type of vessel. Casino owners and manufacturers envisioned a casino built on massive floating barges. Using this design and permanently docking the *Casino Magic* in the waters of Bay St. Louis, Mississippi, the first floating barge casino in the world was born. Other regions in Mississippi quickly followed suit and today most casinos in the state rest on barges.

When first approved in most other states, the casinos were required to actually be located on boats that could sail away from the dock. In fact, in some areas, gambling was only allowed when the boat was sailing. However, over time, regulations began to allow gambling when the boat was docked. Today, legislators in the five Mississippi River states where riverboat gambling is legal, Illinois, Iowa, Louisiana, Mississippi (which had already done so earlier allowed gambling when docked), and Missouri, have accommodated the casino operators by removing all cruising requirements from laws authorizing riverboat gambling. Iowa became the last state to do so, and on October 10, 2007 the ***Mississippi Belle II*** riverboat made its final voyage, bringing an end to cruising gambling boats in America.

RECENT DEVELOPMENTS IN RIVERBOAT GAMBLING

An interesting footnote to the sailing of those modern gambling riverboats happened in 2002. Politicians in Kentucky took a negative view of the gambling going on in neighboring Indiana. They reacted by pointing out that since Kentucky attained statehood in 1792, before Indiana did in 1816, it claimed ownership of the entire Ohio River that borders both states. The politicians had often threatened to stop in some way the operations of the Indiana riverboats. Some politicians felt so strongly about this dilemma that a resolution was proposed in the Kentucky House of Representatives calling for "the purchase of a submarine to patrol the waters of the Commonwealth and search and destroy all casino riverboats." However, the nonbinding resolution never came up for a vote.

The various states with riverboat casinos allow them to offer all the traditional casino games such as blackjack, roulette, and craps. Some boats also offer fine dining and a chance to enjoy a little of the atmosphere of bygone days of early-American-riverboat history. One very important difference between the early riverboats and those of today is the slot machine. This was not a "game" available to the traveling public in those early days. Charles Fey of San Francisco invented slot machine only in 1887, and the machines never appeared on those early boats. But today, slot machines on riverboats play an important part since they alone typically account for over 60% of the total casino revenue. The machines require little maintenance, never call in sick, and do not require any workers compensation or retirement plans. This makes them a high-profit item for modern casino riverboats, and as expected the greatest majority of all the games offered on the boats are slot machines.

The results for the states have been impressive. As of 2007, the riverboat casinos along the Mississippi employed approximately 92,000 people. These are jobs that did not exist prior to 1989. Many of the jobs provide a good income for employees in areas that previously had few jobs, much less good paying jobs. The states reaped $2.6 billion in tax revenues in 2007.[1] These taxes help the states to provide government services without raising taxes or cutting services. Additional economic benefits have been derived due to the multiplier effect.

The results for the casino companies were just as impressive. They added 3.3 million square feet to their inventory. The average riverboat casinos added $140 million dollars to gross revenue or a daily average of $385,000. Entering multiple markets allows a company to counter a downturn in one market with a strong performance in another market.

TABLE 7.1 Riverboat Statistics[2]

State	Number of Casinos	Number of Employees	Square Footage	Gross Revenue (millions)	Taxes Paid (millions)	First Casino Opening
Illinois	9	8,422	285,035	$ 1,958	$ 751	September 1991
Indiana	11	15,672	573,492	$ 2,642	$ 851	December 1995
Iowa	10	9,732	359,438	$ 860	$ 174	April 1991
Louisiana	13	14,545	415,000	$ 1,781	$ 454	October 1993
Mississippi	28	30,970	1,276,512	$ 2,808	$ 332	August 1992
Missouri	11	10,900	699,800	$ 1,599	$ 387	May 1994
Total	83	91,741	3,269,277	$11,649	$2,619	

Conclusion

The role of the gambler on the riverboats of America was an integral part of America's history in the 1800s. What they did or did not contribute to the growth of the country and what impact they have had on today's riverboats is open for discussion by historians as well as laymen. In the end when we look at the expansion of the Louisiana territory and the movement of passengers and commerce on the rivers of that part of the country, we have to acknowledge that for better or worse the gamblers were there and were an integral part of that history.

Key Words

The *New Orleans* 89
Sharpers 91
Constitution 91
Stateroom 92
Poque 93
The *Red Rover* 95
Mississippi Belle II 97

Review Questions

1. Explain the general reasons why riverboat gambling is popular today.
2. Detail the early history of riverboats beginning in 1812 and its effects on the country.
3. Explain the beginnings of gamblers traveling on riverboats.
4. Detail aspects of everyday life on American riverboats in the nineteenth century.
5. Explain how poker was introduced on American riverboats.
6. Explain how sharpers preyed on riverboat travelers.
7. Detail some of the ways that the Civil War affected riverboat gambling.
8. Explain how the westward frontier expansion of the United States affected riverboat gambling.
9. Detail the workings of modern riverboat gambling.
10. Discuss recent developments in riverboat gambling

Endnotes

1. AGA website http://www.americangaming.org/survey/index.cfm. Accessed 7/2/08.
2. Ibid.

CHAPTER 8

OTHER JURISDICTIONS—LAND BASED CASINOS

Soo K. Kang

Learning Objectives

1. To understand the basic situations concerning gambling in Colorado and South Dakota
2. To understand the historical development of gambling in Colorado and South Dakota
3. To learn about surveys of the population of Colorado and South Dakota concerning gambling
4. To understand the reasons why Colorado and South Dakota voted to legalize gambling
5. To understand the different situations concerning gambling in Black Hawk and Central City, Colorado
6. To understand the regulatory environment in Colorado and South Dakota
7. To understand the tax structure concerning gambling in Colorado and South Dakota
8. To learn about tax allocations concerning gambling in Colorado and South Dakota
9. To understand the many social costs of gambling
10. To be familiar with three current issues concerning gambling: competition, target markets, and allocation of revenue

Chapter Outline

INTRODUCTION

As you have read so far, states and tribes needing tax revenue and jobs have increasingly turned to legalized gaming over the past 30 years. We now turn our attention to smaller communities within states. South Dakota and Colorado legalized gaming in specific towns in order to provide economic opportunities for residents. Without these opportunities, the populations of these towns would dwindle to nothing. The following discussion will describe the history of gaming in these towns and its impact.

COLORADO AND SOUTH DAKOTA

As small communities in the United States experienced the loss of federal programs and funding, four gold-mining towns in South Dakota and Colorado turned to the legalization of limited-stakes gambling as a means of economic revitalization and historic preservation. In the 1980s, only Nevada and Atlantic City had legalized gambling; no other small community in the United States had tried such a solution to community revitalization and preservation.

After 15 years of operations, there are 20 casinos in Deadwood, South Dakota, which generated $127.9 million in gaming revenue in 2004. Of this amount, $15.2 million was paid as taxes to the state.[1] In addition, the casinos offered 1,499 jobs and paid $34.1 million in salaries, wages, and benefits. This economic benefit was a result of the 2,926 slot machines and 82 table games in the city. As a result of the casinos, 1.5 to 2 million people visited casinos in Deadwood with an average spending of $688 per year.[2]

By comparison, in 2006, the state of Colorado had 46 casinos with 195 table games and 15,185 slot machines. The total square footage of casinos was 2,323,876 and gaming square footage was 382,942.[3] These casinos generated a total of $106.1 million in taxes on gaming revenue of $765.4 million. Moreover, the casinos employed 7,829 people and spent $222.94 million on wages and salaries including tips and benefits. This was due to the 710,000 travelers who visited the three gaming towns spending approximately $654 per visitor in 2005, making casino trips the sixth most popular marketable trip to Colorado. During the 14 years of operation, casinos in Colorado have paid $934.9 million in gaming-tax revenues to the state and generated more than $7 billion revenue in total.

HISTORICAL DEVELOPMENT

Legalized casino gaming officially began at high noon on November 1, 1989, in Deadwood, South Dakota, which is located approximately 60 miles from Mount Rushmore. This was a result of the 68% of South Dakota voters who approved limited-stakes gaming within the city limits of Deadwood. Three types of games were allowed: slot machines, blackjack, and poker. Each casino operation must offer a facilitating business, such as gift and craft stores, restaurants, or taverns. All of the buildings in the Deadwood area were required to conform

FIGURE 8.1a, b, and c Deadwood was a wild boomtown when Wild Bill Hickok and Calamity Jane lived there. Both are buried there now.

to authentic 1880s architecture. Many of the casinos were located in historic structures, but there were also some new structures that were designed to be compatible with the historic theme of the town.

However, Deadwood's gaming establishments, on average, did not show a profit until 1992. Many landowners, seeing the opportunity for increased profits, quickly turned existing businesses into gambling enterprises, and others sold to investors at prices four to five times the previous appraised values. With the onset of gambling, approximately three-fourths of the businesses on historic Main Street became casinos.

The success of limited-stakes gambling in South Dakota led the state of Colorado to follow suit and it also authorized limited-stakes gaming. On November 6, 1990, the **Colorado Limited Gaming Act** was passed with a 57% voter approval of a statewide constitutional amendment that affected three dried-up mining towns: Black Hawk, Central City, and Cripple Creek. The proposed law was modeled after the gaming laws in **Deadwood, South Dakota**. Gaming started on October 1, 1991 with seven casinos each in Central City and Black Hawk and four casinos in Cripple Creek. By the end of that month, 21 casinos had opened across the three gaming towns; of them, 11 were in Central City and Black Hawk. Gaming had grown to as many as 75 casinos at one time in September 1992.

Survey of Jurisdictions that Legalized Casinos

Published research has reported that gaming impacts on these towns have been enormous in both positive and negative aspects. The positive aspects of gambling have been economic in terms of jobs, taxes, and real estate values. However, Blevins and Jensen[4] reported that retail businesses in all four gaming towns in South Dakota and in Colorado were cannibalized, as gambling became the dominant industry in the communities. However, the resident populations and schools experienced little change; most of the change occurred in vehicular traffic, law enforcement, and the utilization of infrastructure. Patricia Stokowski[5] thought that the two Colorado gaming towns suffered from the consequences of poor organization, planning, and control as the gaming operators served their own interests at the expense of the interests of the residents.

Another study found that although 54% of Colorado residents who participated in the study voted for gambling in the statewide referendum,[6] only 5% of the residents surveyed indicated that they would recommend that other towns legalize gambling. A similar result was reported by residents in Deadwood. Only 10% of the Deadwood residents surveyed indicated that they would recommend that other towns legalize gambling.

What Made Colorado and South Dakota Decide to Legalize Gaming?

South Dakota's and Colorado's decisions to use legalized gambling to revitalize and preserve their historic communities were unique, but necessary because the towns had been designated as national historic landmarks by the National Park Service. Deadwood became the only city in the United States to be named a national historic landmark in 1964. During the 1980s, the question of gaming resurfaced from previous attempts at legalization, and a petition was introduced to reinstate gaming in Deadwood. In 1986, local business owners agreed to lobby for legalized gaming to create economic development for the community. As gaming moved through the state legislature, the Deadwood City Commission established the Historic Preservation Commission in 1987 to oversee the restoration of historic sites in the community.

In Colorado, two dying towns, Black Hawk and Central City, are isolated in the foothills of the Rockies. Both cities had been devastated by the closing of the last gold mines in 1982. The number of tourists who used to come for summer festivals and mining tours had declined until the casinos opened in 1991. Once called the "**Richest Square Mile on Earth**," Central City was known for its old gold mines and hundreds of Victorian buildings. By 1989, the two towns had dwindled to a combined population of less than 350. In order to keep the cities alive, Central City Preservation Inc. (**CCPI**) was founded to facilitate the gaming initiative.

The first year of gaming in Colorado produced wages, revenues, and tax returns in amounts more than double the expectations. Even after the novelty of the first year of gaming ended, revenues continued to rise. However, the Colorado casinos in the first years overbuilt in mainly mom-and-pop establishments, and new casinos were casino and hotel resorts. By 1994, stable, leaner, and larger scale casinos, which combined hotel, parking, and entertainment, had emerged in the Colorado gaming towns. Black Hawk, in particular, has been changed by the gaming industry most dramatically and is the site of major new casino development. The different degrees of community development were reflected on residents' economic status. According to the U.S. Census Data (2001), none of the population and none of the families in Black Hawk were below the poverty line. On the other hand, Central City had approximately 7.4% of families and 12.3% of the population living below the poverty line, including 8.3% of those under age 18 and 5.2% of those ages 65 or over. By comparison, Cripple Creek recorded that approximately 4.7% of families and 6.4% of the population were below the poverty line.

A Tale of Two Cities

Because of their geographic proximity (5 minutes apart, downtown to downtown) and the results of uneven development, Black Hawk and Central City have struggled with each other throughout the development of casino gaming. Historically, Central City was always rich and arrogant, complete with an opera house and beautiful old Victorian homes built with the riches from its Glory Hole gold mine. Black Hawk, on the other hand, was the working-class town at the bottom of the heap. For the first three years of legalized casino gambling, Central City dominated the gaming market in numbers of casinos and gaming devices. Black Hawk and Central City contended for the top position as a major gaming town until 1992, when Central City enacted a moratorium on new development in order to address problems associated with the rapid growth in gaming.

Part of the problem between the two cities was that Central City, because of its opera and tourism base, had few buildings that met the casino building codes. On the other hand, Black Hawk's buildings were falling down, which gave the city the opportunity to build new gambling facilities. Most of the historic properties in Black Hawk have been replaced by large-scale casinos. As a result, Central City accused Black Hawk of abandoning the original purpose of the amendment, namely historic preservation. Black Hawk responded that there was hardly anything left to preserve in Black Hawk. While Black Hawk has prospered from a huge building boom, including projects that required the dynamiting of rocky hills to make room for bigger casinos, Central City has suffered from bankruptcies and closings. Black Hawk, which had a $160,000 municipal budget in 1989, recorded a $22 million budget in 2001, an increase of 13,750%. By 1994, Black Hawk led Central City and Cripple Creek in the Colorado gaming markets.

(a)

(b)

FIGURE 8.2a and b Blackhawk had only a few historic buildings like the Lace House. The new casinos were built to resemble historic buildings.

Source: (b) Copyright © 2008 Steve Durham. Permission is granted to copy, distribute and/or modify the following photos under the terms of the GNU Free Documentation License, Version 1.2 or any later version published by the Free Software Foundation; with no Invariant Sections, no Front-Cover Texts, and no Back-Cover Texts. A copy of the license is included in the section entitled "GNU Free Documentation License".

The feuding continued when Black Hawk casino owners built a parking lot by leveling the top of a mountain to obtain a level surface. Central City casinos were asked to contribute part of the cost, but refused to share the construction expense. Upon their refusal, Black Hawk officials ordered the back gate of the parking lot bolted so that cars could not take

FIGURE 8.3 Residents of Central City felt superior to residents of Blackhawk because they had an opera house among other fine amenities.

Source: Copyright © 2008 Steve Durham. Permission is granted to copy, distribute and/or modify the following photos under the terms of the GNU Free Documentation License, Version 1.2 or any later version published by the Free Software Foundation; with no Invariant Sections, no Front-Cover Texts, and no Back-Cover Texts. A copy of the license is included in the section entitled "GNU Free Documentation License".

the short way to Central City. A 200% increase in traffic during gambling's first month, delivering 15,000 gamblers on weekdays and 35,000 on the weekend, on Colorado State Highway 119 leading to Central City and Black Hawk from the Denver metropolitan area, compounded tensions between the two towns.

Central City, stung by the exodus of casinos while Black Hawk grew like a mushroom, pushed through the Central City Parkway, a four-lane, 8.4-mile parkway, that routes traffic directly from Interstate 70 so that visitors would not be able to drive through Black Hawk first. With its greater financial resources, Black Hawk countered with its own plans to widen Highway 119 to a four-lane autobahn with a tunnel from Interstate 70 through the mountain that would be faster and more direct than Central City's highway.

REGULATORY ENVIRONMENT IN COLORADO AND SOUTH DAKOTA

Both states have adopted land-based casino gaming with limited stakes since 1989 and 1990, respectively. Limited-stakes gambling in both South Dakota and Colorado is unique in the way that it is restricted and regulated. In Colorado, "limited gaming" is defined in three ways: (1) gaming may be conducted only in the historic districts of Black Hawk, Central City, and Cripple Creek for their economic revitalization; (2) only poker, blackjack, and slot machines can be offered; and (3) the maximum amount of any single wager is limited to $5 with no restriction on the amount paid out as a prize. The limit on wagering does not prevent raising in poker, or doubling down in blackjack. However, each single original and subsequent bet may not exceed $5. The business hours in Colorado casinos are restricted from 8 A.M. until 2 A.M. and the minimum gambling age is 21. By Colorado statute, slot machines must pay out between 80% and 100%, with an average payback percentage between 92% and 95%.

South Dakota shares similar legal and operating restrictions like those in Colorado with a few exceptions. First, limited-stakes gambling is allowed only in Deadwood. Like Colorado, only three games (blackjack, poker, and slot machines) are permitted. A maximum bet in South Dakota, however, increased from $5 to $100 in late 2000 as an attempt to attract more visitors and encourage larger-scale businesses. Unlike Colorado, casino operating hours in South Dakota are more flexible. Larger casinos can remain open 24 hours, while most of the smaller ones are open from 8 A.M. until midnight Sunday through Thursday and 8 A.M. until 2 A.M. on the weekends. Casino profit margins are limited by state as mandated payouts. South Dakota state law currently requires that a minimum of 80% of gaming receipts be returned to the bettors. Since the inception of gaming, the average payout to players in Deadwood has averaged 90%.

The gambling industry is strictly regulated by agencies that have been given sweeping powers by both the legislature and the courts to promote the honesty and integrity of the business. The same is true in both Colorado and South Dakota. There are several legal and regulatory systems in place to ensure tight control of gaming businesses in the two states.

First, the **Colorado Division of Gaming**, a division of the Colorado Department of Revenue, and the **Colorado Limited Gaming Control Commission** are two legal entities responsible for the regulation and enforcement of limited gaming in Colorado. One of the duties of the Division of Gaming is the investigation of gaming license applicants. A prospective licensee must demonstrate that he/she possesses "good moral character" in order to obtain a license. Division investigators, who have the powers of police officers, scrutinize personal and financial histories of applicants, including the sources of all moneys applicants plan to invest in a proposed establishment. The division is required to deny licensure when the applicant's background reveals that the applicant has been convicted for gambling and gambling-related offenses.

Once the license is issued, the division's staff monitors licensees for problems such as hidden ownership interests and organized crime involvement. Division investigators also patrol casinos during all hours of operation to handle patron complaints and watch for possible violations of gaming laws, rules, and regulations. In the first 14 years of gaming in Colorado, the division's licensing section processed more than 31,000 new licenses, excluding renewals for casinos and casino employees.

The division's Audit Section conducts regular compliance and revenue audits of casinos to ensure that establishments are following stringent accounting and compliance procedures to ensure proper reporting and payment of gaming taxes. The Emerging Technologies Section oversees the approval of all gaming devices and systems. The Communications Section handles hundreds of information inquiries each year. The Training Section provides training to casinos in all areas of casino operations and regulation.

The Colorado Limited Gaming Control Commission is a regulatory body appointed by the governor. By statute, the commission is responsible for promulgating all the rules and regulations governing limited gaming in Colorado, including the establishment of the gaming-tax rate. The commission also has final authority over all gaming licenses issued in the state and all expenses concerning the regulation of limited gaming in Colorado. Commission members approve the budget for the Division of Gaming as well as allocate money to other state departments, such as the Department of Public Safety, to make sure that the gaming industry is adequately regulated and its patrons protected.

Several nonprofit organizations and programs are available to address problem-gambling issues in the state. The Problem Gambling Coalition of Colorado (PGCC) is the local affiliate of the **National Council on Problem Gambling, Inc**. Its purpose is to increase awareness, advocate treatment, and promote research and education on problem gambling. Gamblers Anonymous (Gam-Anon) has established many groups in Colorado, with meeting locations throughout the state. Gam-Anon is a support group for family members of those with gambling problems.

The South Dakota Commission on Gaming is a legal and regulatory entity in charge of overseeing the regulation and enforcement of limited gaming in South Dakota. The Enforcement Division is responsible for conducting background and criminal investigations relating to limited gaming. Interestingly, South Dakota law limits each casino licensee to a maximum of 30 slot machines and no one is allowed to hold more than three licenses. Some operators combine licenses with other operators to form a cooperative which may look like one casino, but in reality it is actually several licensees operating under one name. The Operations Division conducts regular compliance and revenue audits of casinos within the city of Deadwood. The Operations Division is also responsible for slot machine inspections and the financial portion of background investigations.

Each year, the South Dakota State Legislature appropriates $200,000 from the lottery's operating budget for expenses incurred in developing problem-gambling programs at various drug and alcohol treatment centers throughout the state. A nonprofit organization, the South Dakota Council on Problem Gambling sponsors problem-gambling education and referral services. South Dakota has more Gamblers Anonymous meetings per capita than any other state except Montana, which is the only state with more video gambling machines per capita than South Dakota.

THE TAX STRUCTURE

A percentage of gaming taxes is paid based on the amount of adjusted gross proceeds (**AGP**) a casino brings in. AGP refer to the amount of money wagered by casino patrons minus the amount paid out by casinos in individual winnings.

The Colorado Limited Gaming Control Commission sets the gaming tax rate each year. The commission provides progressive rates based on the level in AGP earned by each casino. A graduated tax starts at 2% of the first $4 million in AGP per location (not machine) and goes up to 20% in AGP of $20 million or over, with a maximum of 40% in AGP. Colorado's gaming-tax rates ranged from 13% to 14% between 2003 and 2006.

Other than gaming taxes based on AGP, casinos also pay miscellaneous fees such as application fees, license fees, and device stamp and renewal fees. In Colorado, gaming-application fees range from $500 to $1,000, a license fee of $1,000, and background deposit from $6,500 to $12,000, depending on the types of gambling offered (see Table 8.1).

State gaming tax in South Dakota was 8% of AGP with a gaming device tax of $2,000 per machine annually. The tax revenues accruing to Deadwood are held by the City of Deadwood and administered by the Deadwood Historic Preservation Commission. The commission allocates these funds to support the preservation of the community environment and to upgrade infrastructure to provide historic architectural resources. South Dakota assesses an application fee of $1,000, license fee of $1,000, and license renewal fee of $200 annually. Also, casinos must acquire a license stamp upon each card game or slot machine with an annual renewal fee of $2,000.

Gaming-tax rates below 20% are said to maximize job creation and capital investment while still generating substantial government revenue. Due to their relative low tax rates, both the South Dakota and Colorado gaming industries have received a steady stream of capital investment since opening. As of 2004, approximately $1.7 billion in capital investment was made in casino gaming since 1989 in Colorado. This capital investment was larger than that invested in Iowa, Illinois, or Michigan. South Dakota received a total of $95.6 million as capital investment since 1989. Those positive flows of financial investment may make residents feel many economic impacts.

TABLE 8.1 Colorado Gaming Tax Structure

AGP (millions)*	2006 Tax Rates (percent)
$0–$2	0.25
$2–$4	2
$4–$5	4
$5–$10	11
$10–$15	16
Above $15	20

*AGP refers to the amount of money wagered by casino patrons minus the amount paid out by casinos in individual winnings.

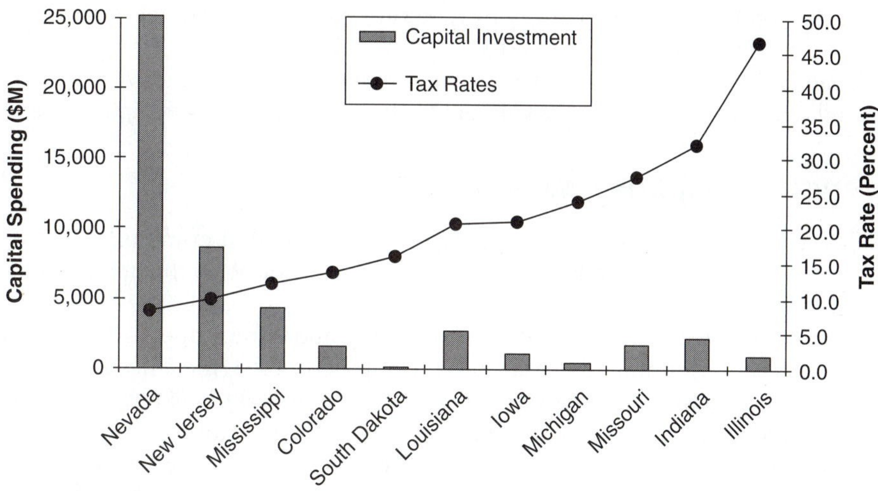

FIGURE 8.4 Gaming-tax rates and capital investment.

TAX ALLOCATIONS

Even though all four casino communities in South Dakota and Colorado used the preservation of their historic Old West images to legitimize gaming, different patterns of development are found depending on where gaming taxes are allocated, as shown in Table 8.2.

As of 2005, the gaming tax distribution in Colorado was as follows: the largest portion of the gaming tax revenue was allocated to general fund (49.8%); historical society (28%); gaming host counties, Gilpin and Teller (12%); gaming host towns, Black Hawk, Central City, and Cripple Creek (10%); and state tourism promotion fund (0.2%).

South Dakota, on the other hand, has a different allocation of its gaming taxes. In 2005, 40% of gaming tax was transferred to the Department of Tourism and 10% was paid to Lawrence County where Deadwood is located. The remaining 50% stayed in the Deadwood Historic Preservation Commission Fund. Of the commission fund, the administrative costs

TABLE 8.2 Gaming-Tax Allocations Comparison Between Colorado and South Dakota

Allocations (2005)	South Dakota (%)	Colorado (%)
State General Fund	None	49.8%
State Tourism Fund	40%	0.2%
State Historical Preservation	0.6% ($100,000) for the State Historical Preservation Loan and Grant Fund 4.3% for Deadwood Historic Preservation Commission	28%
Gaming Host City or Town	45%	10%
Gaming Host County	10% (Lawrence County)	12% (Gilpin and Teller Counties)

of the commission were paid, which amounted to approximately 8.6% of total gaming tax collected in 2005. In addition, $100,000 was distributed as the State Historical Preservation Loan and Grant Fund. All other revenues remaining in the commission fund in 2005, or $6.8 million, were then paid to the City of Deadwood as the net municipal proceeds.

SOCIAL COSTS OF GAMING

The gambling professionals and proponents argue that crime often drops when casinos move in, saying that the low crime rates should account for the upsurge of visitors to gambling locales.

This direct relationship between gaming and crime appears to be true in Colorado, at least, at the beginning of the casino development. First, the cities and towns with casinos that had the highest crime rates per 10,000 population in 1994 listed both Black Hawk with 3,181 and Cripple Creek with 2,195 crime cases. Consequently, the number of police calls in Black Hawk increased from 25 a year before casinos' opening to 15,000 annually after their introduction. In its neighboring city, Central City, the number of arrests rose by 275% the year after casinos arrived. Accordingly, in Gilpin County, where the two cities are located, arrests rose from 185 to 751 in the first two-year period of casinos opening, or a 305.9% increase. Serious crime in Cripple Creek skyrocketed by 287% in the first three years after casinos arrived. In Teller County where Cripple Creek is located, the number of arrests increased from 703 to 1,388, or a 97.4% increase. Despite an overall statewide decline of 5.7% in most crime categories in Colorado between 1989 and 1995, two gaming host counties, Gilpin and Teller, showed an immediate increase of the total offenses and total arrests after the advent of casinos.

However, as the gaming communities have evolved through development phases into a mature stage, the regulatory and monitoring systems by local crime enforcement and various community resources controlled crime rates to a certain degree. As a result, when crime rates were compared with the national average in 2005, violent crime rates in all casino communities except Cripple Creek were similar to the national average. As for property crime, however, all four communities reported a higher rate of property crime than the national average.

City-Data.com compiles city statistics and other data from government and commercial sources. According to its crime statistics, which calculate crime rate per 100,000 inhabitants in the United States, the overall U.S. average-crime–index score was 327.2 per 100,000 residents. Central City in Colorado recorded a significantly low crime-index score of 69.9 in 2003, while Cripple Creek in Colorado showed a much higher crime-index score with 711.2 in 2001, 634.1 in 2002, 914.8 in 2003, and 837.7 in 2004.

In South Dakota, the annual number of felony cases filed in Lawrence County where Deadwood is located increased by approximately 69% in 1996 since the introduction of casinos to Deadwood. By 1991, legalized gambling activities constituted one of the leading causes of business and personal bankruptcies among South Dakota residents, whereas this cause was virtually nonexistent in 1989. When compared to the national average-crime-index score of 327.2, Deadwood experienced a slight fluctuation on overall crime rates with 348.6 in 2002, 284.8 in 2003, and 307.2 in 2004, which were similar to the U.S. average.

According to a study in 1992, approximately, 1,800 jobs in Deadwood were generated because of gaming legalization. Since the population in Deadwood was 1,830, the town welcomed the arrival of commuters and migrants to fill the new jobs. The first outside job seekers arrived from Las Vegas and other cities within the state as well as from states in the surrounding area. In spite of significant increases in employment opportunities, the low-paid, seasonal nature of casino employment had taken its toll on employees' quality of life. The new casino jobs in South Dakota had highly variable hours and frequent turnover between the summer peak tourism season and the rest of the year. Many casino workers could not work as many hours as they wanted or needed. To make things worse, wages of full-time employees were not high enough to keep a family much above poverty. In 1994, there was an average annual wage of $13,494 (not including tips) among gaming employees. In 1998, wages started at about $6 per hour. Not surprisingly, these unfavorable working conditions have resulted in problems such as employee theft. Employees who handled gaming money became subject to criminal background checks.

Casino gaming also has brought numerous changes into the communities in terms of demographics, quality of life, health, and education. Table 8.3 shows each gaming community's various profiles compared to the U.S. national standards. First of all, between 2000 and 2005, except in Central City, the populations of three casino communities in Colorado and in South Dakota decreased. In particular, Black Hawk showed a sharp decrease by 21.58%, indicating a significant emigration of the residents in the last five years. Residents in all four gaming communities were slightly older in median age compared to the national average. The divorce rate in all four communities was reported approximately two to four times higher than the national average.

All health factors including air, water, and superfund quality in all casino communities were superior to those from the national average. However, the number of physicians per capita in all Colorado gaming towns was below the national average. When it came to education spending, Black Hawk was the only community showing higher school expenditure per student than the national average, $8,200 versus $6,058. Even though the education expenditure in Cripple Creek and Deadwood was still below the national average, higher property tax revenues enabled the Lead-Deadwood School District in South Dakota to increase spending per student from $3,340 in 1989 to $4,230 in 1995 and to $5,414 in 2005.

When the cost of living between the four gaming communities and the U.S. average was compared, the overall cost of living-index scores were slightly higher in Black Hawk and Central City than the national average, while the other two, Cripple Creek and Deadwood, showed a lower cost than the national average. Food cost was higher in all four communities than the national average, but housing and utilities costs were all below the national average. Health and transportation related costs were higher in Colorado gaming communities, while in Deadwood, South Dakota, these were slightly below the national average. In general, Deadwood, South Dakota, recorded overall lower living expenses than its counterparts in Colorado (Table 8.3).

CURRENT ISSUES

South Dakota and Colorado each celebrated their fifteenth anniversary of legalized gaming in 2005 and 2006, respectively. Ineffective community planning, unrealized visions of residents and leaders, and the pace and scale of growth in earlier days were lessened, resolved, and accepted by residents in the communities. As the gaming industry has evolved into the maturity stage of its life cycle and nongaming elements have

TABLE 8.3 Gaming Community Profile

		Colorado			South Dakota	U.S.
	As of 2005	Black Hawk	Central City	Cripple Creek	Deadwood	Overall
Demographics	Population	109	486	1,074	1,315	
	Population change[a] (%)	−21.58	0.62	−4.45	−1.87	5.88
	Median age	40.8	39.4	38.5	42.1	37.6
	Household size	2.31	1.92	2.23	1.93	2.58
	Married, no children (%)	31.97	18.16	30.52	25.71	31.04
	Divorced (%)	30.16	26.06	19.78	18.67	7.64
Health	Air quality (100 = best)[b]	93	92	79	71	48
	Water quality (100 = best)[b]	86	87	100	72	55
	Superfund sites (100 = best)[b]	96	97	90	81	71
	Physician per capita[c]	41.2	41.4	105.7	184.4	169.7
Crime	Violent crime[d]	3	3	6	3	3
	Property crime[e]	5	5	5	6	3
Transportation	Car pool[f] (%)	9.28	27.77	16.07	9.29	14.52
Education	School expenditure[g]	$8,200	NA	5,045	$5,414	$6,058
Cost of living	Overall[h]	102.3	101.6	84.6	81	100
	Food	113.3	113.3	102.3	109.6	100
	Housing	97.9	96.1	62	46.6	100
	Utilities	92.8	92.8	79.3	97.9	100
	Health	123.8	123.8	116.1	95.4	100
	Transportation	106	106	103	89.8	100

[a] The percent change in the cities since 2000

[b] Based on annual reports from the EPA

[c] The number of physicians in the county per 100,000 population

[d] Violent crime is composed of four offenses: murder and non-negligent manslaughter, forcible rape, robbery, and aggravated assault

[e] Property crime includes the offense of burglary, larceny or theft, motor vehicle theft, and arson

[f] The percentage of the working population that commutes to work in a carpool

[g] The dollar amount that the local school district spends on each of its students

[h] The total of all the cost-of-living categories weighed subjectively as follows: housing (30%), food and groceries (15%), transportation (10%), utilities (6%), health care (7%), and miscellaneous (32%)

Source: Sperling's Bestplaces (2005).

been introduced, more diverse issues and problems have emerged that need to be addressed in these gaming communities.

Competition

The first issue is related to competition in the gaming markets. Even though gambling came in through a constitutional amendment in Colorado, conservative attitudes of the state residents toward gaming expansion and growth have been observed as state voters, in 1992, 1994, and 1996, overwhelmingly rejected adding new gaming towns, slot machines in airports, and raising a maximum bet. Therefore, it is expected that Colorado is unlikely to change the current offerings or increase stakes.

Increased competition from Native American gaming operations, however, may result in a rapid industry restructuring that could bring changes in its current product offering and market development. Currently, Colorado has only two Native American gaming sites, which abide by Colorado's limited gaming rules, while South Dakota has nine Native American casinos competing for gaming market share in the state. In 2004, the Cheyenne-Arapaho tribes of Oklahoma filed a 27-million-acre land claim, which included all of Denver and Colorado Springs, but offered to drop it in exchange for the approval of a Las Vegas-style casino near Denver International Airport. Even though the plan was initially rejected, the proposed 500-acre casino near the airport will move ahead according to the head of an investment firm. Any new casino project in the region is obviously going to have an impact on the overall market shares and penetration.

Target Market

The second issue is a reexamination of its gaming target markets. The most successful gaming destinations attract tourists, rather than local residents. Unfortunately, the gaming towns in Colorado and South Dakota do not have sufficient markets to draw visitors like the traditional destinations of Las Vegas or Atlantic City, whose successes have been mainly ascribed to being close to major population centers such as California and New York. In particular, Colorado's heavy reliance on the Denver metropolitan market representing 95% of the market base, as opposed to attracting people from outside the state, has been an important concern among gaming officials and business owners.

In earlier days, visitors did not come to hotels, gas stations, or gift shops because gaming was the only activity in these gaming towns. This situation has, however, changed throughout various development stages in Colorado. First, as larger operations came into the market, their revenues stemmed from both an increase in market penetration and from an acquisition of the smaller units' market shares. The first indication of this trend was evidenced by the opening of the Isle of Capri, which invested $29 million on the construction of a 237-room hotel in Black Hawk in 1998. Starting with that, Colorado has experienced the trend toward megacasino-resort projects in Black Hawk as new enterprises modeled after casinos in Las Vegas join the small gambling entities already in place. Additionally, Riviera Casino and the Mardi Gras Casino opened in Black Hawk in 2000. They were expected to boost gambling revenues, not just divert dollars from existing casinos. The changes would also make Black Hawk resemble more traditional casino destinations like Las Vegas and Atlantic City, where the gambling never stops and the high-roller rules. Also, the state's increased tourism budget of $19 million from gaming-tax revenue is expected to attract more non-state visitors to the region.

Allocation of Revenue

The third issue to be addressed is the state's original purpose of legalized gambling and allocation of gaming revenues. Before opening casinos, the gaming promoters suggested that gambling revenues could fund local historic preservation and renovation efforts. Therefore, the overall image of gaming was the harmless entertainment for tourists and substantial benefits for community businesses and residents. When casinos were first developed in Central City and Black Hawk, the cities envisioned that visitors would be interested in the historic ambiance as much as they were attracted to the opportunity to gamble. This proved not to be the case. Their original historic preservation policies and approaches have been challenged by the realities of the towns' heavily gaming-dependent economy, the communities' radical transformation, and the fragile survival of its remaining historic properties, especially at the beginning of the development.

Local zoning regulations required strict adherence to maintaining and restoring the historical elements and, as a result, most of the establishments were relatively small with an average of only 160 devices and limited restaurant, bar, and entertainment amenities. In Colorado, Central City is stricter on historic preservation guidelines and Black Hawk is less stringent in its application of the guidelines. Central City would not allow any developers to tear down entire buildings to construct a new casino. Black Hawk, on the other hand, has given developers almost free rein. Considering the continued conflicts between the two cities, state officials and policymakers should attempt to equalize the development process by investigating residents' opinions and by developing long-term strategies accordingly. Overdependence of South Dakota on gaming also has been a concern for policymakers and the legislature. The state budget of South Dakota relies strongly on gaming tax (13%), which is the highest proportion of tax revenue next to Nevada (42%).

Lastly, most studies of residents' attitudes toward gambling are often conducted in settings in which casinos are being discussed as a development option or right after they open. Residents' support of gambling is a key ingredient to providing high-quality gambling experiences and offering residents an improved quality of life in their communities. Gambling impacts are likely to vary according to the time period; some impacts peak at early stages of a development, while others emerge over time. Therefore, it is necessary to monitor how residents perceive gaming development differently over the various phases of development by using a longitudinal approach both in the short and the long term. Also, addressing safety concerns and involving the community in casino planning and development process are key public relations issues. Continued efforts between community residents and leaders will be necessary and crucial to allow community agencies to work collaboratively to ensure all local needs are being met.

Conclusion

Limited-stakes gambling in Colorado and South Dakota has grown significantly and contributed tremendously in the last 15 years to the development of gaming towns. As Lane Ittelson from Colorado Historical Society remarked, "Gaming has been probably the greatest thing that has happened to historic preservation in the state of Colorado as a whole in the last 20 years."[7] Table 8.4 summarizes the key aspects of legalized casino gaming in both states.

In the early stage of development, casinos are often perceived as economic Harry Potters—magical money pumps exempt from the economic laws that govern other activities—and therefore able to pay whatever taxes are needed to make public budgets balance. In reality, casinos are no different from other business. The law of supply and demand dictates the business. Casinos cost money to build and to operate, and capital will not flow unless they generates acceptable returns.

TABLE 8.4 Summary of Limited-Stakes Gaming in South Dakota and Colorado

Criteria	South Dakota	Colorado
Gaming format	Land-based (limited stakes, $100 maximum bet)	Land-based (limited stakes, $5 maximum bet)
Year of legalization	1989	1990
First casino opening date	November 1989	October 1991
Mode of legalization	Statewide vote, local option vote, legislative action	Statewide vote, legislative action
Voting result	68% approved	54% approved
Location	Deadwood	Black Hawk, Central City, and Cripple Creek
Purpose	Community revitalization and historic preservation	Community revitalization and historic preservation
Operating hours	Vary	8 A.M.–2 A.M.
Allowed games	Slot machines, blackjack, and poker	Slot machines, blackjack, and poker
Gaming-tax rate	8% tax on AGP	See Table 8.1 Graduated rate based on AGP, but not exceeding 40%
Regulatory entity	South Dakota Commission on Gaming	Colorado Division of Gaming and The Colorado Limited Gaming Control Commissions

As the gaming industry enters the maturity stage, weaker competitors will be forced out in already saturated markets and newcomers will join in the undersupplied areas. This trend has been witnessed in the gaming towns in Colorado and South Dakota.

The experiences of bringing limited stakes casino gambling to small communities are dynamic in nature with lots of momentum and constant change. For communities like Colorado and South Dakota that are choosing gambling as a strategy for economic revitalization, the challenge is to effectively plan and manage the growth process so benefits are maximized and social costs are well controlled. A desire to maintain a pristine nature of a historic heritage while meeting fiduciary obligations is not mutually exclusive, but rather complementary with thorough planning and organization. The realization of balanced development is only possible when industry practitioners, academia, and public policy makers work collaboratively to provide a holistic view and analysis of gaming management.

All jurisdictions and constituents still need to resolve unanticipated problems and new market pressures to meet the need for constant monitoring and similar concerns. To build toward long-term success, it is important to monitor a community's ability to handle problems, to focus on the health and integrity of the gaming industry and the value of the experience to the state's visitors, to determine the effectiveness of service delivery to the communities, and to monitor the impacts on other parts of the states. The future direction of limited-stakes gambling hinges on these continuous monitoring efforts to enhance the industry in a rapidly changing business environment.

Key Words

Colorado Limited Gaming Act *103*
Deadwood, South Dakota *103*
The Richest Square Mile on Earth *104*
CCPI *104*
Colorado Division of Gaming *106*
Colorado Limited Gaming Control Commission *106*
National Council on Problem Gambling, Inc. *107*
AGP *108*

Review Questions

1. Explain the basic situations concerning gambling in Colorado and South Dakota.
2. Detail the historical development of gambling in Colorado and South Dakota.
3. Discuss the surveys of the populations of Colorado and South Dakota concerning gambling.
4. Discuss the reasons why these two states voted to legalize gambling.
5. Detail the different situations concerning gambling in Black Hawk and Central City Colorado.
6. Discuss the regulatory environment in Colorado and South Dakota.
7. Explain the tax structure concerning gambling in Colorado and South Dakota.
8. Explain the tax allocations concerning gambling in Colorado and South Dakota.
9. Discuss the many social costs of gambling.
10. Discuss three of the current issues concerning gambling: competition, target markets, and allocation of revenue.

References

Ackerman, W. V. "Deadwood, South Dakota: Gambling, Historic Preservation, and Economic Revitalization." *Rural Development Perspectives* 11, no. 2 (1996), 18–24.

Alberta Gaming Research Institute. Prevalence–United States. Retrieved October 29, 2006, from htp://www.abgaminginstitute.ualberta.ca/nav04.cfm?nav04=42997&nav03=26711&nav02=25776&nav01=25771, 2006.

Calhoun, P. A House Divided. Retrieved August 25, 2006, from http://www.westword.com/issues/2005-04-14/news/feature.html, 2006.

Christiansen, E. The Impacts of Gaming Taxation in the United States. AGA 10th Anniversary White Paper Series. Retrieved August 30, 2006, from http://policycouncil.nationaljournal.com/EN/Forums/American+Gaming+Association/65e43c15-9892-4eba-9915-5e3c383f204c.htm, 2005.

City-data.com Crime Index. U.S. Cities. Retrieved October 27, 2006, from http://www.city-data. com/, 2006.

Colorado Division of Gaming. Gaming in Colorado: Fact Book and Abstract. Retrieved July 15, 2006, from http://www.revenue.state.co.us/Gaming/wrap.asp?incl=publications, 2003, 2005, and 2006.

Eadington, W. R. "The Legalization of Casinos: Policy Objectives, Regulatory Alternatives, and Cost/Benefit Considerations." *Journal of Travel Research* 34, no.3 (1996), 3–8.

Hsu, C. H. C. "A Gaming Management Course and Its Impact on Students' Perceptions." *Journal of Hospitality and Tourism Education* 11, nos. 2 and 3 (1999), 45–49.

Kang, Y. S., P. T. Long, and R. R. Perdue. "Resident Attitudes Toward Legal Gambling." *Annals of Tourism Research* 23, no. 1 (1996), 71–85.

Nelson, T. "S.D. Bankruptcies Down 5 Percent: Judge: Gambling Caused Most Cases." *Argus Leader* (1993), 1.

Perdue, R., P. T. Long, and L. Allen. "Resident Support for Tourism Development." *Annals of Tourism Research* 17, no. 4 (1990), 586–599.

Perdue, R., P. T, Long, & Y. S. Kang, "Resident Support for Gambling as a Development Strategy". *Journal of Travel Research* 34, no. 2 (1995), 3–11.

Perdue, R., P. T. Long, and Y. S. Kang. "Boomtown Tourism and Resident Quality of Life: The Marketing of Gaming to Host Community Residents." *Journal of Business Research* 44, no. 3 (1999), 165–177.

Reuteman, R. They Came, They Saw and They Spent in '05. Retrieved August 31, 2006, from Rocky Mountain News Website: http://www.longwoodsintl.com/cgi-bin/news.cgi?rm=display&articleID=1154352952, 2006.

Sperling's Best Places. Best Places in the United States. Retrieved September 27, 2006, from http://www.bestplaces.net/, 2006.

State's Casinos Set Cash Record (2006). *Gambling Brings in $74.3M in Proceeds*. Retrieved August 21, 2006 from The Coloradoan Newspaper Website: http://www.coloradoan.com/apps/pbcs.dll/article?AID=2006608240315.

Stokowski, P. A. "Undesirable Lag Effects in Tourist Destination Development: A Colorado Case Study." *Journal of Travel Research* 32, no. 2 (1993), 35–41.

Stokowski, P. A. "Crime Patterns and Gambling Development in Rural Colorado." *Journal of Travel Research* 34, no. 3 (1996a), 63–69.

Stokowski, P. A. *Riches and Regrets: Betting on Gambling in Two Colorado Mountain Towns*. Niwot, CO: University of Colorado Press, 1996b.

Stokowski, P. A. (1999a). Economic impacts of riverboat and land-based non-native American casino gaming (Ch. 8). In C. H. C. Hsu (Ed.), *Legalized Casino Gaming in the United States: The Economic and Social Impact* (pp. 155–176). Binghamton, NY: The Haworth Hospitality Press.

Stokowski, P. A. (1999b). Social impacts of riverboat and land-based non-native American casino gaming (Ch. 12). In C. H. C. Hsu (Ed.), *Legalized Casino Gaming in the United States: The Economic and Social Impact* (pp. 233–252). Binghamton, NY: The Haworth Hospitality Press.

U.S. Census Bureau. *Demographic profile: Population Finder*. Retrieved August 21, 2006, from U.S. Census Bureau Website: http://factfinder.census.gov/home/saff/main.html?_lang=en, 2001.

Wielgosz, R., T. Brown, and A. R. Lategola. Rural Boomtowns: The Relationship Between Economic Development and Affordable Housing. Retrieved October 29, 2006, from http://www.ruralhome.org/pubs/hsganalysis/boomtowns/ruraltoc.htm, 2000.

Endnotes

1. South Dakota Commission on Gaming (2005). The 2005 Deadwood Gaming Abstract. Retrieved June 2, 2008 from http://www.state.sd.us/drr2/reg/gaming/CY2005%20Gaming%20Abstract.pdf
2. Analysis of Current Market (2004). Analysis of the Current Markets for Gaming in South Dakota, with Projections for the Likely Impacts of New or Enlarged Facilities. Cummings Associates. Arlington, MA. Retrieved June 2, 2008 from http://www.state.sd.us/drr2/reg/gaming/Analysis.pdf
3. Colorado Division of Gaming (2003, 2005, 2006). *Gaming in Colorado: Fact Book and Abstract.* Retrieved July 15, 2006 from http://www.revenue.state.co.us/Gaming/wrap.asp?incl=publications
4. Blevins, A., and Jensen, K. (1998, March). Gambling as a community development quick fix. *Annals of the American Academy*, 556, 109–123.
5. Stokowski, P. A. (1993). Undesirable lag effects in tourist destination development: A Colorado case study. *Journal of Travel Research, 32*(2), 35–41.

   Stokowski, P. A. (1996a). Crime patterns and gambling development in rural Colorado. *Journal of Travel Research, 34*(3), 63–69.

   Stokowski, P. A. (1996b). *Riches and Regrets: Betting on Gambling in Two Colorado Mountain Towns*. Niwot, CO: University of Colorado Press.

   Stokowski, P. A. (1999a). Economic impacts of riverboat and land-based non-native American casino gaming (Ch. 8). In C. H. C. Hsu (Ed.), *Legalized Casino Gaming in the United States: The Economic and Social Impact*. Binghamton, NY: The Haworth Hospitality Press, 155–176.

   Stokowski, P. A. (1999b). Social impacts of riverboat and land-based non-Native American casino gaming (Ch. 12). In C. H. C. Hsu (Ed.), *Legalized Casino Gaming in the United States: The Economic and Social Impact*. Binghamton, NY: The Haworth Hospitality Press, 233–252.
6. Long, P. T. (1996). Early impacts of limited stakes casino gambling on rural community life. *Tourism Management, 17*(5), 341–353.
7. AGA Report (2001). State of the State: The AGA Survey of Casino Management (p. 7). The American Gaming Association. Retrieved Nov. 25, 2006 from http://www.americangaming.org/assets/files/AGA_SOS_2001.PDF

CHAPTER 9

THE COSTS AND BENEFITS OF LEGALIZED GAMBLING

STEVE DURHAM

Learning Objectives

1. To understand the general points of debate between the positions of legalizing and not legalizing gambling
2. To learn the details and history of the National Gambling Impact Study Commission (NGISC)
3. To understand the definition of crime in relation to legalized casinos
4. To learn the relationship of crime rates to legalized gambling
5. To understand the use of longitudinal studies in relation to crime and gambling
6. To understand any connections and relationships between bankruptcy and gambling
7. To learn about the existence of disordered gambling and how it relates to legalized gambling
8. To understand the levels of disordered gambling
9. To understand the various treatments for disordered gambling

Chapter Outline

INTRODUCTION

You have just read eight chapters on the history of gaming in America. As you can see, the path to today's gaming industry was not a straight path. Gaming has been legal, illegal, or tolerated for most of American history. It was not until Nevada legalized gaming in 1931 and seriously began to regulate it in the 1950s that gaming became a legitimate industry in the eyes of the public. Once Nevada eliminated the influence of organized crime in its gaming industry and New Jersey established its gaming industry without criminal influence, other jurisdictions rushed to consider gaming as a source of economic activity and tax revenue.

THE GENERAL DEBATES

The debates over legalizing gaming are vigorous and often heated. Much information was disseminated along with much disinformation. Much of the disinformation came from a lack of knowledge. Very little research assessed the impact of legalized gaming on a community where it was offered. For decades, the experiment with gaming in Nevada was considered an anomaly. Nevada's small and sparse population somehow made it different from any other state. Its comparatively "Wild West" lifestyle added to the perception that gaming could work there, but nowhere else. There was no reason to study the impact of gaming on Nevada. What few studies available were frustratingly inconclusive.

Part of the debate is fueled by religious and moral considerations. Some people take their religion seriously. They make every effort to live a life worthy of the moral teachings of their religion. This often spills over into their approach to public policy. Most organized religions emphasize an orderly and responsible life. Tossing money onto a "21" table or slipping $20 bills into an electronic gaming device is not viewed favorably when the money could be used for food, shelter, or clothing for family members. Sometimes, these views are dismissed as naïve, from another era, or repressive by gaming proponents. However, many Americans share this worldview. As such, their opinions will exert an influence on public policy.

Third, there will always be opposition to legalized gaming. To think that the debate is over once casino gaming is legalized is naïve. The history of gaming in America has seen it alternately banned, legalized, and tolerated. The pendulum can swing back toward prohibition just as it has swung toward legalization over the past 30 years. The opposition should be acknowledged and brought into the debate in order to neutralize its effectiveness in influencing the debate.

The strongest portion of the anti-gaming argument had been the likelihood that organized crime would infiltrate and dominate casinos. There was truth to this argument in the early days of modern gaming. As you have read, Las Vegas was rife with organized crime money from the 1940s to the 1980s. No voter would knowingly vote for a measure that would encourage organized crime to flourish, especially in their state or municipality.

However, with the cleansing of Nevada in the 1980s and the success of New Jersey in establishing a gaming industry without organized crime influence, this argument no longer holds true. In fact, the ability of the multiple jurisdictions to establish casinos without criminal influence has demonstrated that the industry has a proven method for running clean and untainted casinos.

With the specter of organized crime not a factor, opponents to gaming have focused on other negative impacts of gaming. They have raised the issues of bankruptcy, domestic violence, crime, suicide, divorce, substance abuse, and pathological gambling. They claim that all these social problems increase dramatically when gaming is introduced into a community. Unfortunately, there is a lack of solid and conclusive research. However, in recent years there has been an increasing amount of research done so the quality of information is much improved. But, much is still needed.

In this chapter, we will review the various social problems that are attributed to gaming. The latest research will be analyzed for insights into what a community can expect if it legalizes gaming.

NATIONAL GAMBLING IMPACT STUDY COMMISSION

From 1931 to 1976, only Nevada allowed legal casino gaming. Between 1976 and 1988, only Nevada and New Jersey allowed legal casino gaming. The opportunity to legally wager was not widely available or utilized for most of the twentieth century. Nevertheless, in 1988, the Indian Gaming Regulatory Act (**IGRA**) was passed by Congress. Suddenly, casinos across the nation were a real possibility. In the early 1990s, eight states spread across the midsection of the country legalized some form of casino gaming. Casinos seemed to be springing up everywhere. This caught the attention of those opposed to gambling.

In 1996, Congress authorized the National Gambling Impact Study Commission (**NGISC**) to study gambling's impact on American society and report back to the Congress on their findings and conclusions. The opening meeting of the NGISC was held in 1997. The report was delivered to Congress in June 1999.

Because gaming businesses were concerned about their rights, the industry formed the American Gaming Association (AGA) as its own lobbying organization. They hired Frank Fahrenkopf, former chair of the Republican National Party, to be the association's executive director. Just as the impact from the wave of legalization beginning with IGRA and riverboats along the rivers of the Midwest was being felt, the U.S. Congress authorized a study of legalized gaming across America. The study was to be completed by the NGISC. The stated intent was to determine the impact on communities where gaming had been legalized. Many in the industry perceived this study as nothing more than an attempt to smear the industry's reputation. The rush of legalized gaming was less than a decade old when the NGISC held its hearings. In fact, gaming was still expanding and establishing itself throughout the 1990s and the early twenty-first century. It is very difficult to collect data on a moving, changing object much less study its impact.

The commission was composed of nine individuals representing differing viewpoints on the issue of gaming. In part through the AGA's effort, those on the commission studying gaming included industry representatives. J. Terrence Lanni of the MGM organization, John W. Wilhelm of the Hotel Employees and Restaurant Employees International Union (**HERE**), and William A. Bible, with a background on the Gaming Control Board of Nevada, sat on the commission. Opponents of legalized gaming including Dr. James C. Dobson of **Focus on the Family** also sat on the commission. The commission held meetings around the country, heard testimony from experts and members of the public, commissioned research, and performed an extensive review of the literature. The result of the commission was a 132-page report not including appendices. The NGISC looked at all forms of gaming—lotteries, casinos, horse and dog racing, sports wagering, and Internet gambling. They also examined pathological gambling, regulation, and the social and economic impacts. It was a thorough effort.

There were many recommendations. The majority fell into two categories. Many called for more research to perform studies on the impact of gaming. However, the rest were cautionary in nature. The NGISC advised a "go slow" approach to jurisdictions considering gaming. They pointed to the social and economic costs of gaming as incentive to be thorough in deciding to legalize gaming and to set in place mechanisms to minimize the negative aspects.

As stated earlier, the commission was composed of nine individuals representing differing viewpoints on the issue of gaming. Individuals who worked in the industry such as J. Terrence Lanni of the MGM Grand Resorts were impaneled along with long-time gaming opponents like Dr. James C. Dobson of Focus on the Family. It may seem odd to have such diversity. Isn't it likely that each commission member perceived the findings of the commission through a filter biased by their personal experience and beliefs? Actually, that was the point. Public policy debates are based on the fundamental question: What kind of society do we want to live in? Will we allow discrimination based on class, but not on ethnicity? Will we allow alcohol consumption or will we limit such activity? Should the government provide health care to all citizens?

The question of gambling is no different. What kind of society allows gambling? What kinds of gambling do we allow? What limitations do we place on it? The two extreme positions would be a total ban on one end of the continuum and total government disengagement at the other. The problem with a total ban is enforcement. How do you enforce a total ban when gambling is a natural impulse and considerable amounts of money can be made offering a gambling experience? On the other hand, the social and economic costs of wide-open gambling are too disruptive to the social order to allow the government to sit by idly.

The composition of the NIGSC makes perfect sense if every segment of society is to be represented in the debate. Democracy allows everyone to participate, either directly or through representatives. In this way, all views are taken into account and one extreme is not forced onto the society at large. A middle ground or compromise is required.

The conclusions reached by the NIGSC did not provide the knockout punch opponents had wished. However, neither did it unconditionally endorse the gaming industry. Rather it called for a moratorium on further gaming expansion until more research was completed. In reality, the most significant conclusion of the report was that there was not enough information. Very little research had been completed by the mid-1990s on the impact of gaming on a community. What research had been done was contradictory and hard to reconcile.

Let's turn our attention to the problems that legalized gaming creates or exacerbates.

CRIME

It is often asserted by opponents of legalized gaming that crime increases when a casino is introduced into a community. The type of crime is rarely specified or quantified in these assertions. We must have a definition of crime in order to examine it properly. Without a definition we cannot know where to look for the information we need to analyze whether crime comes with casino gaming.

Before we define what we mean by crime, exploring a theory of criminal activity will help us understand the circumstances under which crime occurs. The routine activity theory of crime states that for crime to occur three conditions must exist.[1] There must be motivated offenders, suitable targets, and an absence of capable guardians. In the case of crime, we are essentially saying that we need criminals, victims, and no security or law enforcement personnel in the immediate vicinity.

Clearly, casinos attract tourists who are suitable targets. Tourists are not familiar with the physical layout of the area. They carry large amounts of cash and other valuables compared to local residents. They do not know the availability of law enforcement or lack thereof.

Most criminals are opportunistic. They look for relatively easy targets that require little effort to plan and execute a crime. Even low-level criminals recognize that there are many suitable targets in and around casinos. The casinos attract local as well as out-of-town criminals.

When a community first opens a casino, the security force and law enforcement agencies are in a new situation. Typically, the local police department does not add officers until the casino has been open a while, after the scope of the need is known. Since the casino is new, they are inexperienced with how the casino will affect the quality and quantity of their workload. Security officers employed by the casino are typically local residents with no experience in casino work. They lack the expertise to take precautionary steps to minimize crime. These factors limit the number of capable guardians.

With the introduction of casino gaming, there is an increase in suitable targets, an increase in the number and level of motivation of potential offenders, and a reduction in the coverage and expertise of guardians. In other words, you have the perfect situation for an increase in crime.

Definition of Crime

Let's return to the definition of crime. For ease of analysis, we will use the Federal Bureau of Investigation's definition and statistics. Two key categories of crime used by the FBI are violent crime and property crime. Violent crime includes murder, non-negligent manslaughter, forcible rape, robbery, and aggravated assault. These crimes have a personal nature to them and inflict harm on the victim. Property crime includes burglary, larceny theft, and motor vehicle theft. These crimes involve strictly physical possessions; no physical harm comes to the victim.

Every year, the FBI issues a statistical tally of crime in the United States under the **Uniform Crime Reporting Program**. The report is available on the Bureau's Web site. The report provides the information in numerous formats. For our purposes, we are going to look at the data for Metropolitan Statistical Areas. These areas surround an urban core and share an identity based on that urban core. For example, the information on Las Vegas includes Clark County. A little-known fact is that The Strip and its casinos are actually in Clark County, not Las Vegas. Therefore, it is important to capture the entire area's information when analyzing crime data.

Table 9.1 shows the population and crime rates in 2006 for the 15 largest Metropolitan Statistical Areas (MSAs) in America. Table 9.2 shows the population and crime rates in 2006 for MSAs within a population range of 500,000 on either side of Las Vegas. As you can see, Las Vegas had 5,362 total crimes per 100,000 in population in 2006. This rate is fairly high. Only San Antonio (5,600), Seattle-Tacoma (5,425), and Phoenix (5,388) were higher. Ironically, New York City and environs had the lowest crime rate at 2,343.

TABLE 9.1 Crime Rates for the 15 Largest Metropolitan Statistical Areas in the United States Based on 2006 Census Estimates. Crime Rates are per 100,000 of Population

Rank	MSA	Population (000's)	Total Crimes	Violent Crime Rate	Property Crime Rate	Total Crime Rate
1	New York	18,819	440,209	438.4	1,905.0	2,343.4
2	Los Angeles	12,950	410,347	562.9	2,583.9	3,146.8
3	Chicago	9,506	n/a	n/a	n/a	n/a
4	Dallas-Fort Worth	6,004	296,427	534.3	4,419.0	4,953.3
5	Philadelphia	5,827	207,849	659.2	2,903.4	3,562.6
6	Houston	5,540	263,244	707.2	4,122.6	4,829.8
7	Miami	5,464	284,395	790.0	4,368.1	5,158.1
8	Washington, D.C.	5,290	177,617	478.2	2,888.5	3,366.7
9	Atlanta	5,138	n/a	527.3	n/a	n/a
10	Detroit	4,469	194,786	757.0	3,593.6	4,350.6
11	Boston	4,455	n/a	n/a	n/a	n/a
12	San Francisco	4,180	191,314	635.9	3,929.9	4,565.8
13	Phoenix	4,039	216,212	509.9	4,878.1	5,388.0
14	Riverside-San Bernardino	4,026	154,679	489.2	3,431.5	3,920.7
15	Seattle-Tacoma	3,263	176,751	415.9	5,008.6	5,424.5

TABLE 9.2 Crime Rates for Metropolitan Statistical Areas Within a Population of 500,000 for Las Vegas Based on 2006 Census Estimates. Crime Rates are per 100,000 of Population

Rank	MSA	Population (000's)	Total Crimes	Violent Crime Rate	Property Crime Rate	Total Crime Rate
1	Portland (OR)	2,138	84,548	323.8	3,644.6	3,968.4
2	Cleveland	2,114	76,437	459.7	3,130.8	3,590.5
3	Cincinnati	2,104	84,191	364.7	3,690.6	4,055.3
4	Orlando	1,985	102,229	879.2	4,321.0	5,200.0
5	Kansas City	1,967	93,612	595.9	4,176.0	4,771.9
6	San Antonio	1,942	108,832	497.0	5,103.2	5,600.2
7	San Jose	1,787	53,724	316.6	2,717.3	3,033.9
8	Las Vegas	1,778	94,783	877.2	4,484.7	5,361.9
9	Columbus	1,726	87,687	426.3	4,699.5	5,125.8
10	Indianapolis	1,666	77,995	546.9	4,175.9	4,722.8
11	Virginia Beach-Norfolk	1,649	64,309	462.3	3,402.4	3,864.7
12	Providence	1,613	n/a	n/a	n/a	n/a
13	Charlotte	1,583	n/a	n/a	5,248.1	n/a
14	Austin	1,514	64,049	345.3	3,942.7	4,288.0
15	Milwaukee	1,510	68,420	579.6	3,926.5	4,506.1
16	Nashville	1,455	67,707	857.7	3,842.0	4,699.7
17	Jacksonville	1,278	n/a	n/a	4,526.9	n/a

Crime Rates

Looking at the components of the total crime rate, Las Vegas had 877 violent crimes per 100,000 in population. Only Orlando, Florida had a higher rate of 879. San Jose had the lowest rate at 317. Likewise, Las Vegas' property crime rate was also among the highest. In descending order, Charlotte (North Carolina), San Antonio, Seattle-Tacoma, Phoenix, Columbus (Ohio), and Jacksonville (Florida) were higher. New York City's property crime rate was the lowest at 1,905.

What can we conclude from these numbers? Unfortunately, not much. The FBI has identified 13 different factors that can impact the level of crime in a community. The list appears in Table 9.3. By cross-referencing this list with the crime rates of the cities on the lists, we can partially explain the higher crime rates. For example, Charlotte, Phoenix, and Las Vegas have all experienced a tremendous influx of new residents in the past two decades. The lack of social cohesion means fewer residents looking out for their neighbors' property and well-being. A transient population also increases the likelihood of criminals moving to the community. This transiency is a factor identified by the FBI as influencing crime rates. These three cities also enjoy a warm climate that encourages criminal activity. Criminals are less active in cold winter weather. Another factor is the effective strength of law enforcement agencies. New York City's crime rate in the 1980s and early 1990s was skyrocketing. With the inauguration of Rudy Giuliani as mayor in 1994, his strong emphasis on enforcing the law and the introduction of new policing methods resulted in an exemplary crime situation.

Although no firm conclusions can be made, it does appear that crime is higher in Las Vegas than most other cities. Perhaps this is partly due to the many tourists and the criminals who prey upon them. Of course, any fight between intoxicated casino patrons from out of town shows up as an aggravated assault statistic for Las Vegas. Regardless, we will

TABLE 9.3 The Federal Bureau of Investigation has Identified 13 Factors that Affect the Level of Crime in a Community

Factors Affecting Crime Rates

- Population density and degree of urbanization
- Variations in composition of the population, particularly youth concentration
- Stability of the population with respect to residents' mobility, commuting patterns, and transient factors
- Modes of transportation and highway system
- Economic conditions, including median income, poverty level, and job availability
- Cultural factors and educational, recreational, and religious characteristics
- Family conditions with respect to divorce and family cohesiveness
- Climate
- Effective strength of law enforcement agencies
- Administrative and investigative emphases of law enforcement
- Policies of other components of the criminal justice system
- Citizens' attitudes toward crime
- Crime reporting practices of the citizenry

have to wait for a comprehensive study of crime rates in gaming jurisdictions in order to settle this question.

Longitudinal Studies

There are flaws to the approach discussed earlier. To determine the impact gaming has on crime, a **longitudinal study** of a community that introduces gaming should be performed. A baseline would be established prior to the existence of casinos. An analysis of crime statistics over a period of years would yield the answer as to whether crime increased, decreased, or remained the same due to gaming. In addition, the population affected by crime should include tourists. Casinos attract a large number of visitors, and visitors presumably would be the victims of most of the crime committed in and near a casino. Finally, the types of crime more likely to result from casino activity (public drunkenness, credit card fraud, embezzlement, prostitution, etc.) are not included in the FBI's statistics. Data on these crimes are available only from the local law enforcement agency.

Fortunately, such a study taking these factors into account has been conducted. In 1998, B. Grant Stitt, David Giacopassi, and Mark Nichols published a study of seven casino jurisdictions: Sioux City (Iowa), Biloxi (Mississippi), St. Louis (city), St. Louis (county), Alton (Illinois), Peoria (Illinois), and St. Joseph (Missouri).[2] The jurisdictions ranged from a large metropolitan area to mid-size cities. Biloxi had nine casinos while Alton had a single riverboat. Each had legalized gaming in the 1990s.

The authors established a baseline of crime based on the four years prior to the opening of the casino. They then compared the baseline to the crime levels for a period of up to three years after the opening of the casinos. They categorized the change in crime rate as a significant increase, a significant decrease, or no change based on statistical analysis of the data. Table 9.4 shows the results of the analysis. As is readily apparent, the results vary widely from one jurisdiction to another. Some jurisdictions like Alton experienced an overall significant decline in its crime rate while others like Peoria and Sioux City saw their crime rate soar. No conclusions can be drawn regarding the impact of casino gaming on the overall crime rate.

TABLE 9.4 Stitt, Giacopassi, and Nichols Found No Pattern to the Overall Change in Crime when Casino Gaming was Introduced into a Community

	Significant Increase		Significant Decrease		No Change		Crime
	Categories	Proportion	Categories	Proportion	Categories	Proportion	Categories
Sioux City	12	54.5%	4	18.2%	6	27.3%	22
Biloxi	10	45.5%	5	22.7%	7	31.8%	22
St. Louis (city)	6	27.3%	11	50.0%	5	22.7%	22
St. Louis (county)	6	31.6%	11	57.9%	2	10.5%	19
Alton	2	12.5%	10	62.5%	4	25.0%	16
Peoria	9	75.0%	2	6.7%	1	8.3%	12
St. Joseph	4	23.5%	2	11.8%	11	64.7%	17

Source: U.S. Dept. of Justice.

Even looking at the individual crimes provides little insight. The only offense, which increased in all jurisdictions, was drug violations. The crime with the most dramatic increase was credit card fraud, though it did not increase in all jurisdictions. While there is an inherent logic to associate these crimes with the casino environment, a compelling argument could be made that introducing any economic activity that raises the disposable income of the population, could lead to an increase in crime. In other words, opening a car manufacturing plant or technology campus could lead to the same results.

One of the assumptions behind this study was that any change in crime statistics would be attributed to the opening of a casino. However, the warning provided by the FBI regarding the multiplicity of factors affecting crime statistics applies here as well. The opening of a casino increases the transient nature of the population. An initially understaffed and inexperienced police force is temporarily weak; this encourages criminals to victimize patrons and residents alike. In other words, it may not be the casino itself, but the introduction of any large and new business which employs many people and attracts tourists into the jurisdiction that impacts crime rates.

As we have seen, crime may go up. It may go down. The impact of casino gaming on crime rates probably is similar to any other large-scale business, especially one that attracts a lot of tourists, and does not in and of itself create more crime purely due to the gaming activity.

BANKRUPTCY

The connection between bankruptcy and gambling is intuitively appealing. After all, if a gambler bets more than he can afford, even only occasionally, it can lead to dire financial stress. Major payments such as rent or mortgage and car payments can go unpaid leading to the use of credit cards for daily expenses. The balance on credit cards can mount and incur large interest payments that only exacerbate the situation. Eventually, the gambler is buried in debt and turns to the legal system for relief through the bankruptcy process.

Unfortunately, there have been no studies that firmly establish this link. In 1999, the United States Department of the Treasury produced a report that tried to determine the strength of the link, if any, between casino gambling and bankruptcy. It was directed by Congress to perform the study and report back to Congress. The final report was delivered to Congress in July 1999.

The Treasury Department reviewed three major studies and several minor studies. SMR Research Corporation[3] studies the issues surrounding bankruptcy in response to the rise in the national bankruptcy rate. The authors of the study theorized that because the availability of casino gaming had risen at the same time as the bankruptcy rate there must be a causal connection. However, the results of their study are mixed. They found that easy credit, unemployment, lender marketing, consumer debt, and other factors contribute to the bankruptcy rate.

They found a small relationship between access to casino gaming and bankruptcy. As can be seen in Table 9.5, counties with no gaming facilities had a bankruptcy rate of 3.96, or lower by 18% than counties with some gaming facilities. Counties with five or more gaming facilities had a bankruptcy rate higher than nongaming counties by 35%. Clearly, there is a relationship, but is it causal in nature? We cannot tell unless we look at all the other factors to determine their impact. In addition, the counties with gaming may have had higher rates before the introduction of gaming facilities. Typically, gaming is

TABLE 9.5 SMR Research Corporation Found a Small Relationship between the Rate of Bankruptcies and the Presence of Gambling Facilities

	Number of Counties	Population	1996 Bankruptcy Filings	Filings per '000 Residents
All Counties with Gambling Facilities	298	97,385,935	454,384	4.67
Counties with 5+ Gambling Facilities	23	16,391,661	87,435	5.33
Counties with 1–4 Gambling Facilities	275	80,944,274	366,949	4.53
Counties with No Facilities	2,844	166,526,572	358,724	3.96

introduced into economically distressed jurisdictions. It is likely the bankruptcy rates were high beforehand.

The study notes much evidence to counter the position that gambling causes bankruptcy rates to rise. Of the 24 counties with the highest bankruptcy rates, only 9 contained or were near gaming facilities. If there was a strong cause-and-effect relationship, certainly a majority of those counties would have high rates. In addition, South Dakota, Minnesota, and Iowa have gaming and low bankruptcy rates while Hawaii has no gaming and high bankruptcy rates. The other factors that impact bankruptcy rates must be at play.

A study by Tahira K. Hira of Iowa State University[4] was focused specifically on finding a connection between gaming and bankruptcy. Her subjects were individuals who had sought bankruptcy protection through the courts and who had responded to a questionnaire that they were gamblers. She found that there were four main predictors of bankruptcy: number of credit cards, amount of credit card debt, income level, and marital status. Gambling was not a major factor according to this study.

A University of Minnesota Medical School study analyzed 1,342 individuals in pathological treatment centers in Minnesota over a four-year period. They found that 21% had declared bankruptcy and 94% reported that they had had at least one gambling-related problem in their life. Many had debt well in excess of their income's ability to repay it. While the study could not conclude that gambling caused bankruptcy, it is easy to conclude that pathological gambling leads to debt buildup and can lead to bankruptcy.

While pathological gambling can lead to bankruptcy, the Treasury Department noted that more relevant factors include the 1978 Bankruptcy Reform Act which liberalized bankruptcy processes, higher levels of debt relative to income in general, increasing availability of credit card debt, increase in the number of divorces, high medical expenses, unemployment, and increases in the number of uninsured motorists. Again, the conclusion that casinos create social costs is not supported entirely by the data.

DISORDERED GAMBLING

Our final topic is the one topic that can be laid squarely at the doorstep of casinos. After all, you cannot have disordered gamblers without gambling. However, the situation is not that straightforward. Gambling is available in many forms, both legal and illegal. Casinos may not be the only source of increased opportunity for gambling available to the person suffering from disordered gambling.

Before we examine disordered gambling as a social problem, we must define what we mean by the term. In general, a person is said to suffer from **disordered gambling** if they experience a persistent and recurring failure to resist gambling behavior that is harmful to the individual and concerned others. They find it difficult to limit the amount of time and money spent on gambling, and suffer adverse effects due to this activity.

Levels of Disordered Gambling

There are actually three levels used in diagnosing this condition. Each level is defined by the behavior of the gambler and the consequences. The list of behaviors in Table 9.6 is used for assessment purposes.

Level 1 represents those individuals who can gamble without experiencing any adverse effects from their gambling. This is not to say they do not experience discomfort. After all, losing more than your budget for gambling during a trip to Las Vegas or Atlantic City can cause feelings of anger, frustration, and disappointment. However, these are not severe enough to warrant the label of "adverse effects." The vast majority of people fall into this category. In addition, those who do not gamble at all clearly fall into Level 1.

Level 2 are people who gamble, but exhibit fewer than five of the criteria from Table 9.6. They do not experience dire financial and relationship consequences. However, they are not fully in control of their gambling behavior.

TABLE 9.6 The *Diagnostic* and *Statistical Manual of Mental Disorders, 4th Edition* or *DSM-IV* Recommends Using These Criteria in Diagnosing Someone with a Disordered Gambling Problem

Criteria for diagnosing pathological gambling

1. Preoccupation. The subject has frequent thoughts about gambling experiences whether past, future, or fantasy.
2. Tolerance. As with drug tolerance, the subject requires larger or more frequent wagers to experience the same "rush."
3. Withdrawal. Restlessness or irritability associated with attempts to cease or reduce gambling.
4. Escape. The subject gambles to improve mood or escape problems.
5. Chasing. The subject tries to win back gambling losses with more gambling.
6. Lying. The subject tries to hide the extent of his or her gambling by lying to family, friends, or therapists.
7. Stealing, in order to feed their gambling addiction.
8. Loss of control. The person has unsuccessfully attempted to reduce gambling.
9. Illegal acts. The person has broken the law in order to obtain gambling money or recover gambling losses. This may include acts of theft, embezzlement, fraud, forgery, or bad checks.
10. Risked significant relationship. The person gamble despite risking or losing a relationship, job, or other significant opportunity.
11. Bailout. The person turns to family, friends, or another third party for financial assistance as a result of gambling.

Source: American Psychiatric Association, *The Diagnostic and Statistical Manual of Mental Disorders,* 4th edition, *American Psychiatric Association,* 1994, and reprinted with permission.

Level 3 gamblers are often labeled pathological gamblers because they exert little control over their gambling behavior. A person is categorized as a Level 3 gambler if he/she exhibits at least five of the criteria listed in Table 9.6. As you can see, some of these behaviors are obviously destructive. The loss of a job or significant relationship in the pursuit of any single activity is not healthy for an individual. Lying, stealing, and other illegal acts are not recommended for a wholesome, beneficial lifestyle. The gambler's behavior affects not only themselves, but also others in their lives. Loss of rent or mortgage money will obviously imperil spouses and children dependent on the gambler for financial support.

There have been various studies conducted to determine the prevalence of Level 3 disordered gambling. The results vary, but the general consensus is that between 0.4% and 1.5% of the adult population experiences severe disordered gambling behavior. An additional 1.0% to 3.0% experience Level 2 gambling disorders. The remaining 96% experience no problem when gambling. They are able to control the amount of time and money spent on gambling activities and they do not experience any adverse effects from their gambling.

The question arises of why some people exhibit this behavior and not others. Opponents of gaming generally propose that it is a moral failing, fully within the control of the individual, brought on by the availability of gambling venues. They argue that limiting the venues will reduce the number of disordered gamblers. This approach ignores the reality that there is something inherent in a disordered gambler which makes him/her more likely to gamble than others. Someone with the proclivity for this behavior will seek out the opportunity to gamble, regardless of whether it is legal or illegal, a casino or a lottery, local or distant.

Causes of Disordered Gambling

The scientific community has not fully determined the root of disordered gambling behavior, but experiments to date indicate that there could be a biological and genetic basis. Dr. Donald W. Black of the University of Iowa studied 31 disordered gamblers and their parents, siblings, and children.[5] He also studied a group of 31 individuals who did not exhibit disordered gambling behavior as a control group. Through detailed interviews, he determined that a pathological gambler's relatives exhibited an 8.3% rate of disordered gambling. The rate among the control group was 2.1%. While not identifying the exact mechanism or gene sequence, the study clearly shows a connection between genetic heredity and gambling behaviors.

Dr. Black also found that there was a higher rate of other impulse-related disorders such as alcoholism and substance abuse within the families with a disordered gambler. This condition is called comorbidity. It is not unusual for an individual who suffers from one impulse disorder to exhibit another. This would suggest that there is an underlying cause to all the behaviors. Therefore, while limiting the number and availability of gambling venues would help minimize the incidence of disordered gambling, it would ignore a possible problem, which is internal to the individual. Further research is needed to understand the nature of all addictions fully so that treatment programs can be made more effective.

Treatment of Disordered Gambling

Current options in treatment for disordered gambling are varied. Counseling provided by a psychologist or social worker provides a one-on-one situation where the gambler receives intense treatment from a professional who understands impulse disorders. Peer support methods rely on groups of gamblers advising and encouraging each other to refrain from gambling. Self-help approaches allow the gambler to deal with his/her behavior through the use of reference materials and telephone support.

The most well-known approach is step-based programs such as **Gamblers Anonymous**. Gamblers Anonymous has the gambler answer the 20 questions listed in Table 9.7. A disordered gambler will answer affirmative to at least seven of these questions. These questions reflect the criteria for determining if an individual suffers from disordered gambling as listed in Table 9.6.

A member of Gamblers Anonymous will follow a process based on successive activities, listed in Table 9.8. One of the basic premises of the organization is that a gambler cannot be treated until he/she wants to be treated. Until the gambler realizes the impact his/her behavior has on his/her life, relationships, job, and other areas, there is nothing the organization can do. Hence, the first step is to admit powerlessness over the behavior and that life is unmanageable as a result.

The effectiveness of treatment is still being debated. In part, the definition of success must be determined. Is it considered a failure if a disordered gambler gambles once after completing treatment? Is it considered a failure if a disordered gambler relapses periodically, but always returns to the program? Even if we were to define success, the reality is that no one treatment is 100% effective. Not all disordered gamblers correct their behavior.

TABLE 9.7 These Questions are Asked by Gamblers Anonymous to Determine if Someone Will Find the Organization Helpful

Twenty Questions asked by Gamblers Anonymous

1. Did you ever lose time from work or school due to gambling?
2. Has gambling ever made your home life unhappy?
3. Did gambling affect your reputation?
4. Have you ever felt remorse after gambling?
5. Did you ever gamble to get money with which to pay debts or otherwise solve financial difficulties?
6. Did gambling cause a decrease in your ambition or efficiency?
7. After losing did you feel you must return as soon as possible and win back your losses?
8. After a win did you have a strong urge to return and win more?
9. Did you often gamble until your last dollar was gone?
10. Did you ever borrow to finance your gambling?
11. Have you ever sold anything to finance gambling?
12. Were you reluctant to use "gambling money" for normal expenditures?
13. Did gambling make you careless of the welfare of yourself or your family?
14. Did you ever gamble longer than you had planned?
15. Have you ever gambled to escape worry, trouble, boredom or loneliness?
16. Have you ever committed, or considered committing, an illegal act to finance gambling?
17. Did gambling cause you to have difficulty in sleeping?
18. Do arguments, disappointments or frustrations create within you an urge to gamble?
19. Did you ever have an urge to celebrate any good fortune by a few hours of gambling?
20. Have you ever considered self destruction or suicide as a result of your gambling?

TABLE 9.8 The Steps toward Recovery for a Disordered Gambler are Very Similar to the Steps of Other 12-Step Programs

THE RECOVERY PROGRAM
Here are the steps which are a program of recovery
1. We admitted we were powerless over gambling—that our lives had become unmanageable.
2. Came to believe that a Power greater than ourselves could restore us to a normal way of thinking and living.
3. Made a decision to turn our will and our lives over to the care of this Power of our own understanding.
4. Made a searching and fearless moral and financial inventory of ourselves.
5. Admitted to ourselves and to another human being the exact nature of our wrongs.
6. Were entirely ready to have these defects of character removed.
7. Humbly asked God (of our understanding) to remove our shortcomings.
8. Made a list of all persons we had harmed and became willing to make amends to them all.
9. Make direct amends to such people wherever possible, except when to do so would injure them or others.
10. Continued to take personal inventory and when we were wrong, promptly admitted it.
11. Sought through prayer and meditation to improve our conscious contact with God as we understood Him, praying only for knowledge of His will for us and the power to carry that out.
12. Having made an effort to practice these principles in all our affairs, we tried to carry this message to other compulsive gamblers.

Further research into the true nature of the behavior will lead us to the answers for more effective treatment.

In the meantime, the casino industry clearly presents a temptation to those who are disordered gamblers. Like the alcohol service industry, where the responsibility for not serving intoxicated guests is placed squarely on the establishment, the casinos are in a position to cut off disordered gamblers. While bartenders and cocktail servers can be trained to identify the symptoms of an intoxicated guest, casinos have very little criteria to determine if a guest is a disordered gambler. The gambler who is playing the nickel slots is just as likely to be a disordered gambler as the craps player who is betting $100 per bet. There is very little evidence to tell the casino employee if someone has ruined personal relationships, lost a job, sold an asset to finance gambling, and so on. Until there is a generally accepted protocol for determining who is a disordered gambler, the industry will continue to fund the research needed to identify the sources of the behavior and to create effective treatment regimens.

In light of the research on pathological gamblers, individual casinos as well as the casino industry have worked hard to develop responsible gaming. These efforts support associations like Gamblers Anonymous, but also develop new avenues to handle gambling problems. The casino industry, especially the AGA has developed and sponsored research agendas to identify ways to help. In fact, the AGA created a special branch of the organization devoted to studying these very issues.

Conclusion

The introduction of casino gaming into a community is a major consideration. The impact is positive and negative. This chapter has addressed some of the negative aspects as put forth by opponents to gambling.

The National Gambling Impact Study Commission addressed many of these topics in the mid-1990s. Their most significant conclusion was that more research was needed in order to identify the magnitude of the problems, the sources of the problems, and the strategies to cope with the problems. While there has been considerable research conducted since the commission's report was presented to Congress in 1999, there are still no firm answers.

As we look at crime, bankruptcy, and disordered gambling, we see that casinos are only partially to blame for these side effects. Crime rates are impacted by numerous factors. A rise in bankruptcy does not appear to follow when casino gaming is legalized, but a certain degree of correlation is evident in the data. Disordered gambling is certainly encouraged by the availability of casino gaming, but the condition appears to be innate to certain individuals who will seek out opportunities to gamble with or without legalized gaming in their jurisdiction of residence.

This is not to say that the gaming industry should ignore the protests of opponents and the obvious impact of its business on communities. The funding the industry provides for research and treatment will allow the scientific community to make progress toward a definitive answer as to what exactly is the social impact of legalized gaming. Without the industry's support, this research would not be funded. It is in everyone's best interest—individuals, the industry, communities, and society at large—to find the information needed to minimize the negative impact on individuals and communities by legalized gaming.

Key Words

IGRA *120*
NGISC *120*
HERE *120*
Focus on the Family *120*
Uniform Crime Reporting Program *122*
Longitudinal study *125*
Disordered gambling *128*
Gamblers Anonymous *130*

Review Questions

1. Explain the general points of debate between the positions of legalizing and not legalizing gambling.
2. Discuss the details and history of the National Gambling Impact Study Commission (NGISC).
3. Explain the definition of crime in relation to legalized casinos.
4. Explain the relationship of crime rates to legalized gambling.
5. Detail some of the uses of longitudinal studies in relation to crime and gambling.
6. Discuss if there are any connections and relationships between bankruptcy and gambling.
7. Define disordered gambling and explain how it relates to legalized gambling.
8. Detail the levels of disordered gambling.
9. Detail the various treatments for disordered gambling.

Endnotes

1. Cohen, L. & Felson, M. (1993). Social change and crime rates: A routine activities approach. *American Sociological Review*, 44, 588–607.
2. Stitt, B. G., Giacopassi, D., & Nichols, M. (1998). *The Effect of Casino Gambling on Crime in New Casino Jurisdictions*. U.S. Department of Justice, p. 6.
3. SMR Research Corporation (1997). *The Personal Bankruptcy Crisis, 1997: Bankruptcy Report.*
4. Hira, T. (1998). *Bankruptcy and Gambling: Is There a Connection?* Iowa State University.
5. Black, D. W., M.D. (2006). *Pathological Gambling and Family Background*. University of Iowa.

CHAPTER 10

ECONOMIC BENEFITS

STEVE DURHAM

Learning Objectives

1. To understand the basic overall economic benefits of casino gambling
2. To learn the details and extents of the benefits of additional jobs that casino gambling brings to a community
3. To understand the effects that casinos have on welfare programs
4. To understand the role that additional taxes brought in by a casino has to a community and its economy
5. To learn the specific examples of the economic benefits of additional taxes in the Nevada and Illinois markets
6. To understand the casino industry's impact on job creation in the local community
7. To learn how other governments' (such as Great Britain's and Russia's) actions have affected their local casino industries

Chapter Outline

Introduction
Jobs
Multiplier Effect
Welfare to Work
Taxes
  Nevada's Tax Rate
  Illinois' Tax Rate
Impact on Job Creation
Other Governments' Actions
  Great Britain
  Russia
  Atlantic City
Summary
Conclusion

INTRODUCTION

Chapter 9 cataloged a number of social impacts that accrue to a community when it legalizes casino gaming. There are many factors which, both positively and negatively, change the community when a casino is introduced. For example, with all the new jobs created, people move to the area to work. This influx creates a more transient community. Transiency is identified by the Federal Bureau of Investigation as a factor that positively correlates with increases in crime rates. Transiency would have the same effect if a Toyota plant or a Google campus were brought into the community. Therefore, in general, increases in new jobs would swell the population density in the area which in turn would raise the crime rate. Therefore, the gambling allowed in a casino does increase the crime rate, but perhaps not totally in the way people might think. Although none of the social impacts can be totally attributed to casino gaming, residents of a community need an incentive to allow casino gaming, especially if some of the social impact is negative.

As you have read in many previous chapters, proponents for legalized gaming have emphasized the jobs created and the tax revenue generated as the primary benefits. In this chapter we are going to explore these factors in more detail. What kinds of jobs are created? How do they impact the local economy? What kinds of taxes are generated? How much money is collected? What are the tax rates in different jurisdictions? What are the political attitudes toward the casinos in a community?

JOBS

It is obvious that a casino creates jobs. According to the American Gaming Association,[1] commercial casinos employ over 354,921 people in America. There are an additional 450,000 jobs in related businesses. That means that over 800,000 people owe their livelihood to the casino industry. From 2004 to 2005, the industry created 5,000 new jobs. Every time a new casino opens, more jobs are created. With the advent of gaming in Pennsylvania and other new jurisdictions, we can expect additional jobs. This is particularly important in areas of high unemployment.

What is not so obvious are the types of jobs that are created. Casinos actually create three categories of jobs: direct temporary, direct permanent, and indirect jobs. The construction jobs created when the casino is designed and built are a form of **direct temporary jobs**. Architects and interior designers, plumbers and electricians, and steel framers and concrete pourers are all needed to build the casino. These jobs are created solely to benefit the casino, but are temporary in nature. Once the casino opens, these jobs end.

Jobs that are paid directly by the casino and are created solely for the benefit of the casino are called **direct permanent jobs**. These jobs include dealer, hotel front desk clerk, cook, and so on. The people who supervise and manage these positions are also working at a type of direct permanent job. These jobs did not exist before the casino was built. These jobs are ongoing and do not end. The casino continues to need someone to perform these duties in order to serve the guests, maintain the facilities, create a secure environment, and so on.

A third category created is indirect jobs. **Indirect jobs** are created due to the infusion of money into the local economy. Every $100 million in casino revenues results in $21.7 million in direct supply purchases.[2] Indirect jobs are created by the presence of the casino, but not paid by the casino directly. A new delivery person is hired by the local food supplier to handle the increased work load supplying the casino. A new dry cleaner opens up and hires a clerk because the new dealers, managers, supervisors, and so on, need their clothes cleaned. The local fire department hires additional firemen due to the increased number of homes that need fire protection. The number of examples is endless.

The first jobs created due to the casino are the construction jobs. According to a study by Arthur Andersen for the American Gaming Association in 1996, for every $1 million

FIGURE 10.1a, b, and c Casinos bring three types of jobs to a community—direct temporary, direct permanent, and indirect.

Source: (a) © Lisa F. Young. Image from BigStockPhoto.com. (b) © Robert Lerich. Image from BigStockPhoto.com. (c) © Dragan Frifuovic. Image from BigStockPhoto.com

invested in building a casino, renovating a casino, or adding on to a casino between 10 and 15 jobs are created.[3] For example, a casino that costs $1 billion to build will create between 10,000 and 15,000 construction-related jobs. That is a significant number, particularly in an area of high unemployment. Not only does the construction of the casino employ these individuals, but these employees can use the experience they gained in building the casino in the construction of other types of buildings. This experience enhances these individuals' ability to obtain further employment and their lives are improved accordingly.

The casino industry is one of the more labor-intensive industries. It takes a lot of people to staff a hotel/casino. Desk clerks, dealers, slot change personnel, food servers, cooks, and more are needed to run a casino. Although technology has made inroads, guests still prefer to interact with a person rather than a machine. It is estimated that 13 jobs are created for every $1 million in revenue.[4] Although the actual number will vary depending upon the size and amenities offered by a casino, you can see this is a significant number of jobs.

According to the American Gaming Association, the 354,921 employees of casinos were paid a total of $12.6 billion including tips and benefits in 2006.[5] That is, an average compensation package of $35,600. In other words, casinos employ many people and they pay them well. The Arthur Andersen study referenced earlier found that the casino industry on average paid better wages than the motion picture industry, the hotel/motel industry, and the amusement/recreation industry.

MULTIPLIER EFFECT

As stated earlier, indirect jobs are needed to service the needs of the casino as well as its employees. The money spent by the casino on payroll, supplies, and services spreads throughout the community. This is called the **multiplier effect**. Multipliers are used to determine the total impact of each dollar of direct spending on the local economy. For example, a dollar is spent by a tourist at a local store (direct). Then the store owner pays his/her employee with part of that dollar (indirect). The employee uses the dollar to buy groceries (indirect). The grocery store sends that dollar to their corporate offices. That means the original dollar has been circulated through the local economy two times. The higher the number of times of circulation, the better the economic worth of the transaction. Generally the multiplier is around two.

The term **leakage** refers to the phenomena when parts of that dollar are exported outside the local economy, such as when the dollar is sent to corporate offices. When casinos are locally owned, the money tends to stay longer within the local economy and the money benefits the local community with more investments, which results in a higher multiplier. However, it is more likely that the casino is owned by an outside corporation that siphons most of the money out of the community and back to their home offices. This results in a lower multiplier and more leakage. Therefore, depending on the type of ownership, casinos can have a stronger or weaker economic impact on the local economy.

Another question regarding leakage refers to states that do not have casinos. However, in this case, citizens simply drive across the border to a state that does have a casino. The question thus arises whether a non-casino state does better economically if its citizens stay home to gamble. Would a state capture more money if the leakage occurred from a local casino, or from the export of money going to an out-of-state casino? Another aspect of leakage relates to the customer base. If clients come from outside the local community, they bring fresh money from outside, which fuels the economy, and the money that is exported to the corporate offices has less impact. However, if the client base consists of mainly locals, then casinos may take local money and export it, immediately decreasing the economic impact and increasing the leakage rate. For example in Illinois, around 58% of the players are locals, which means that the casinos are taking money that could be spent locally and exporting it outside the community. Grinols[6] explains that only when gambling is able to tap outside markets will the casinos have a positive economic impact; otherwise gambling results in inefficient transfers from one business to another. This results in less money available for local development.

This impact is best understood by looking at how $100 moves from the casino to an employee to the community. Let's say that the casino pays a hotel desk clerk $100 in his/her paycheck. That employee uses part of his/her paycheck to pay for groceries. The store uses part of that money to pay the stock clerk. The stock clerk uses part of his/her money to pay his/her rent. The landlord uses part of that money to pay for his/her dry cleaning. The dry cleaner pays the clerk's wages out of that money. As you can see the $100 spreads around the community several times. Eventually it dissipates like a ripple on a pond, but not before creating economic activity several times its original value. This is the *multiplier effect*.

PricewaterhouseCoopers[7] conducted a survey of casino employees entitled "1997 Gaming Industry Employee Impact Survey." The survey includes responses from 178,000 employees from 97 casino companies in ten states. Some of the findings reflect the impact of direct employment. Each month casino employees purchase 840,000 meals in local restaurants on top of 1.4 million fast food, take-out, or delivered meals. Each year casino employees purchase 66,000 homes, 176,000 automobiles, and 173,000 major appliances. This activity alone generates a large number of indirect jobs. And the multiplier effect spreads that value even farther into the community.

WELFARE TO WORK

Because casinos are often legalized in jurisdictions with high unemployment, casino jobs have a material effect on welfare programs. Of the 178,000 responding to the survey, 8.5% reported getting off welfare due to obtaining employment with the casino. Approximately 16% stopped receiving unemployment benefits because of their casino jobs and 9% no longer received food stamps.

According to Arthur Andersen's[8] "Economic Impacts of Casino Gaming in the United States, Volume 2: Micro Study" from May 1997, three specific jurisdictions benefited from legalized casino gaming. Biloxi/Gulfport, Mississippi saw 18,100 jobs created from 1990 to 1996. Of those, 62% or 11,200 were direct casino jobs. The number of Aid to Families with Dependent Children (AFDC) recipients declined by 9% in 1995 and 15% in 1996. Food stamp recipients declined every year after 1993. A similar story is told for Shreveport/Bossier City, Louisiana. Just over half of the 10,000 jobs created between 1993 and 1994 were attributed to casinos. **AFDC payments** fell 14% in 1995 and 15% in 1996. The number of food stamp recipients declined by 15% in 1996. Joliet, Illinois saw similar declines—14% in AFDC recipients between 1994 and 1996 and 14% in food stamp recipients between 1993 and 1996. It would appear that casinos help take people from welfare and unemployment to employment and independence.

TAXES

The benefit to jurisdictions is not only an increase in economic activity and a reduction in people on assistance. The taxes generated by casinos are often a large portion of the local and state budget. In some states such as Nevada, gaming-related taxes allow the state to forgo a state tax on personal and corporate income. In other states, the tax is marked for specific purposes. In most cases, it goes into the general fund which is allocated each year by the state legislature (Table 10.1).

The amount paid in taxes is dependent upon the gaming revenue generated in a state as well as the tax rate. Nevada has the highest number of casinos. Consequently, it has the highest gaming revenue and the highest tax revenue. South Dakota allows gaming in only Deadwood and has enacted some very strict limits on gaming such as a low maximum bet, and a low number of table games and electronic gaming devices per gaming facility. As a result, its gaming revenues and tax receipts are very low.

Nevada's Tax Rate

The tax rate among these states varies widely. Nevada has a top rate of 6.25% of gaming revenue. Its tax rate has been low from the beginning. The state has a tradition of minimal taxes. Fortunately, the casino industry has grown throughout its history in Nevada, which has caused tax receipts to continually climb. Because of this, there has been no significant movement to increase the tax rate. Conversely, the consistent and low tax rate has encouraged companies to invest in Nevada. Any economist will tell you that investors look for political stability as part of their investigation when deciding where to invest. Political stability includes transparent government activity, an absence of corruption, and slow, measured change in the regulations and laws affecting business.

Nevada has demonstrated these traits. By ridding the industry of organized crime influence, the state showed it was serious about eliminating even the possibility of

TABLE 10.1 The Tax Revenue Generated by Casinos is a Leading Reason States Legalize Gaming. Tax Revenues for 12 States in 2006

State	Tax Revenue (hundreds of thousands of dollars)
Nevada	1,034.0
Indiana	842.0
Illinois	833.9
Louisiana	559.2
New Jersey	474.7
Pennsylvania	472.8
Missouri	417.3
Michigan	365.6
Mississippi	350.4
Iowa	314.8
Colorado	115.4
South Dakota	14.9

corruption among public officials. All government business is transacted according to open meeting laws and there is a system of checks and balances to ensure transparency. The fact that the tax rate has changed little for over 70 years provides the stability investors seek. It is doubly attractive that the rate is low. The number of casinos, the increasing size and dollar value of new investment, and the number of investors interested in moving into the market are just a couple indicators of investors' confidence in Nevada.

Illinois' Tax Rate

Illinois shows another side of the story. There are many people in jurisdictions considering the legalization of gaming who believe a casino is a magical goose that lays golden eggs. Because casinos deal in cash, there is a general feeling that casinos are profitable without effort. Even those knowledgeable about casinos feel the profit margins are large enough that casinos can afford high tax rates. Of course, these jurisdictions are looking for a tax source and view casinos as merely a cash source.

The initial tax rate in Illinois was effectively 35%. Clearly, it is much higher than Nevada's rate. However, the state limited the number and location of casinos. There is a single casino at each site. It is not a wide-open market like Nevada. Because of the near-monopoly nature of the Illinois market, casinos could expect much higher revenue per unit. Therefore, they could afford a higher tax rate and were willing to enter the market.

However, the state legislature became aggressive when it needed tax revenues to balance the state budget. The tax rate was raised four times in five years.[9] At the peak, the tax structure for casinos had a top rate of 75% on revenues over $250 million. Casinos began to create strategies to prevent their revenues from exceeding $250 million. With the additional labor and other variable expenses, the additional revenue generated a net loss to the casino. The casino companies also diverted investment dollars to other markets with better returns and a more reasonable and more stable tax environment.

FIGURE 10.2 Many people think a casino is like a goose that can lay golden eggs. They do not realize that casinos are businesses that are sensitive to tax rates.

Source: © Jeffrey Collingwood. Image from BigStockPhoto.com

The Illinois legislature's mistake was not only raising the tax rate to extraordinary levels, but raising it so rapidly. The lack of stability, regardless of the tax rate, would have spooked investors. The state legislature soon realized their mistake when they saw the measures the casinos took. The casinos were also forthright in their dealings with the state. They took a public stance explaining their position. They would not abandon their investments, but they informed the public that there were better venues for their investment dollars. The state legislature revised the tax rates and structure to encourage the industry, not penalize it for succeeding. Today the effective rate is 50%.[10] That is still very high, but one with which the casino industry can continue to do business and make profits.

IMPACT ON JOB CREATION

One lesson to be drawn from this examination of tax rates is the impact on job generation by the industry. Clearly, the low and stable tax rate of Nevada has helped to foster a competitive industry that provides the majority of jobs in the state. The reader needs to be cautioned that other factors are involved when investment decisions are made, but the stability of the government and the tax rate are key factors. When looking at jurisdictions with higher tax rates, the investment in the market is more limited. Again other factors come into play, but the tax rate and stability, especially of a new jurisdiction, are key variables in the investment analysis. By setting tax rates high, a state is automatically limiting the growth of the industry. Fewer jobs will be created than are possible. Essentially, the higher tax rates create a tradeoff between tax revenues and job creation. In their quest to balance the budget, the state legislatures decide without knowing it that they will sacrifice jobs for tax receipts.

Ironically, this may satisfy legislators opposed to casinos. Sensing they cannot prevent gaming becoming legal, they may agree in the legislative negotiating process to vote for legalizing gaming if the tax rate is high enough to make operating a casino less attractive. They can tell their supporters they extracted a high tax rate as a condition of legalization. It is not a win, but it is not a loss either.

OTHER GOVERNMENTS' ACTIONS

Great Britain

There are other examples of government action which can affect the desirability of the market as an investment venue. Great Britain, where the gaming laws were last revised in 1969, is a good example. The focus was on limiting gaming while still making it available. The size and location of the gaming clubs were limited. A customer had to become a member in order to play. Other restrictions were also instituted.

In the late 1990s, a government commission was assembled to study the gaming laws and the industry in the country. The purpose was to make recommendations on revising the law and finding the right balance for a legal gaming industry. The resulting report was called **The Budd Report** after the chairman of the commission. The report basically proposed an open-market solution with strict regulation along the lines of Nevada. The Labor government of Tony Blair began the process of studying the report and developing legislation to implement its recommendations.

Political and economic dynamics interfered with this process. The Iraq War diverted attention from the project. Tony Blair stepped down as Prime Minister. His replacement, Gordon Brown, was less enthusiastic about gaming and free markets. Internet gaming exploded and increased the availability of gaming to the general population. Gordon Brown's popularity plummeted and his leverage with Parliament declined as a result. The free-market approach was changed to a two-tier structure based on the size of the casino. A cap on Las Vegas-style casinos was included. Then the number of Las Vegas-style casinos was limited to just one and the government went about the business of deciding the site of this casino. As of the writing of this text, the government has quietly tabled any plans for revising the gaming statutes or awarding the site of the lone super casino.

Again, we see the impact of an unstable legal and political environment. The fickleness of the British government has scared off all foreign gaming companies except Harrah's Entertainment. Harrah's is taking a wait-and-see attitude. Their pronouncements state they are in the United Kingdom to stay, but they will divert investment dollars to other markets if the return is better.

Russia

Yet another example is Russia. In late 2006, President Putin signed a bill from the Duma (Russia's parliament) that restricted the gaming industry to just four zones within the country: the Kaliningrad region enclave near the Baltic Sea, Primorsky region on the Pacific coast, the Altai region in Siberia, and near the southern cities of Krasnodar and Rostov.[11] None of the zones are located near the country's two most populous cities, Moscow and St. Petersburg. In addition, any gaming operation with assets worth less than $23 million was forced to close in 2007. The vast majority of these operations were slot parlors. They were more akin to mom-and-pop operations that employed thousands of people and provide a living for numerous small-time entrepreneurs. The remaining operations were required to move their operations to one of the four zones. The effective date for the completion of this radical change was July 2009.

Politics in Russia are not as transparent as in Western Europe or the United States. The reasons for the legislation were not clear. Most likely different politicians backed the bill for different reasons. However, where transparency is lacking, insidious reasons are attributed to the action by the public and political analysts alike. Regardless, the effect on the industry and employment has been devastating. Not only were the smaller operations legislated out of existence, but larger operations were forced to find new locations and pay to move. In addition, suppliers to the industry, electronic gaming device manufacturers in particular, were presented with a drastically smaller market for their products in locations far from their distribution facilities. Reevaluating whether to continue their operations in Russia and the size of their operations was an unwelcome event. The disruption to the industry will be felt for many years as investors remain cautious as they wait to see if stability returns to the market.

Atlantic City

Sometimes the governmental action can be something popular, but ultimately detrimental. Atlantic City has slowly approached a ban on smoking in the casinos. The number of

FIGURE 10.3 Political processes are not readily transparent in Russia. Investors are wary of a jurisdiction where the rules are not always followed.

Source: © Elena Elisseeva. Image from BigStockPhoto.com

smoking bans either statewide or city-specific in the United States has increased tremendously in recent years. The public is increasingly aware of the potential damage sustained by nonsmokers who are consistently in the presence of cigarette smoke. Although customers are affected by the smoking of other customers, the employees who cannot remove themselves from the smoke are the most vulnerable. Through legislative activity or referendum votes, the public has placed restrictions on where smokers may smoke.

A large segment of casino patrons are smokers. There is currently no explanation for this correlation. However, casinos have gone to great expense to purchase and install air handling systems that minimize the impact of cigarette smoking. Some casinos have set aside nonsmoking sections of their casinos to accommodate both types of gamblers. Despite these efforts, nonsmokers still complain about the smell and danger of cigarette smoke. And many are fearful of the health risks associated with secondhand smoke. It is in this atmosphere that the Atlantic City Council has faced the issue of a smoking ban.

The ban took a long time to enact. The state of New Jersey banned smoking statewide with an exemption for the casinos of Atlantic City.[7] However, the city council took up a measure to ban smoking throughout the city. As you can imagine, the casinos weighed in on the issue. Knowing that they stood to lose a good portion of their customer base either to casinos in competing jurisdictions or to a decision by the gamblers to stop gambling, they participated actively in the debate. The initial phase of the ban required casinos to set aside a part of their casinos as nonsmoking. But the final phase required an entire ban on smoking. The impact on the casino industry operating results and investment plans is yet to be seen, but the uncertainty of a political environment that jeopardizes jobs and profits will produce caution on the part of industry participants at the least.

SUMMARY

The impact of the casino industry on a jurisdiction is significant. The number of jobs created is higher for casinos than other businesses because they are labor intensive. It takes a lot of employees to serve the customers. Of course the jobs created by the casinos themselves are the largest number at over 354,000.

However, other jobs are created. There are the direct temporary jobs involved in the construction of a new casino or in the renovation or addition of an existing casino. These are typically high-paying jobs for skilled tradesmen and professionals. The experience gained on the job is transferable and makes the employee more valuable.

The spending on the construction and the ongoing expenses of operating the casino are spread throughout the community due to the multiplier effect. The impact is reflected in part in the indirect jobs that are created. There is a need for more sales clerks, dry cleaners, doctors, and policemen to service the employees of the casino. There is also a need for more delivery persons, sales people, accounts receivable clerks, and distribution managers to service the supply needs of the casino. Of course, outside the community there is an increase in employment as electronic gaming device manufacturers, uniform manufacturers, furniture makers, and other suppliers increase their staff to meet demand.

These indirect jobs are just as important to the economy as the direct jobs created by the casinos. As we saw, many people are able to go off public assistance because a casino creates a direct or indirect job where there were no employment opportunities previously. And, naturally, politicians are anxious to give their voters job opportunities.

Politicians are also interested in the taxes generated by gaming. They know that their obligation to voters and their ability to get reelected is dependent upon them delivering the essential services deemed important by the voters. Of course, voters do not want to pay more in taxes than they consider reasonable. Therefore, the taxes paid by casinos allow politicians to provide these services with raising taxes on constituents.

The amount paid in taxes by casinos is considerable. In the case of Nevada, the gaming revenue tax has allowed the state to refrain from instituting a personal and corporate income tax. In Pennsylvania, the gaming bill was passed in part because the taxes expected from gaming will allow the state to reduce the property tax rate. While our discussion covered taxes paid directly by the casinos on gaming revenue, we did not address the additional tax revenue generated by the multiplier effect. Primary among these taxes is the sales tax on economic activity outside the casino. Increase sales by just $1 million and a sales tax of 5% will generate an additional $50,000 for a community. Clearly, the economic impact of casinos is sizable.

A jurisdiction can choose any tax rate it wishes. Nevada's rate at 6.25% is the lowest among American states. Pennsylvania's at an effective 52% is the highest. While the temptation by states is to view gaming as a cash machine, it is better to relate the tax rate to the level of monopolistic conditions in a market. In Nevada, there is no monopoly and there are numerous casinos. Gaming companies will not pay a premium in taxes to enter that market. However, in Illinois and Pennsylvania, single casinos are designated for specific sites. There will be no competition in the immediate area which guarantees monopoly-like profits. Casinos recognize this and are willing to pay a higher tax rate. Whether rates in the area of 50% are reasonable is determined through the give and take of the marketplace and between the government and the casinos. But one result of a high tax rate is investment dollars gravitate to the markets where the gaming companies can make the best return. A lower rate will attract more investment dollars that generate jobs than a higher rate.

Another impact government can have on casinos' decision to invest in a market is the stability of the government. We are not talking about whether the government will continue to exist as is the case in some third-world countries, but whether the government's policies toward gaming remain constant or are changed gradually with transparency. As we saw in the case of Illinois, raising the tax rate four times in five years had almost as big an impact as the size of the tax rate after the final increase. Likewise, the fickleness of the British government toward gaming law reform and the sudden restructuring of the Russian casino market have made gaming companies cautious about investing there. Stability and predictability are valued highly by business people.

Conclusion

As you have read, casinos provide many economic benefits to a community. Jobs and taxes are the primary benefits. This allows people to make a living without government assistance. It also allows politicians to deliver services to their constituents. While casinos can introduce negative social impacts into a community, the economic benefits help offset these and in many cases outweigh them.

Key Words

Direct temporary jobs *135*
Direct permanent jobs *135*
Indirect jobs *135*
Multiplier effect *137*
Leakage *137*
AFDC payments *138*
The Budd Report *141*

Review Questions

1. Detail the basic overall economic benefits of casino gambling.
2. Explain the details and extents of the benefits of additional jobs that casino gambling brings to a community.
3. Explain the effects that casinos have on welfare programs.
4. Elaborate on the role that additional taxes brought in by a casino plays in a community and its economy.
5. Detail the specific examples of the economic benefits of additional taxes in the Nevada and Illinois markets.
6. Explain the casino industry's impact on job creation in the local community.
7. Elaborate on how other governments' (such as Great Britain's and Russia's) actions have affected their local casino industries.

Endnotes

1. American Gaming Association. Retrieved July 15, 2008. http://www.americangaming.org/Industry/factsheets/index.cfm.
2. American Gaming Association. Retrieved March 23, 1999. www.americangaming.org/media/Myth_Facts/index.html.
3. Arthur Andersen. (December 1996). "Economic Impacts of Casino Gaming in the United States, Volume 1: Macro Study," p. 28.
4. Ibid., p. 28.
5. American Gaming Association. Retrieved July 15, 2008. http://www.americangaming.org/Industry/factsheets/index.cfm.
6. Grinols, Earl and Omorov, J. D. (1996). Who loses when casinos win? *Illinois Business Review,* 53(1), 7–11.
7. Arthur Andersen. http://www.hotel-online.com/Trends/Andersen/index.html
8. Arthur Andersen (December 1996). "Economic Impacts of Casino Gaming in the United states, Volume 1: Macro Study," p. 28.
9. Paul Dworin (February 2007). Killing the golden goose. *Global Gaming Business,* p. 4
10. Ibid., p. 4.
11. "Putin Pulls Plug on Russian Casinos, Slots." *Global Gaming Business,* February 2007, p. 6.

CHAPTER 11

ACCEPTANCE OF GAMING

WILLIAM N. THOMPSON AND STEVE DURHAM

Learning Objectives

1. To understand the general reasons for the public's acceptance of gambling
2. To learn about the situations in Nevada that led to a greater public acceptance of casino gambling
3. To learn about the situations in New Jersey that led to a greater public acceptance of casino gambling
4. To understand the changing social norms that led to a greater public acceptance of casino gambling
5. To understand the economic trends that led to a greater public acceptance of casino gambling
6. To understand how a greater mobility led to a greater public acceptance of casino gambling
7. To learn about the forces that work against casino promotions
8. To learn about the forces that helped establish casinos
9. To understand the importance of casino investments in the public's acceptance of casino gambling
10. To understand the political factors that help in legalizing casino gambling

Chapter Outline

INTRODUCTION

Chapters 9 and 10 covered the costs and benefits of legalized gaming. It should be clear that a position can be staked out on either side of the issue with legitimacy. On several occasions in American history, the debate over legalizing gambling has surfaced. At times gambling activity was prohibited when the voices against gambling prevailed while at other times it was legalized or tolerated when the voices of acceptance prevailed.

The shift from prohibiting gaming to legalization is a major change. Rarely do major changes in society occur unassisted and outside the context of other changes at work on the society. Such is the case with casino gaming. As you learned earlier in this book, no form of gambling was legal in the United States in 1931 except betting on horse racing. Once Nevada legalized casino gaming, it remained alone among states until New Hampshire started a state lottery in 1964. Even as lotteries proliferated among the states, no additional state legalized casino gaming until New Jersey voters approved a referendum in 1976.

REASONS FOR THE ACCEPTANCE OF GAMBLING

There were 45 years between Nevada and New Jersey. It was only 12 years from New Jersey to the passage of Indian Gaming Regulatory Act (IGRA) and another three years until other states legalized riverboat and land-based casinos. What was a stigmatized activity spread rapidly due to a rush of legalization. Today there is casino gaming in over 30 states, lotteries in over 40 states, and more forms of gaming in the pipeline. What was once a remote pleasure is now available within a short drive of practically most Americans. How did this reversal occur?

There are many forces that contributed to this drastic change. Although it is difficult to assign the exact amount of responsibility to each factor, the successful regulation of gaming by governmental entities must be considered a significant force. All gaming prior to Nevada was left unregulated by the state where it was legal. Laws governing liability and business practices that were already on the books were left to handle any disputes or problems that might arise between the customer and the casino. Because most gambling activity was small stakes and untaxed, the government did not feel a need to intervene or regulate it.

Nevada

This was the situation in Nevada between 1931 and the end of World War II. The county sheriff issued licenses and collected the taxes. When both the casino owners and the players were local residents, there was no reason to set up extensive regulatory mechanisms. Any problems could be handled through the existing laws or through informal processes among people who knew each other.

However, with the construction of casino resorts on the Las Vegas Highway and the influx of out-of-state owners, the ballgame changed. Although the state of Nevada was slow to react and needed prodding by the federal government, it assumed the role of regulator. Through the creation of the Nevada Gaming Commission and the Gaming Control Board, the state set increasingly strict licensing requirements for the casinos to meet. The state recognized that they needed to ensure the integrity of the industry to forestall a federal ban on gaming, to reassure public confidence in the casinos, and to ensure the state received its due in taxes. The legitimate casino owners saw the value in this role for government. They not only accepted the new role, they welcomed it. They saw how it was good for business.

(a)

(b)

FIGURE 11.1a and b The construction of resorts on the Las Vegas Strip in the 1950s such as The Dunes and The Stardust signaled the entry of organized crime into Nevada.

While the infiltration of organized crime into Las Vegas casinos was substantial, Nevada persisted in efforts to clean up the industry. The process began in the 1950s and was not completed until the early 1980s. But by the early 1970s, Nevada had established that state-regulated gaming could be an industry run like any legitimate business. Organized crime played an increasingly smaller role in the industry. Publicly traded companies owned and operated casinos. Casinos set up formal policies and procedures to ensure internal controls. The public's acceptance of state-regulated casinos as legitimate businesses was reflected in the year-on-year increases in visitors to Las Vegas and in casino gaming revenue.

New Jersey

The reality that state-regulated casino gaming could have integrity and the perception of it were essential to the passage of the casino referendum in New Jersey in 1976. By that time, Nevada was into its third decade of active regulation and had successfully put organized crime on the run. However, it was not a given that New Jersey voters would pass the referendum. The citizens of New Jersey voted down a referendum on casino gaming just two years earlier. The previous measure would have allowed casinos in any county where the voters would vote their approval. The new referendum limited casinos to Atlantic City. This clearly had a beneficial effect on the vote. State residents were willing to allow casinos, but they wanted them geographically limited. In part this was symptomatic of the "not in my backyard" mentality. But it also was a cautious approach to casinos. The voters seemed to say that they believed organized crime could be prevented from infiltrating the gaming industry, but, just in case, the problem should be physically isolated.

The referendum passed and in 1978 the first casino opened. The Casino Control Commission took a tough stance on each applicant for a casino license. There were individuals who had passed muster in Nevada, but who ran into difficulty in New Jersey, largely due to past associations with undesirable characters. They were not accused of direct participation in illegal activities. These individuals, who were associated with license applications, removed themselves from all gaming activity with their companies or terminated their employment in order for the company to obtain a license. This further accelerated the cleansing process occurring in Nevada and ensured the integrity of Atlantic City casinos. New Jersey, whose image as a haven of criminal activity was cemented in the public imagination, proved that criminal activity could be prevented from entering the gaming industry.

With two states in the gaming business and proving daily that the criminal element can be eliminated, the public increasingly saw legalized casino gaming as a legitimate leisure activity. As other jurisdictions approved casino gaming, including Indian reservations, the stigma traditionally attached to gambling weakened considerably. This contributed to the rush of legalization in the 1980s and 1990s.

Changing Social Norms

But there was another force impacting the public's perception of gaming. The 1950s and 1960s saw a loosening of societal norms for individual behavior. The civil rights movement, the Vietnam War protest movement, and the sexual revolution all contributed to a relaxation of strictures. The stage was set for examining all aspects of social strictures including the stigma attached to gambling. What had been right was now questionable, if not outright wrong. Questioning presidential authority led to questioning all authority—academic, religious, parental, and so on. Within this context, why exactly was gambling a bad thing?

The generation that came of age in the timeframe from the 1950s to the 1970s experienced all this without experiencing the forces behind their parents' worldview. Their parents' arguments rang hollow on so many fronts that everything was called into question. When a parent warned of the pitfalls of gambling, it was questioned as well. By the 1970s, Nevada had proven its seriousness in establishing the integrity of state-regulated gaming. Looking at the hard evidence of Nevada casinos versus warnings of crime and personal ruin against the backdrop of their youthful optimism and belief in personal invincibility, many young people began to view state-sanctioned casino gaming as one of numerous entertainment options.

Economic Trends

Aiding these political and societal forces were economic trends. America had become a world power at the turn of the twentieth century through industrialization. However, wealth was not evenly spread among the population. There was still a great deal of poverty outside the upper and middle classes. Progress in reducing the unequal distribution of income was reversed with the onset of the Great Depression. After World War II, the redistribution of income regained momentum.

The median family income in 1946, the first full year after the war ended, was $27,490 in 2006 dollars. By 1976, the median family income had grown to $42,223, or a 53% increase. By contrast, the increase from 1976 to 2005 was only 10%. This remarkable increase in post-war income and wealth provided a greater number of Americans with **discretionary income**. This is income not dedicated to necessities such as housing, food, and clothing. With this added income, families found they could afford items that had been luxuries previously. Among those luxuries were vacations. With more income, more and more people were able to take vacations. We will return to this in a moment (Table 11.1).

TABLE 11.1 Median Family Income Rose Dramatically in the Two Decades after World War II

1946	1976	Dollar Variance	Percentage Variance
$27,490	$42,223	$14,733	53.6%
1976	2005	Dollar Variance	Percentage Variance
$42,223	$46,326	$4,103	9.7%

Also as a result of the additional discretionary income Americans had, more families owned a car. When the automobile was invented at the end of the nineteenth century, it was affordable only to the very wealthy. It was not until Henry Ford perfected the assembly line and the increased wealth of the nation after World War I that car ownership spread to the middle class. However, the Great Depression severely limited people's ability to afford a car. However, the explosion of wealth after World War II, led to increased car ownership. Increasingly, American families owned two cars. One was for the husband to use for transportation in his work and the other was for the wife to use for household chores and family responsibilities.

Greater Mobility

With greater car ownership and increased income, Americans took more vacations to farther destinations. The interstate highway system, begun in the mid-1950s, facilitated this phenomenon. A trip from Los Angeles to Las Vegas in 1940 took six hours on a two-lane highway through the Mojave Desert in a car without air conditioning. Today that trip is four hours on a limited access highway in air conditioned comfort with CD and DVD entertainment available.

In addition to automobile travel, air travel also exploded in the post-war years. With the introduction of jet engines, airplanes were more economical to operate. They could carry more passengers and could fly farther distances without stopping for refueling. Increased wealth and the availability of reasonably priced airfares worked together to increase vacations utilizing the airlines. People in the Midwest and on the East Coast could now consider a trip to Las Vegas without facing a four or five day drive in the car.

All these factors—government-regulated gambling, economic trends, societal changes—made gambling accessible and acceptable. The American public slowly shifted its view of gaming from vice to entertainment option. All the pieces for widespread legalization of gaming were in place by the 1980s except the legislation.

The rest of the chapter was written by noted casino expert and author Professor William Thompson, PhD. He delves into the actual legalization processes. He describes the forces that came to bear on those processes and how we arrived at the situation we have today.

CASINO STATUS

Over the past two decades, the United States has witnessed a massive expansion in all forms of gambling activity. The expansion has been punctuated by an explosion of new casino facilities. Just 30 years ago while the nation was in the midst of a rapid spread of state lotteries, only one state, Nevada, permitted casinos to operate every day. Even

20 years ago there were only two casino states, Nevada and New Jersey. Then the casino floodgates opened with a proliferation of riverboat casinos, small-stakes casinos, and Native American casinos.

We will first examine forces that stymied the promotion of casino gambling throughout the land while at the same time fostered lottery development, and then examine the forces that helped establish casinos in over 30 states today.

John Dombrink and I explored these forces in a 1990 book entitled *The Last Resort: Success and Failure in Campaigns for Casinos.*[1] At the time we were amazed that lotteries had won approval almost everywhere they were advocated, while casinos had been successfully adopted only in New Jersey.

Forces against Casino Promotion

We suggested that two political models were at work. Lotteries were subject to a typical model of policymaking where leaders (and voters) balance the pros and cons of an issue and then lean toward the direction that seems to carry the greatest weight—a **gravity model**. When lotteries were adopted they were of a passive variety, and they were not associated with problems such as crime or compulsive gambling. The always present moral opposition could not outweigh proponents' claims that the lotteries would bring "easy money" to good causes such as education for little children or help with paying heating bills for the elderly.

Casinos were special, however, and at the start of campaigns, political leaders and voters started with but one fixed idea in their minds—the corrupt lifestyle of the Las Vegas casino establishment—its crime, its Mafioso origins, and its proclivity to producing ruined lives. Casino proponents started way behind, and they had to successfully jump each one of the many hurdles—as they did in New Jersey, the second time around in 1976—for them to win the day. We called this a **veto model**.

Any one of several vetoes could kill the issue: (1) crime emerging as a dominant campaign issue instead of the economy, (2) a history of bad experiences with gambling in the venue deciding the issue, (3) the bad character of campaign proponents, (4) opposition from local business elites, or (5) the opposition of a key political actor, particularly a governor or attorney general. All the factors could be favorable but one and the issue would fail. Gubernatorial opposition killed casinos in Arkansas (it was Bill Clinton and his young wife who led the opponents in 1984) and Florida (1978), and an attorney general in New York (1981). On the other hand, lotteries won in the face of gubernatorial opposition in many places such as California in 1984.

A good economic climate for state governments also put the damper on casino expansion, as voters were not ripe to endorse "sin" in order to get taxes if the taxes were not needed. The 1970s and early 1980s was the period of revenue sharing in America. The philosophy of **New Federalism** was ushered in by President Richard Nixon. His notion was that the federal government had lots of money, indeed with the income tax they could get lots more money, and moreover, they were not seriously constrained by requirements to balance the public budget. States on the other hand could not rely on income taxes for unlimited wealth; moreover they could not engage in deficit spending. Under revenue sharing formulas the states and their communities received automatic grants from the federal government each year. Essentially, the federal government was raising money for the states.

FIGURE 11.2 As governor, Bill Clinton worked against the legalization of casinos in Arkansas.

Source: Copyright © 2008 Steve Durham. Permission is granted to copy, distribute and/or modify the following photos under the terms of the GNU Free Documentation License, Version 1.2 or any later version published by the Free Software Foundation; with no Invariant Sections, no Front-Cover Texts, and no Back-Cover Texts. A copy of the license is included in the section entitled "GNU Free Documentation License".

When the revenue-sharing process was phased out during President Reagan's first term in office, the state budgets were generally in very good financial shape. However, Reagan's military build up, and his unwillingness to endorse Budget Director David Stockman's severe cutting program for domestic spending led to severe federal deficits that worried many economists. They worried Congress enough that the lawmakers passed the Graham-Rudman Budget Act which restricted spending. During these Reagan years, states felt little inclination to grasp the golden ring of "free money" via casino taxation. Then Reagan did a turnabout on the states. Not only did he lead the effort to end revenue sharing, but he started to eliminate some federal programs, or at least funding of the programs. But the programs had constituencies, so he took an alternative path to keep them going. He mandated that the state governments take responsibilities for the programs and fund them. The most onerous of these obligations on the states came with the mandates for states to fund Medicaid—medical assistance for poor people. A recovering economy began to bring prosperity to the nation as a whole, but now state after state was suffering a severe budget crisis. The formula for casino expansion was being set into place.

Forces that Helped Establish Casinos

Proponents of casinos also sought to take the edge off of the notion that they were bringing "Las Vegas" to the heartlands. Casino gambling was promoted as an amenity for riverboat cruises on the Mississippi—like in the good ole days with Huck Finn and

Tom Sawyer. The words "Las Vegas" were banned from all pro-casino literature in Iowa. South Dakota pushed games with five-dollar betting limits in order to restore the "Old West" mining town of Deadwood. The word "casino" was banned from the campaign. The success of these two ventures in 1988 and 1989 found themselves imitated with Illinois, then Missouri, Indiana, Louisiana, and Mississippi legalizing riverboat casinos, and Colorado agreed to let three historical mining towns have limited-stakes casinos (or fun halls for playing games with prizes of money, or some such euphemism). Louisiana also agreed to let New Orleans have a land-based casino, while Michigan voters approved land-based casinos for Detroit—after five unsuccessful tries, but following the creating of a land-based casino in Windsor, Ontario, only a mile from downtown Detroit. Some minor elements of the veto model appeared in some of these campaigns—for instance passive gubernatorial opposition in Colorado and Michigan, but more concerted opposition—a veto of legislation in Indiana. Many of the bills passed at late-night legislative sessions on the last day such as in Louisiana, Iowa, and Indiana, with some strange unexplained switches in votes.

Another line of casino expansion occurred on Native American lands. Tribal reservation lands were unique political entities. They were subject to some state laws—generally all criminal laws, but not most of the civil regulatory laws. So ruled federal courts several times, following tribes' establishment of bingo halls that did not follow state rules on hours of operation and prize limits. When the U.S. Supreme Court concurred that tribes did not have to follow state edicts on gambling as long as gambling was not illegal, the commercial casino industry panicked. They insisted that tribal gambling be regulated. Led by Nevada's Senator Harry Reid, Congress enacted the Indian Gaming Regulatory Act of 1988. The federal government had ultimate authority over tribal matters and the new law created some federal regulations of tribal bingo, but it also created a mechanism for tribes to negotiate agreements with states for regulation of casino-type gambling. Reid enunciated the idea that his bill had brought tribes under strict regulations that all gambling needed. His bill had a directly opposite effect. The bill gave the tribes the incentives and the legal and political means to establish not only bingo halls but major casinos. His bill said the tribes could offer "any" game allowed by the state for "any" organization, at "any" time. Many states allowed charities to have fund-raising events using casino games. The tribes did not pass up their chance. In state after state they won the right to have casinos.

Developments in the United States were being prodded by the fact that Canada was following a similar pattern of expansion. In 1969, the national law of Canada permitted provincial lotteries and "**lottery schemes**." In the 1980s, several provinces experimented with charitable casinos under the rubric of "lottery schemes." In 1990, Manitoba Lottery Foundation opened a permanent casino in Winnipeg. Six other provinces followed with casinos, many of which have the appearance of Las Vegas–style operations, although the government is involved in their essential managerial functions. There were other forces behind the spread of casino gambling.

Besides the Indian Gaming Regulatory Act of 1988, two pieces of "national" legislation from the 1990s sparked the expansion. One of the "national" bills of interest was not passed by Congress, but rather by the Nevada state legislature. In 1993, the casino state took the shackles off its own owners and operators and repealed the essential parts of their state "**Foreign Gaming Law**."

FIGURE 11.3 Thanks to Indian gaming, many Americans can visit a casino in remote locations such as Harrah's Rincon in Valley Center, California.

The foreign gaming law had been promulgated in the 1950s at a time when the state was being criticized for not effectively controlling its casino owners. In building a new system for strict regulation, the state decided that its license holders had better not conduct operations beyond Nevada's control in any other state or country. After New Jersey legalized casinos and established its own "strict" regulatory system, the law was modified a bit. Nevada companies could seek New Jersey licenses after they received permission from Nevada authorities to apply for licenses. Later, prior approvals were allowed for applications into other jurisdictions as well, and some companies were granted general prior approvals to seek licenses. In all cases when a Nevada company received a "foreign" license, they had to make reports for the Nevada Gaming Control Board and Commission. The rules were still quite restrictive and stifling in 1988 when Native American casinos began to open on a large scale and as South Dakota and then Iowa ushered in the new era of commercial casino expansion. Then in 1993, the casinos won a wholesale reversal of the law. The wraps were off. They could now seek opportunities for licenses anywhere, with the proviso that they report back to Nevada regarding their foreign operations. The Nevada companies were now free to promote the legalization of casino gambling elsewhere and to assist Native American tribes in winning agreements with states to open casinos.

Casino Investments

In 1994, Las Vegas casinos invested nearly $17 million in a failing voter campaign to legalize casinos in Florida. In 1998, they placed over $25 million into a campaign to defeat Native American gaming in California. They also lost that try as the tribes invested over $70 million to get the voters to go the other way.

A 1994 legislative effort led to the creation of a national lobbying group for casinos. Provisions of the **Graham-Rudman Act** of 1986 required that any appropriation made that was not within a spending cap set by the Congressional Budget Office had to be balanced by an equal spending cut in an existing program, or by a new tax. The Clinton Administration sought an appropriation for a new child-welfare program above the spending cap. They needed to cut either one billion dollars from another program or to raise a billion with a new tax. They pursued the latter course, proposing a 4% federal tax on all casino winnings—from both commercial and Indian casinos. Tribes across America rallied in unified support with lobbying funds and funds for congressional campaigns. The National Indian Gaming Association immediately became a very visible organization on Capitol Hill.

Commercial casinos did not sit idly by either. The tax was a major threat to their bottom lines. Las Vegas casino companies took the lead and founded the **American Gaming Association**, headquartered in Washington, D.C. The new association selected former chair of the Republican National Committee, Frank Fahrenkopf, to be their executive director and chief lobbyist. He delivered the casino's message very well—that casinos were good for America, good for employment, and good as a source of taxes for financially strapped state governments fulfilling their federal mandates and educating all their little children. Not to be lost in the whirlwind of new activity in Washington was the fact that the casino tax bill died in committee without a vote being taken in either house.

FIGURE 11.4 Unlike Las Vegas, what happens in Washington, D.C., does not stay in Washington, D.C.

Source: © Afsar Husain. Image from BigStockPhoto.com

Political Factors

Bill Clinton was the consummate politician. Was it all by design? He now had two major lobbying organizations pouring money into his reelection campaign. Native American casinos became the third or fourth leading contributor to Democratic Party campaigns. But it was not just Clinton who got cover from casino industry money. So too did state leaders who were pushing casinos.

Governors could no longer simply oppose casinos and expect them to be defeated. Indeed, governors saw a new wisdom in jumping on the bandwagon and supporting casinos. Casinos also were able to gain the upper hand after Congress authorized a national commission to study gambling. Four of the nine members of the commission had ties to the casino industry. Their 1999 report had cutting criticism for lotteries, but only praise and mild suggestions for change for the casino industry.

As the twentieth century ended, a new form of casino gambling appeared. Its growth outside the law—as far as U.S. authorities were concerned—has caused more than a small wave warning existing operators of casinos. Internet gambling appeared on the scene in the mid-1990s and by 1998 there were 50 online casinos in operation. By 2006 over a thousand Web sites offered real-money wager opportunities to players everywhere. The Internet gambling sites were located throughout the world, but outside the United States. Many were in the Caribbean and in Central America, particularly Costa Rica. Multiple sites were headquartered on an Indian (First Nation) reserve near Montreal, Canada. While not operating from the United States, over 60% of the players on these sites are in the United States, although their play is "probably" illegal.

The **1961 Wire Act** prohibits interstate and international gambling on sports events over wires—then considered telephone lines. While Internet casinos provide regular casino games in addition to sports betting, and while the gambling is not strictly over telephone lines, U.S. courts have determined that the gambling is illegal. Prosecutions, however, have been rare—only one player has been prosecuted in the United States. Effective prosecution would demand severe invasions of privacy and would not likely have wide public support. Congress nonetheless considered and passed the **Unlawful Internet Gambling Enforcement Act** of 2006. The Act made the ban in the Wire Act more specific and clear, and provided greater penalties for parties helping Internet gaming operators with financial services.

There is still ambivalence regarding this form of gambling. The American Gaming Association has advocated legislation creating a commission to study Internet casinos. AGA members are divided. Some want to participate as operators; they want Internet gambling legal also so that it can be regulated to assure integrity of the games. Other casinos want the Internet games banned as they fear competition from this growing casino sector. Internet sites made over $10 billion in 2005, more than all of the casinos in Las Vegas, and the Internet casinos do not have to build massive physical palaces, nor hire many workers. Over 25% of bricks-and-mortar casino budgets go for workers.

Thus far the competition has not hurt non-internet casinos while the new law has stifled further Internet growth. All commercial casinos except those on the Gulf Coast saw profits go up in 2006. Commercial casinos now win over $40 billion a year from players. Native American casinos have revenues above $25 billion.[2] Growing competition in gambling need not mean a game where one casino takes profits from the existing player base of another casino. Thus far good competition has proven only to be a way of growing the numbers of patrons for all casinos.

Conclusion

In the last 20 years of the twentieth century, we saw an explosion of gaming in the United States. Legislatures at the state and federal level legalized gambling in a wide variety of venues. The battle was different in each case, but common themes were exhibited. The state budget is in deficit. Voters are not in the mood for additional taxes. A group organizes to legalize gambling. An opposition with visions of Las Vegas and ruined lives arises. The battle is engaged and the economic benefits outweigh the increasingly hollow claims of sin and vice. A new gaming jurisdiction is born.

The proliferation of gaming could not have occurred without a change in Americans' attitude toward gambling. Their perspective saw a dramatic shift in the last half of the twentieth century. The view that gambling was a vice that caused personal ruin was based on illegal gaming activities as experienced by the generation that fought World War II. Without government oversight, organized crime could operate illegal gaming activities with disastrous results for individuals.

However, in post-war Nevada, gaming regulation took a strong stance opposed to organized crime or any business irregularities. With the taming of gaming activity, integrity was state enforced and the public recognized the change.

The public was also wealthier and traveling more in the post-war years. Access to Nevada and Las Vegas in particular improved dramatically with the building of the interstate highway system and with the upgrading of air transportation. The greater exposure to gaming in person and via media occurred at the same time societal changes were loosening the strictures on individual behavior.

All these forces coincided to create a backdrop in the 1980s to enhance the chances of legalization efforts in states throughout the country. Introducing casino gaming with its attendant flow of tax revenue was a very appealing prospect. With the assurance that gaming would not bring organized crime and other unsavory side effects, voters and legislatures approved gaming. Indian gaming, which followed a different route, would not have been legalized by Congress without the same forces that enabled its proliferation at the state level.

In less than 40 years, we have gone from one state with gaming to gaming within a short drive of most Americans. This explosion of gaming continues with new jurisdictions considering adding casino-style gaming to racetracks and with the debate over legalizing Internet gambling. America has gone through cycles of prohibition and legalization. There is no guarantee that gaming will continue to be so widely available. But state-regulated gaming has a better chance of survival than previous incarnations of gaming.

Key Words

Discretionary income *150*
Gravity model *152*
Veto model *152*
New Federalism *152*
Lottery schemes *154*
Foreign Gaming Law *154*
Graham-Rudman Act *156*
American Gaming Association *156*
1961 Wire Act *157*
Unlawful Internet Gambling Enforcement Act of 2006 *157*

Review Questions

1. Explain the general reasons for the public's acceptance of gambling.
2. Detail the situations in Nevada that led to a greater public acceptance of casino gambling.
3. Detail the situations in New Jersey that led to a greater public acceptance of casino gambling.
4. Explain some of the changing social norms that led to a greater public acceptance of casino gambling.
5. Explain some of the economic trends that led to a greater public acceptance of casino gambling.
6. Discuss how a greater mobility led to a greater public acceptance of casino gambling.
7. Detail some of the forces that work against casino promotions.
8. Detail some of the forces that helped establish casinos.
9. Explain the importance of casino investments in the public's acceptance of casino gambling.
10. Explain some of the political factors that help legalize casino gambling.

Endnotes

1. Dombrink, J. & Thompson, W. N. (1990). *The Last Resort: Success and Failure in Campaigns For Casinos* (Nevada Studies in History and Political Science). Reno, NV: University of Nevada Press.
2. National Indian Gaming Associaton web site. http://www.indiangaming.org/library/indian-gaming-facts/index.shtml, Accessed 3/13/09.

CHAPTER 12

REGULATIONS

STEVE DURHAM

Learning Objectives

1. To understand the analogy that some people make between gambling and alcohol
2. To understand the analogy that some people make between the illegality of controlled substances and prostitution
3. To understand how Nevada's experimentation with legalized gambling affected the decisions of other jurisdictions to legalize gambling
4. To learn about the history of the spread of casino gambling throughout the country
5. To learn the factors that enter into the decision as to whether casinos should be legalized
6. To understand some of the problems of legalized casinos
7. To learn about the responsibilities of the gaming industry
8. To learn about some of the future trends of the casino industry

Chapter Outline

Introduction
Analogy with Alcohol
Controlled Substances and Prostitution
The Nevada Experiment
Spread of Gambling
Why Legalize Casinos?
Problems of Legalized Casinos
What is the Responsibility of the Gaming Industry?
Future Trends
Conclusion

INTRODUCTION

Gambling is an activity inherent to humans. It has been documented throughout history from ancient civilizations to today. Gambling took different forms during different eras, but the impulse was the same. Some people gamble rarely while others gamble frequently. As you learned in this book, different people gamble for different reasons. Some hope to win while others enjoy the social or entertainment value of gambling. Others are attracted by the exhilaration of the action. Of course, there are those who suffer from disordered gambling and cannot control their gambling.

The history of gaming shows a close relationship with crime. The Louisiana Lottery in the wake of the Civil War was corrupt almost from the beginning. Card sharps on the riverboats were in business to cheat unsuspecting victims. Organized crime transferred its business acumen from its illegal activities to Nevada where casino gaming was legal. However, they brought their other nefarious habits with them, namely skimming, murder, and intimidation.

You also learned that in early American history, gambling laws were enacted in part to prevent disruption to the social order. A man who owned a substantial amount of land was wealthy by the standards of the day and was a pillar of the community. Social class was more rigidly defined. Greater rights such as voting were assigned to those who owned land. Such a man and his family could lose everything if gambling took hold of his life. In turn, the community would be placed in turmoil and social relationships disrupted.

ANALOGY WITH ALCOHOL

Because the stability of personal and social relationships is necessary to the well-being of a community, it behooves the government to intervene. In this regard, gambling is similar to alcohol, controlled substances, and prostitution. Alcohol can have a deleterious effect on a community due to the alcoholism of some individuals predisposed to it. Alcohol can also impact the community negatively if consumption is not strictly controlled. We are all familiar with the death, injury, and destruction possible when an individual consumes too much alcohol.

Because of its potential negative impact, the sale of alcohol as packaged goods and as a consumable is restricted by age and strictly enforced. Only an individual who passes a thorough background check is licensed to sell alcohol. The license can be revoked for even the slightest infraction. Some communities restrict the number of licenses available in order to limit the number of legal outlets for alcohol sales. Some states limit the sale of packaged goods to state-owned stores. Hours of operation for bars and liquor stores are legislated rather than left to the free market.

The state also determines the legal definition of **inebriation**. We have seen in recent years most states reduce the blood alcohol content (**BAC**) criteria to 0.8%. For most people, a single shot of liquor, a beer, or a glass of wine consumed within an hour will produce a BAC of 0.8% or more. Clearly, the will of the people as expressed through the government is to limit the amount of alcohol consumed in public settings.

On top of these strictures, the courts have weighed in on the responsibility of bar owners and bartenders in preventing alcohol-related impacts. A bartender and the bar owner are considered partially responsible if a bar patron consumes alcohol and then proceeds to injure himself or another. Bar employees are trained extensively to identify the

FIGURE 12.1a and b Our approach to alcohol has evolved since the days of Prohibition. Will our approach to gambling follow in those footsteps?

Source: (a) © Dana Rothstein. Image from BigStockPhoto.com. (b) © Igor Terekhov. Image from BigStockPhoto.com.

signs of inebriation. Slurred speech, reduced inhibitions, lack of coordination, and so on are among the clear signs that a patron has been overserved. The employees have certain strategies to reverse the impact of the alcohol. They slow down service, offer food, suggest and serve a non-alcoholic alternative, notify the manager, and in extreme cases confiscate the patron's car keys.

We arrived at these restrictions on the consumption of alcohol after a national experiment between 1920 and 1933 when the production and sale of all alcohol was banned. The ban resulted from popular agitation over the concern of the impact alcohol had on communities with limited restrictions and enforcement. The experiment was called **Prohibition** and it was a dismal failure. People still wanted to drink. The production and sale of alcohol was taken over by organized criminal organizations. The rise of the Federal Bureau of Investigation and its young director, J. Edgar Hoover, was directly linked to its fight against gangsters involved in the alcohol trade. By 1933, the nation realized the folly of a total ban on alcohol. The federal government repealed Prohibition and left it to each state to decide its own approach to alcohol.

If you have traveled around the country, you know that different states have widely varied approaches. It was not too long ago that some counties in the southern states were dry. There was no sale or consumption of alcohol allowed. Many northeastern states allow the sale of alcohol only through state stores that are limited in their numbers and in their hours of operation. The state of Utah severely restricts alcohol. To consume alcohol in a restaurant, one must purchase the alcohol at a state store. It can only be a single-serving bottle of liquor or a full bottle of wine. The customer must take the bottle to the restaurant where the waiter will open the bottle of wine or take the liquor to the bartender who then mixes the drink. The restaurant charges a fee for the service, but not the drink itself.

CONTROLLED SUBSTANCES AND PROSTITUTION

Alcohol consumption moved from a total ban to a tightly controlled substance. By contrast, controlled substances such as heroin, LSD, marijuana, and PCP are under a total ban. Like the prohibition of alcohol, the production and sale of these substances is controlled by organized criminal elements. There is a tremendous amount of violence committed in the market that crosses borders. At the writing of this book, Mexico is in the throes of a spasm of violence committed by the drug cartels against federal officials.

Like alcohol, the use of drugs can be very disruptive to the social fabric of a community. There are those who become addicted and lose everything. Even those who use a drug recreationally without addiction can find their worlds turned upside down if they are arrested and convicted. Their ability to support their families and participate in society becomes limited. While a larger share of the population is susceptible to becoming addicted to drugs as opposed to becoming alcoholics, the situations are analogous.

Prostitution also deals with a basic human urge. It is also under a total ban. Unlike alcohol and drugs, there is no production process. It is not as easy for criminal elements to control the total supply. However, it requires a criminal element to market the product. And violence associated with prostitution is common.

(a)

(b)

FIGURE 12.2a and b Prostitution and controlled substances share similar sociological traits with alcohol and gambling.

Source: (a) © Evgeny Kan. Image from BigStockPhoto.com. (b) © Bernardo Martino. Image from BigStockPhoto.com.

When we look at controlled substances, prostitution, alcohol, and gambling, we find similarities. There is a ready demand for all these activities because the urge is inherent in people. A legal ban on any of these activities reduces the supply while leaving the level of demand in place. By definition, only criminals enter these markets to supply the demand. The amount of violence associated with any activity is directly related to the degree in which criminal elements are involved in the production and sale of the activity.

As we see in alcohol and gambling, legality with tight controls on who produces and sells the product results in a healthy industry without violence and a limited impact on society. By contrast, the illegality of drugs and prostitution has continued the violence and social disruption associated with these activities. This is not an argument for legalizing either drugs or prostitution, but to point out the impact of legality on a particular market and that market's impact on the community.

THE NEVADA EXPERIMENT

The experiment with legalized casino gaming in Nevada started like all previous attempts at legalization in America. The activity was legalized, but with minimal supervision by government. This worked adequately and gambling did not disrupt the social fabric of communities so long as the gambling was controlled by local owners in saloons across the state. However, when organized crime moved into Las Vegas in the 1940s and 1950s, the problems of legalized gaming came to the fore.

The state of Nevada responded to this situation with a strong push from the federal government. **The Kefauver Committee's** investigation into organized crime threatened Nevada with the specter that the federal government would ban gambling nationwide. Gambling was one of only a few economic activities that the citizens of Nevada relied on for employment. Nevada tightened its laws and created enforcement mechanisms such as the Gaming Control Board. The state established the right to deny a gaming license to anyone based on the premise that a license is a privilege, not right. The courts upheld this right and the Gaming Control Board strictly limits access to the industry.

The evolution of Nevada's regulatory environment created a template for state-sponsored gaming. It proved that the criminal element could be eliminated from and prevented from entering the gaming industry within a state. The link between gaming and crime was broken in Nevada.

At the same time that Nevada was tightening its control on the gaming industry, there were social forces in play that removed the stigma of gambling activity. It was no longer viewed as a vice. Increasingly, it was considered just another entertainment option. There was still a hint of the forbidden fruit to gambling as demonstrated in the Las Vegas slogan, "What happens in Las Vegas stays in Las Vegas." But, it is considered socially acceptable to spend money on gambling.

SPREAD OF GAMBLING

With a loosening of social strictures on gambling and an example of successful state-sponsored and regulated gaming, legalization of gaming spread across the country. First, New Jersey legalized gaming in Atlantic City in 1976. New Jersey showed that it is possible to replicate Nevada's success in preventing organized crime from infiltrating the industry. This was particularly impressive given the proximity to New York, Philadelphia, and other east coast metropolises known to have significant organized criminal elements.

Other states followed suit in the late 1980s and early 1990s. Funding available to states from the federal government declined in this period as Congress increased the number of mandates for which states were responsible. Raising taxes on citizens is limited by their reluctance to accept higher taxes. State legislatures and governors needed to find alternative tax sources. The tax on gaming revenue did not affect any particular tax payer and voter. The economic activity casinos generated through the multiplier effect also boosted other tax revenues such as sales tax and income tax. Casino legalization was the perfect solution.

Riverboats and land-based casinos spread quickly in the early to mid-1990s. Most of these were located in the states along the Mississippi River. However, at the same time commercial casinos were spreading, Native American gaming was taking hold. Tribes had operated bingo halls for years. In the 1970s and 1980s, some tribes expanded these operations. Most notable among these tribes were the Seminoles of south Florida and the Cabazon Band of Mission Indians in the Palm Springs, California area. Their size drew the attention of the state government that tried to limit or eliminate them. Based on the sovereign nation concept first espoused by Chief Justice Marshal in 1836, tribes used the court system to establish their rights to offer gaming on reservation land. When the Supreme Court upheld this right in 1987, Congress acted quickly and passed the Indian Gaming Regulatory Act (**IGRA**) in 1988. It created a legal framework for gaming on Indian reservations.

The passage of IGRA set the stage for the massive expansion of Indian gaming. Today there are over 400 casinos on reservations across America. Most are located near an urban area or along a well-traveled highway. These casinos provide a source of economic development where other attempts failed. The poverty on reservations is legendary. There are multiple causes, but the lack of available jobs is significant. Casinos are labor intensive. They need many people to serve customers. Opening a casino on a reservation goes a long way to reducing poverty among Native Americans.

WHY LEGALIZE CASINOS?

Any jurisdiction that is considering legalizing casino gaming is hoping to create jobs and generate tax revenue. As you learned, there are three categories of jobs created by casinos. First are the temporary direct jobs. Primarily related to construction of the facility, these include architects, carpenters, plumbers, foremen, and so on. These jobs exist only as long as it takes to build the casino. Permanent direct jobs are the positions inside the casino. Managers, dealers, housekeepers, and hotel desk clerks are just a couple of the hundreds of jobs needed in a casino. The third category is permanent indirect jobs. There are those jobs created by suppliers to the casino such as added deliverymen hired by the food supplier. There are also those jobs created to service the casino employees like added firemen and checkout clerks at the grocery store. The multiplier effect creates the economic activity that requires these indirect jobs.

Of course, casinos generate opportunities for increased tax revenue. Taxing casinos directly is one source. This is typically in the form of a tax on gross gaming revenue. The government takes its share before the casino deducts expenses. In essence, state tax revenue is not affected by the ability of the casino to control its expenses. However, other tax revenues also increase. The increased economic activity will affect sales tax and income

FIGURE 12.3 When a community decides to legalize gaming, the deal is that tax revenues and the number of jobs will increase.

Source: © Gino Santa Maria. Image from BigStockPhoto.com.

tax. As value of land under and near the casinos increases, property tax collections increase as well. All these taxes assist the government in meeting its obligations to tax payers without increasing the individual taxpayer's taxes.

Jobs and tax revenue are the main selling points for legalizing casino gaming. Opponents to gaming raise the issue of negative social impacts that come with gaming. The specter of organized crime associated with casinos has been tamed. Nevada and every subsequent jurisdiction has proven that government can ensure the integrity of casino gaming. However, there are other potential negative impacts.

PROBLEMS OF LEGALIZED CASINOS

We have looked at crime, bankruptcy, and disordered gambling in this book. As you will recall, there were no firm conclusions regarding the causal relationship between crime and casinos. The Federal Bureau of Investigation has identified 13 factors that have an effect on a community's crime rate. Among these were the level of transiency of the population and the number of people living in a square mile. The fact that a casino increases the transiency and population density of an area suggests it increases the crime rate. But a new manufacturing plant or high-tech campus would also increase these factors. It is not the gaming per se that increases crime, but a change in population traits caused by the introduction of any new business enterprise.

Likewise, conclusions about bankruptcy are hard to make. Opponents argue that people living in the vicinity of the casino will gamble more than they can afford. This will lead to financial stress and eventually bankruptcy. The logic can be compelling on the surface.

However, studies show mixed results by jurisdiction. While there was some correlation between the presence of gaming venues and bankruptcy, there was evidence to the contrary. And different studies found different reasons for the bankruptcy rate—amount of credit card debt, marital status, income level, and more. Perhaps one explanation of the data is that some people find financial salvation when a casino is built. They can find a job and can raise themselves economically. Others are tempted by the gambling and overindulge. This leads to problems including bankruptcy. Further studies are needed to better understand the phenomenon.

Finally, we looked at disordered gambling. This problem is clearly the result of the introduction of gaming into a community. Forty years ago only 10% of the American population lived within a four-hour drive of a casino. Today that ratio has been reversed. Ninety percent live within a four-hour drive. With greater availability, a greater incidence of disordered gambling can be expected. After all, someone living in Michigan in 1970 would not have ready access to Las Vegas. Travel by car would take a few days and airfares were expensive and prohibitive. Today, someone in Michigan can visit the casinos in Detroit or any number of Native American casinos within the state. In addition, a flight to Las Vegas is very reasonably priced.

Disordered gambling is the inability of a person to control his/her gambling. The person finds he/she cannot adequately resist gambling and the impact on his/her personal and professional lives is deleterious. Disorderd gamblers lose jobs, destroy relationships, and create financial hardship. The percentage of the population predisposed to disordered gambling is less than 1.5%. Naturally, if these individuals were not exposed to casino gaming, they might find other ways to gamble. But easy access to gaming clearly increases the number of people with a gambling problem.

WHAT IS THE RESPONSIBILITY OF THE GAMING INDUSTRY?

America has taken the leap to legalizing casino gaming. Like alcohol before it, legalization entails many controls and restrictions to minimize the impact on society. However, like the inebriated bar patron or alcoholic poses a problem, the disordered gambler poses a problem for the casinos. The casino industry has responded.

The industry, through the American Gaming Association and the National Center for Responsible Gaming, has started to address this issue. The American Gaming Association (**AGA**) is an industry association. Among its foci is the issue of disordered gambling. The AGA has funded research into the causes prior to the establishment of the National Center for Responsible Gaming (**NCRG**). Currently, the NCRG funds research into the cause and treatment of disordered gambling. Progress over the past ten years has been remarkable, but much is still needed in order to assist the industry in minimizing its negative impact on society.

The AGA has also encouraged its members to promote problem gambling hotlines in their casinos. Brochure racks are located at each cage counter and other easily noticed spots. If a patron suspects he/she has a problem, he/she can call the number in the brochure and obtain help. Most of the time this help is at no expense to the gambler. This system relies on a self-reporting model. In other words, the gambler has to recognize he/she has a problem and seek help. If the gambling behavior is addictive in nature, the likelihood someone will seek help is greatly reduced.

When we look at the alcohol industry, we see that the bar owner and bartender are partially liable for their customers' consumption. They are charged with the duty to slow

FIGURE 12.4 Non-profit organizations like the Arizona Council on Compulsive Gambling have sprung up in jurisdictions with legal casino gaming to handle one of the negative impacts of gambling.

down or refuse service to someone who is intoxicated. Unfortunately, there is no way to know for sure if someone is overindulging in gambling. The dollar amount of bets is not a reliable indicator because different people can afford to gamble different amounts. There are no obvious signs as there are with inebriated guests. There is no slurred speech, lack of coordination, or lowered inhibitions to tell a dealer or cage cashier that someone needs to be cut off from gambling. It is hoped that more research will give casinos practical information they can use to prevent disordered gamblers from destroying their lives.

All casinos have a self-exclusion list. Someone with a gambling problem can place their name on the list. The casino is then obligated to prevent that person from entering the casino. These lists can be fairly effective in keeping these self-excluded individuals out of the casino. However, here again the industry is relying on a self-reporting model which is not going to ensure that everyone who suffers from disordered gambling will be kept out of casinos. At some point, it may become the responsibility of casino employees to identify and cut off disordered gamblers the way bartenders cut off bar patrons. For a more detailed discussion on responsible gaming, see the *Casinos: Organization and Culture* title in this series.

FUTURE TRENDS

The industry faces an exciting future. There is the further legalization in jurisdictions not currently offering casino gaming. Pennsylvania legalized casinos and racinos in 2004 well after the rush to casinos in the Midwest in the 1990s. These facilities are just starting to come online as of the writing of this book. Other states and countries will also consider gaming in the future.

Macau opened up its gaming industry in the 1990s. Stanley Ho had had a state-granted monopoly on casinos prior to the government opening licenses to others. Today the Venetian, Sands, and Wynn have opened next to Mr. Ho's casinos. Incredibly, in just five years, Macau has grown to produce more gross gaming revenue than Las Vegas. It is the largest gaming market in the world.

Technology will continue to shape the industry. Electronic gaming devices have come a long way from the slot machine invented by Charles Fey. They will continue to evolve as server-based gaming becomes technologically possible and gains licensing approval by gaming jurisdictions. Server-based gaming will allow customers to change the slot machine software on a whim. If a guest tires of playing "Wheel of Fortune," they can switch their unit to "The Munsters" or "Texas Tea." Server-based gaming will also allow a gambler to play on a handheld device that gives them the mobility to move around the casino floor, eat in a restaurant, lounge by the pool, or sit in their room, all the while playing their favorite slot machine.

Of course, Internet gaming is already making an impact. We do not hear much about it here in America because it is illegal. Congress has taken steps to prevent Americans from gambling on the Internet. Their most notable effort was making it illegal for credit card companies and financial institutions to pay gambling debts. The Internet relies on credit cards to establish a player's credit. Without credit cards, the industry is hamstrung in its ability to attract customers. However, Barbuda and Antigua, two small island nations in the Caribbean Sea, brought suit against the United States before the World Trade Organization (WTO). These two countries have a thriving Internet gaming industry. The ban on Internet gaming in America was found to be a violation of the WTO's regulations against tariffs and other impediments to imports and exports. It is still unresolved what, if anything the U.S. will do in response.

But elsewhere in the world, Internet gaming is a $15 billion-plus business and growing. It is regulated by European countries as they apply the lessons of Nevada to this emerging sector. Whether America can comply with its international obligations and ban Internet gaming is yet to be seen.

Of course, all these changes are challenges for the bodies that regulate the industry. How is the integrity of a handheld device maintained when a guest can take it out of sight of a surveillance camera and employees? Are there enough qualified employees to staff regulatory bodies as more and more jurisdictions legalize gaming? Is there a point of saturation beyond which there are diminishing returns for expanding gaming? Regardless of the answers to these questions and more, the future is quite exciting.

Conclusion

This book has covered a lot of territory. You have been exposed to the history of gambling in America. You have read several chapters, each devoted to a specific gaming market, as well as chapters on the costs and benefits of legalized gaming. An entire chapter focused on the reasons and mechanics of the spread of gaming in America.

This book has given you a good base of knowledge on the casino industry. You understand casinos and the environment in which they operate better than the vast majority of Americans. You are prepared to move on and learn more. As you take the courses associated with the other books in the *Casino Essentials* series, you will learn how casinos market themselves in order to generate astounding revenues. There is a whole book devoted to controls that maximize profit. The criteria for granting complimentary goods and services and for extending credit to high-limit players cover several chapters because of their significance to casino profitability. A whole book on the organizational structure of casinos has been written because of the uniqueness of casinos. Of course, the most unusual aspects of casinos are the gaming departments. You will be fascinated by the information on managing a table games or slot department.

Good luck on your journey through these books and your career in the casino industry. You could not have picked a more interesting topic to study or a more exciting industry to join.

Key Words

Inebriation *161*
BAC *161*
Prohibition *162*
The Kefauver Committee *164*
IGRA *165*
Disordered gambling *167*
AGA *167*
NCRG *167*

Review Questions

1. Explain the analogy that some people make between gambling and alcohol, and discuss its validity.
2. Explain the analogy that some people make between the illegality of controlled substances and prostitution and discuss its validity.
3. Discuss how Nevada's experimentation with legalized gambling affected the decision of other jurisdictions to legalize gambling.
4. Detail the history of the spread of casino gambling throughout the country.
5. Discuss the factors that enter into the decision as to whether casinos should be legalized.
6. Explain some of the problems of legalized casinos.
7. Discuss some of the responsibilities of the gaming industry.
8. Discuss some of the future trends of the casino industry.

CONTRIBUTOR'S BIOGRAPHIES

Daniel Heneghan has followed the casino industry for 30 years, first as a journalist and later as a state gaming regulator. Dan joined the Press of Atlantic City in June 1975 and was one of a team of journalists who covered the effort to legalize casinos in Atlantic City in 1976. In January 1979, he was assigned to cover the business and regulation of casinos full time. In that position, he wrote about virtually every aspect of the construction, opening, licensing, and ongoing operations of each of the first dozen Atlantic City casinos. As a journalist, he did freelance work for most of the major news services and his work appeared in numerous trade magazines and newsletters.

In March 1996, Dan became the Public Information Officer for the New Jersey Casino Control Commission. In that capacity, he is in charge of all media relations and is the chief spokesman for the regulatory agency. As a member of the Directors Advisory Team, he is a senior advisor to the chair and members of the commission. He has often been a panelist at various gaming conferences and a guest lecturer at gaming-related courses at several universities.

A native of New York, Dan holds a degree in communications from Fordham University.

Soo K. Kang is associate professor of Restaurant and Resort Management at Colorado State University in Fort Collins, Colorado. She earned her master's and Ph.D. in Hotel, Restaurant, Institution Management, and Dietetics from the Kansas State University.

Dr. Kang has published articles in numerous periodicals including *Tourism Management*, *Journal of Travel Research*, and *Journal of Korean Academic Society of Hospitality Administration*. She has been a visiting scholar in the School of Hotel and Tourism Management at the Hong Kong Polytechnic University and participated in the 2006 Marriott Faculty Internship.

Her research interests include the traveler decision-making process, quality of life in tourism management, gaming impact studies, and cross-cultural tourism management.

John Marchel, owner of *John Marchel Enterprises*, has gambled successfully throughout the world for over 25 years. Since 1988, he has combined his experience as a manager, teacher, and player to present winning gambling seminars and lectures throughout the United States. John is a graduate of Richard Canfield's Expert School of Blackjack and Frank Scoblete's Golden Touch Blackjack School where later he was an instructor. In addition to the seminars, lectures, and private tutoring on winning gambling, John also publishes *The Gaming Bulletin*, a monthly e-mail newsletter on casino gambling.

In 1998, John wrote his first book, *101 Casino Gambling Tips*. This book presents casino gambling tips for both the novice as well as for the seasoned player. John's latest book, *KISS Guide to Gambling*, published by Dorling Kindersley Publishing of New York, released in the fall of 2001, covers all the who, what, when, where, and why of gambling.

John was born in New York City and has traveled throughout the world and now makes his home in Northern California. John continues to be an active and regular visitor to casinos.

William N. Thompson is a professor in the Public Administration Department at the University of Nevada, Las Vegas. He received B.A. and M.A. degrees in political science from Michigan State University. His Ph.D. is from the University of Missouri-Columbia.

Since coming to Nevada in 1980, Dr. Thompson has been actively studying public policy and gambling. He and John Dombrink of the University of California-Irvine collaborated in writing *The Last Resort: Success and Failure in Campaigns for Casinos*. Thompson's articles on gambling have appeared in numerous publications, including the *Annals of the American Academy of Political Science, Indian Gaming, Journal of Gambling Studies, Casino Executive, Gaming Law Review*, and *International Gaming and Wagering Business*. He also coauthored with Michele Comeau *Casino Customer Service: The WIN WIN Game*. He is also the author/editor of *Gambling in America: An Encyclopedia*, author of *Legalized Gambling: A Reference Handbook*, and *Native American Issues*, and coauthor with Tony Cabot of *International Casino Law*.

He has appeared on numerous news programs on television including *The Today Show, Frontline*, and *World News Tonight* and has been quoted in such publications as the *New York Times*, the *Economist*, and *Fortune*.

INDEX